Health Laws in India

Health Laws in India

Edited by

Dr. Caesar Roy
LL.M, PGDCFS, Ph.D (Law)
Assistant Professor
Midnapore Law College
West Bengal, INDIA

Routledge
Taylor & Francis Group
LONDON AND NEW YORK

Manakin
PRESS

First published 2023
by Routledge
4 Park Square, Milton Park, Abingdon, Oxon OX14 4RN

and by Routledge
605 Third Avenue, New York, NY 10158

Routledge is an imprint of the Taylor & Francis Group, an informa business

British Library Cataloguing-in-Publication Data
A catalogue record for this book is available from the British Library

Library of Congress Cataloging-in-Publication Data
A catalog record for this book has been requested

ISBN: 9781032379852 (hbk)
ISBN: 9781032380278 (pbk)
ISBN: 9781003343127 (ebk)

DOI: 10.4324/9781003343127

Typeset in Times New Roman
by Manakin Press, Delhi

Manakin
PRESS

Contents

Preface

The relationship between health and law in not new but the relation is multifaceted. Law and health are both subjects with an inherent dynamism. Health and well being are deeply personal matters but being on the receiving end of it is what gives us new awareness on various aspects related to health. Every human has a right to highest attainable standard of physical and mental health. This right to health has thus evolved a whole system for protection of health. It ensures that every human has equal access to good quality of services for maintenance of sound health. Right to Life does not connote merely animal existence rather it has a much wider meaning which includes right to health and medical care being essential for making the life of every person meaningful and purposeful with dignity of person. Right to health is not included directly in as a fundamental right in our Constitution. The obligation of the State to ensure the creation and the sustaining the conditions congenial to good health is cast by the Constitutional directives contained in Part IV of our Constitution. But the Supreme Court has brought the right to health under the preview of Article 21 by widening the scope of this Article. Thus right to health was held as an as integral part of right to life and government has constitutional obligations to provide health facilities and medical services. At the same time, implementation of right to health has its own highest challenges. Besides the Constitutional provisions, there are various statutes which also deal with 'health.' There are many international instruments also which are relating to 'health.' This edited book will be helpful to prepare a foundation for understanding and analysis of advanced knowledge in the field of health and its relation with law.

Health and law as a curricular subject of law is a recent addition and is taught in law colleges under many universities in India. But beyond the law college curriculum, many more topics are there relating to law and health. Thus keeping in mind the broad perspectives of health laws in India, this edited book tries to focus on intersection between law and health.

This edited book is divided into five extensive sections. Various authors have contributed their valuable writings for the book. The first section is "Concept of Health." It contains four chapters. The second section "Medical Profession,

Patient and the law" includes two chapters. "Organization of Public Health Care and Medical Jurisprudence", the third section contains three comprehensive chapters. Fourth section is on "Insurance and Victim Compensation" with two chapters. Last section of the book is on "Health Legislative Perspective" with seven wide-ranging chapters.

This edited book will be helpful to prepare a foundation for understanding and analysis of advanced knowledge in the field of health and its relation with law. This edited book has been explained in simple style so that all the readers could grip the subject easily widely cited in and referred in numerous Supreme Court and High Court judgments.

The salient feature that distinguishes this edited book from others is the clear exposition of law, its systematic arrangement and simple and lucid language. This edited book is humble attempt of editor to discuss all the aforesaid issues and its legal implications.

This edited book will be helpful for the teachers, students, researchers, lawyers, Judges, law firms, medical professionals, academicians, libraries, national and state Bar Associations, Law Universities and College and persons interested in the subject.

I acknowledge my humble gratitude and indebtedness to the contributors who have contributed their valuable writings for this edited book. I convey my sincere thanks to them for providing such type of thought-provoking writings.

This book would not have come such a long way but for the blessings of my parents. I pay my respect to them through this edited book. It is only because of their inspiration and enthusiasm that this edited book could take the final shape. I express my thanks to my wife for her support and encouragement during preparation of this book and to my son Drishan who sacrificed his claims to the time spent in editing this book.

I express my heartiest warm gratitude to all my well wishers for providing me moral support.

In spite of my best efforts some errors might have remained undetected in the book and therefore, I will highly appreciate the comments which may be made by the readers from time to time so that those may be removed in the next edition. I sincerely appeal and request the readers for constructive criticism and corrective suggestions for the improvements of the book.

Last but not the least; I take this opportunity to express my thanks to Manakin Press Pvt. Ltd. for placing the book in the present shape.

Dr. Caesar Roy

List of Contributors

1. **Dr. Liji Samuel:** Assistant Professor & Director (i/c), Centre For Health Law and Policy, The National University of Advanced Legal Studies, Kalamassery, Kochi, Kerala – 683503.
2. **Dr. Bhavana Sharma:** Assistant Professor of Law, *Lingaya's university,* Nachauli, Jasana Road, Old Faridabad, Faridabad, Haryana – 121002.
3. **Mr. Samuel Molsom:** Guest Faculty, Tripura Law College.
4. **Mr. Sajal Sharma:** Assistant Professor, School of Law, Presidency University, Itgalpur, Rajanakunte, Yelahanka, Bengaluru, Karnataka – 560064.
5. **Dr. Nirmala Kumari K:** Assistant Professor, Vaikunta Baliga College of Law, Kunjibettu, Udupi, Karnataka – 576102.
6. **Dr. Suneet Kashyap:** Senior Assistant Professor, School of Law, Indira Gandhi National Open University, Block – G, Zakir Hussain Bhawan, Academic Complex, Maidan Garhi, New Delhi – 110068.
7. **C. E. Pratap:** Research Scholar (Part-time), Tamil Nadu Dr. Ambedkar Law University, 5, Dr. D.G.S. Dinakaran Salai, Poompozhil, Raja Annamalai Puram, Chennai, Tamil Nadu – 600028 & Advocate, High Court, Madras, Tamil Nadu.
8. **Dr. Meena Ketan Sahu:** Reader, P.G. Department of Law, Sambalpur University, Jyoti Vihar, Burla, Odisha – 768019.
9. **Dr. Caesar Roy:** Assistant Professor of Law, Midnapore Law College, Midnapore, Paschim Medinipur, West Bengal – 721507.
10. **Shreya Mishra:** Assistant Professor of Law, Maharashtra National Law University, Moraj Design and Decorator (DnD) Building, Near Oil Depot, Mihan Fly Over, Wardha Road, Khapri, Nagpur, Maharashtra – 441108.

11. **Dr. Sukdeo Ingale:** Assistant Professor, Deccan Education Society's Shri. Navalmal Firodia Law College, Gate No. 3, Fergusson College Campus, F. C. Road, Pune, Maharashtra – 411004.

12. **Dr. Aneesh V. Pillai:** Assistant Professor, School of Legal Studies Cochin University of Science and Technology, University Road, South Kalamassery, HMT Kalamassery, Ernakulam, Kerala – 682022.

13. **Mrs. Soumya James:** Research Scholar, School of Legal Studies, Cochin University of Science and Technology, University Road, South Kalamassery, HMT Kalamassery, Ernakulam, Kerala – 682022.

14. **Dr. Aparna Singh:** Assistant Professor of Law, Dr. Ram Manohar Lohiya National Law University, Sec- D1, LDA Colony, Kanpur Road Scheme, Lucknow, Uttar Pradesh – 226012.

15. **Diksha Dubey:** Student of B.A LL.B(H), Maharashtra National Law University, Moraj Design and Decorator (DnD) Building, Near Oil Depot, Mihan Fly Over, Wardha Road, Khapri, Nagpur, Maharashtra – 441108.

16. **Anjali Dixit:** Assistant Professor, Shaheed Bhagat Singh Law College, Peshwa Nagar, Bithoor, Opposite Bithoor Police Station, Kanpur Nagar, Uttar Pradesh – 209201.

17. **Dr. Deepom Baruah: Assistant Professor, Centre for Juridical Studies, Dibrugarh University,** Nagakhalia Gaon, Dibrugarh, **Assam – 786004.**

18. **Sridip S. Nambiar: Assistant Professor,** Sree Narayana Law College, Kanjiramattam Road, Poothotta, Kanjiramattom, Manakunnam, Kerala – 682315.

19. **Dr. Radheshyam Prasad:** Associate Professor (Law), UPES School of Law, Dehradun, Uttarakhand 248007.

List of Cases

A.S. Mittal & Ors. v State of Uttar Pradesh & Ors., AIR 1989 SC 1570, p.34.

Abdul Sayeed v. State of M.P., (2010) 10 SCC 259, p. 142

Abhilasha Garg & Another v. The Appropriate Authority, WP(C) 182/2010, p. 216.

Anand Manharlal Brahmbhatt v. State of Gujarat, Special Cr. Appeal No.4204/2015, p. 204.

Aparna Dutt .v. Apollo Hospital Enterprises Ltd, 2002 ACJ 954 (Mad. HC), p. 104.

Aruna Ramchandra Shanbaug v. Union of India, (2011) 4 *SCC* 454, p. 239.

Ashok Kumar v. Anupama Sharma, FAO-M No.29/2018, p. 201.

B. K. Parthasarthi v. Government of Andhra Pradesh, AIR 2000 AP 156, p. 261.

Baby M case, 537 A. 2d 1227, p. 262.

Baby Manji Yamada v. *Union of India and Another*, (2008) 13 SCC 518, p. 187.

Bandhua Mukti Morcha v. Union of India, AIR 1984 SC 802, p. 33.

C. Jagadeeshwar v. State of Andhra Pradesh, 1998 Cri.L.J 549 (AP), p. 238.

CECS v. Subhash Chandra Bose and other, AIR 1992 SC 573, p. 110.

CEHAT v. UOI, [(WP(C) No.344/2002; (2003) 8 SCC 412, p. 217.

Center for Enquiry into Health and Allied Themes v. UOI, AIR 2003 SC 3309, p. 218.

CERC v. Union of India, (1995) 3 SCC 42, p. 33.

CESC Ltd. v. Subash Chandra Bose, AIR 1992 SC 573, p. 52.

Chandrakanth Jayanthilal Suthar & Another v. State of Gujarat, (2015)8SCC 721, p. 212.

Lakshmi mandal v. Deen Dayal Harinagar Hospital, (WP(C) 8853/2008, p. 220.

Laxmi v. Union of India and others, (2014) 4 SCC 427, p. 165.

M. Kala v. The Inspector of Police, WP-8750/2015, 24th March, p. 215.

M/s. Cosmopolitan Hospitals & Anr. v. Smt. Vasantha P. Nair & Ors., (1992) 1 CPJ 302 (NC), p. 35.

Madan Gopal Kakkad v. Naval Dubey, (1992) 3 SCC 204 : 1992 SCC (Cri) 598, p. 142.

Mahendra Pratap Singh v. State of Orissa, AIR 1997 Ori 37, p. 52.

Maneka Gandhi v. Union of India, AIR 1978 SC 597, p. 83.

Maneka Gandhi v. Union of India. AIR 1978 SC 597, p. 237.

Manoj Kumar Singh v. State of U.P. & Others, CRL. Misc. App. No. 67 of 2013, p. 170.

Maruti Sharipati v. State of Maharashtra, 1987 (1) Bom.CR 499(1986) 88BOMLR 589, p. 238.

Maruti Shripati v. State of Maharashtra [1987] (1) BOMCR 499, p. 252.

Mohini v. *The State (Govt. of NCT of Delhi),* W.P. (C) 3754/2015 decided on 14.09.2015, p. 174.

Mrs. X v. *Union of India,* Writ Petition (Civil) No. 81 of 2017, p. 305.

Municipal Council, Ratlam v. Vardhichand others, 1980 Cri LJ 1075, p. 52.

Munn v. Illinois, 94 U.S. 113 (1876), p. 69.

Murari Mohan Koley v. State of West Bengal (2004) 3 CALLT 609 HC, p. 207.

Murli S. Deora v. Union of India, (2001) 8 SCC 765, p. 39.

N.D. Jayal & ors. v Union of India, 2003 Supp (3) SCR 152, p. 40.

Naresh Marotrao Sakhare v. Union of India, 1996 (1) Bom. C.R. 92, 1995 Cri.LJ 96 (1994) (2) Mh. LJ 1850, p. 237.

Nilabati Behera Alias lalit v State of Orissa & ors, AIR 1993 SC 1960, p. 236.

P. Geetha v. The Kerala Livestock Development Board Ltd. & Others, 2015 SCC On Line Ker 71, p. 190.

P. Rathinam v. Union of India, AIR 1994 SC 1844 : (1994)3 SCC 394, p. 238.

Parivartan Kendra & Anr v. U.O.I & Ors, 2016(1) R.C.R. (Criminal) 336, p. 165.

Sheetal Shankar Shelvi v *Union of India,* Writ Petition (Civil) No. 174 of 2017, p. 305.

Solanki Chimanbhai Ukabhai v. State of Gujarat, AIR 1983 SC 484 : 1983 Cri.L.J. 822, p. 141.

State of Haryana v. Bhagirath, (1999) 5 SCC 96 : AIR 1999 SC 2005, p. 142.

State of Haryana v. Smt Santra, AIR 2000 SC 3335, p. 103.

State of Karnataka v. Manjanna, 2000 (6) SCC 188, p. 114.

State of Karnataka v. Manjanna, AIR 2000 SC 2231, p. 114.

State of Maharashtra v. Chandrabhan, AIR 1983 SC 549, p. 245.

State of Punjab and ors. v. Mohinder Singh Chawla etc., AIR 1997 SC 1225, p. 38.

State of Punjab v. Ram Lubhaya Bagga, (1998) 4 SCC 117, p. 38.

State of Punjab v. Ram Lubhaya Bagga, AIR 1998 SC 1703, p. 38.

State of U.P. v. Dinesh, (2009)11 SCC 566, p. 141.

State v. Riyazuddin & others, Cr.Appeal.No.577/2013, p. 209.

State v. Sanjay Kumar, 1986 (10) DRJ 31, p. 238.

Suchita Srivastava & another v. Chandigarh Administration, SCP(C) 5845/2009, 28th Aug. p. 203.

Sunil Batra v. Delhi Admn. AIR 1978 SC 1675, p. 44.

Supreme Court Legal Aid Committee v. State of Bihar, (1991) 3 SCC 482, p. 58.

Sweetha v. State of Haryana & others, (2015) CWP 19343/2015, p. 213.

T. Damodarand others v. Special Officer, Municipal Corporation of Hyderabad, AIR 1987 AP 171, p. 54.

T. Ramakrishna Rao v. Hyderabad Development Authority, Writ Petition 36929/1998, p. 54.

Tamil Nadu in re v. Union of India, (2002)3 SCC 31, 246.

Union of India (UOI) and Ors. v. Jan Balaz and Ors., MANU/SC/1362/2015, p. 195.

Unnikrishnan, JP v. State of A.P, AIR 1993 SC 2178, p. 55.

Upendra Baxi v. State of Uttar Pradesh (1983) 2 SCC 308, p. 245.

Veena Sethi v. Union of India, AIR 1983 SC 339, p. 246.

Velusamy v. State, 1985 Cr. L.J 1981, p. 125.

*Vincent Panikurlangara v. Union of India, (*1987) 2 SCC 165, p. 21.

Vincent Panikurlangara v. Union of India, AIR 1987 SC 990, p. 21.

Virendra Gaur v. State of Haryana, 1995 (2) SCC 577, p. 55.

Voluntary Health Association of India v. UOI, WP(C) 349/2006, p. 218.

Wake v. Northern Territory, (1996), 109 NTR 1, p. 233.

Washington v. Glucksberg, 521 U.S.702,117 S.Ct. 2258 (1997), p. 235.

1

Concept of Health

Right To Health: A Human Right Perspective

Dr. Liji Samuel

Abstract

Various international and national instruments have encapsulated the much celebrated words the 'right to highest attainable standards of health and wellbeing'. But still people in both developed and developing countries die either because of unavailability or inaccessibility of health care. The inadequate Government resources and mushrooming growth of private health care sector are major hurdles in the way of realizing right to health. There is no right based approach in preparing and implementing health policies in many States including in India. A right based approach on health only ensures availability, accessibility, acceptability and quality.

Keyword: *right to health, fundamental right to health, obligations of the State.*

INTRODUCTION

Good health and its natural corollary defence against illness are fundamental to everyone, not only for their well – being, but also for their very survival. It assumes the highest value in every society because it is an important contributor to productivity and economic growth of a country. Right to health is a judicially recognized human right in India and this brings the State under the obligation to provide adequate measures for protecting and promoting the health of people.

Health has a wide variety of meanings and the concept of health varies in accordance with the opinion of experts from different disciplines. Though there is a conceptual conflict on health, the health of people is determined by multitude of factors like physical, environmental, political, cultural, family and individual factors. But the very concept of health has undergone drastic change in the wake LPG programmes and the market economy is trying to redefine the scope and ambit of human right to health. In this juncture this paper tries to analyze the basic concepts and norms relating to health and also intends to point out the legal content of right to health and basic obligations of State in implementing right to health.

MEANING OF HEALTH

Health, which is the derivation of old English '*hoelth*' and '*hale*'[1] simply means soundness and strength. But it is difficult to define health precisely by synchronizing different aspects and perspectives on health

Health has a wide variety of meanings ranging from an ideal state to the absence of medically defined and certified disease. The dictionary meaning of health is that 'it is the soundness of body or the condition in which its functions are duly and efficiently discharged'[2]. Health may be defined, negatively and positively. There is also a middle path between these two concepts.

DEFINITION OF HEALTH IN THE NEGATIVE SENSE

In the negative sense health is defined as the absence of 'ill health'. Ill health is a complex notion comprising of disease, illness, handicap, injury and other related ideas[3]. This is the traditional concept of health.

1 Susan Kun Leddy. (2003)Integrative Health Promotion .U.S.A: SLACK Incorporated.

2 Oxford English Dictionary 53(5th ed., 1989).

3 Roger, Detels., Walter, Holland, W., James Mc Ewen., & Gilbert, S. Omenn. (1997) Oxford Textbook of Public Health .New York :Oxford University Press.

DEFINITION OF HEALTH IN THE POSITIVE SENSE OR POSITIVE HEALTH

Positive definition of health or the concept of positive health is considered to be germinated from the definition given in the preamble to the Constitution of WHO. As per this definition 'health is a state of complete physical, mental and social well – being and not merely the absence of disease or infirmity[4]. This is later amplified to include 'socially and economically productive life'[5]. This is the most widely accepted definition of health and almost all member States of WHO have already adopted it for health policy planning and programming[6].

---

4 Preamble to the Constitution of the World Health Organization 1948.

5 Para V of Declaration of Alma – Ata – International Conference on Primary Health Care, 1978.

6 Criticisms have already been levelled against the concept of positive health put forward by WHO definition and are the following;

- The definition identifies health as a state, although health is not a static entity but a dynamic condition which is ever changing under the influence of multiple factors related to agent, host and environment.
- The definition equates health with well-being, which is by itself an abstract concept. Conventionally, well – being is not only related to health, but also socio-economic achievements of individuals.
- The definition gives a qualitative concept of health and, therefore, does not propose any basis whereby health could be quantified and expressed in concrete mathematical units.
- The definition envisages only three dimensions of health: physical, mental and social. It fails to perceive the moral dimensions of health which is related to soul.
- The definition presents health as a wide spectrum with negative health or absence of disease or infirmity at one end; and positive or complete physical, mental and social well-being, at the other end.
- The definition presents an 'idealistic' rather than a 'realistic' image of health, which is not attainable within the existing means available to man.

Facing the criticism of an unrealistic definition of health the WHO study group devised an operational definition of health. It identifies two dimensions of health: broad and narrow view. In a broader sense, health means the condition or quality of the human organism expressing the adequate functioning of the organism in given conditions, genetic or environmental. In a narrow sense, health means :

DEFINITION OF HEALTH IN TERMS OF FITNESS – THE MIDDLE WAY

The third important definition of health is that it is equal to 'fitness'[7]. The concept of fitness has two aspects: one which is related with the co – relation between heart and lungs and the other is sociological. Here it seems that sociological view deserves more attention and it means people have the necessary health if he is able to perform a job or task adequately. So fitness cannot be classified either in terms of positive health or health in the negative sense because there is no absolute well – being or absence of disease. This is the middle way which encloses the essential conditions for being fit.

MODERN DEFINITION OF HEALTH

In the opinion of many modern market oriented health reformers health is more like a commodity which can be provided or even bought in discrete packages[8]. This definition is the bye product of modern market driven medical care. It clearly negates the concept of health in its very positive sense and the health care services are confined to certain packages of medical care especially curative care and it can be availed only by those who can afford the cost. It is a common phenomenon in most of the countries including in India that millions of people die without proper

---

(*a*) there is no obvious evidence of disease, and that a person is functioning normally, i.e., conforming within normal limits of variation to the standards of health criteria generally accepted for one's age, sex, community and geographic region; and

(*b*) the several organs of the body are functioning adequately in themselves and in relation to one another, which implies a kind of equilibrium or homeostasis – a condition relatively stable but which may vary as human beings adapt to internal and external stimuli.

See, Dhaar, G.M., & Robbani, I.(2006) Foundations of Community Medicine. India: Reed Elsevier India Pvt. Ltd.

7 Supra n. 3.

8 Robert, Beaglehole., & Ruth, Bonita. (2004). Public Health at the Cross Roads – Achievements and Prospects. Cambridge: Cambridge University Press.

health care at the same time the medical tourists avail luxurious medical treatment basically because of the disparity in income.

The modern definition of health is linked with the private health care sector and it considers health as a commodity rather than public good. As far as private health care sector is concerned there is only one category of people or principle, consumers or consumerism.

CHANGING CONCEPTS OF HEALTH

Health is multifaceted and multidimensional[9], and it is not perceived in the same way by all members. In a world of continuous change, new concepts are bound to emerge based on new pattern of thought. Health has evolved over the centuries as a concept from an individual concern to a worldwide social goal and encompasses the whole quality of life[10]. The changing concepts of health can be analyzed by concentrating on seven important areas.

---

9 Physical dimension: It conceptualizes health biologically as a state in which every cell and every organ is functioning at optimum capacity and in perfect harmony with the rest of the body

Mental dimension: It says that mental health is not mere absence of mental disease. Mental health is the ability to respond to the varied experiences of life with flexibility and a sense of purpose.

Social dimension: It is the quantity and quality of an individual's interpersonal ties and the extent of involvement with the community.

Spiritual dimension: It refers to that part of the individual which reaches out and strives for meaning and purpose in life. It is the intangible something that transcends physiology and psychology.

Emotional dimension: Emotional health of a person relates to the feelings of a person.

Other dimensions include: Philosophical dimension, cultural dimension, socioeconomic dimension, environmental dimension, educational dimension, nutritional dimension, Curative dimension and preventive dimension. See, Park, K. (2002) Park's Textbook of Preventive and Social Medicine. India: M/s Banarsidas Bhanot.

See also, Misra, R.P. (2007) Geography of Health – A Treatise on Geography of Life and Death in India. India: Concept Publishing Co.

10 Supra n.9.

BIOMEDICAL CONCEPT

This concept is same as the traditional definition of health that it is the absence of disease and it based on germ theory of disease[11]. So it viewed human body as a machine, disease as the consequence of the breakdown of the machine and the doctor's task is to repair the machine. The germ theory provides the two ways to keep human body disease free: one is to strengthen the immunity of the body so that the germs fail in their mission and the second one is to kill the germs when they attack human body. By adopting this concept the responsibility for health shifted from the individual and community to the physicians, surgeons and hospitals[12].

The other side of this concept is that it ignored the importance of environmental, psychological and cultural aspects of health. The germ theory also faced the criticism of inadequacy, that it is not able to tackle the health problems arising out of malnutrition, mental illness etc.

ECOLOGICAL CONCEPT

According to the opinion of ecologists health is a dynamic equilibrium between man and his environment and disease is the result of maladjustment of the human organism to his environment. Human ecological and cultural adaptations do determine not only the occurrence of disease but also the availability of food and the population explosion[13]. This concept is considered as an answer to the drawbacks of germ theory.

PSYCHOLOGICAL CONCEPT

The psychological concept of health has two dimensions. One is mental health and the other is the approach of patients and their families towards health and diseases. Psychological factors have great bearing on the overall

11 By the middle of the 19th century, the etiology of disease converged on a single factor i.e. Germ. It was widely accepted that when microbes invaded human body, they disturbs the normal functioning of the system causing various kinds of diseases. Modern medicine with its antibiotics, sterilization kits, chemotherapy, and sophisticated techniques of surgery represents further improvements, expansion and application of germ theory. Ibid.

12 *Ibid.*

13 *Ibid.*

health and feeling of being healthy or unhealthy. A good number of people feel sick, without being sick[14].

SOCIOLOGICAL CONCEPT

The sociological concept considers health as a human construct, which exists without someone describing or recognizing it. It does not deny the scientific basis of disease but interprets health in the light of the social realities as exhibited by religion, community, gender, natural, and environment. So health can be considered to be a process with several stages ranging from complete health (ideal) to death (no health)[15].

HOLISTIC CONCEPT

This model is the synthesis of all the above discussed concepts. It recognizes the strength of social, economic, political and environmental influences on health. This view corresponds to the view held by the ancient philosophers that health implies a sound mind, in sound body in sound family, in sound environment. The holistic approach implies that all sectors of society have an effect on health, in particular, agriculture, food, industry, education, housing, public works etc[16]. But it is true that we are missing this link by adhering to new medical model of health.

ECONOMIC CONCEPT

It treats health as a commodity, people should posses because it gives them satisfaction; it enables them to work to their optimum capacity and produces goods and services. Health can be purchased in the market from doctors, hospitals and medical stores. All that is need is to have enough resources. The price one pays for the factors of health such as hospitals, doctors, medicines etc. are determined by the market forces of demand and supply[17].

---

14 *Ibid.*

15 *Ibid.*

16 *Ibid.*

17 *Ibid.*

But this approach is totally antithesis to the basic concept of health. Here the determining factor is the capacity of payment, ignoring all other elements of health. Poor who are, unable meet the demands of modern market medicine or unaware of modern technologies, might be kept away from health care services. Here the goal of health care services would be the maximization of profit and not the universal goal of health for all.

HUMAN RIGHT CONCEPT

Health and human rights are inextricably interrelated. This approach tries to devise health as a basic human right and thereby propagates the idea of indivisibility and universality. The theories of right to health proclaim the inherent rights of human being for their survival and this in turn it makes the Sate to protect and promote the public health.

EVOLUTION OF STATE'S RESPONSIBILITY IN HEALTH CARE

Health for a long time considered as the responsibility of individual and later the burden shifted to the community. State's responsibility evolved mostly as an outcome of extreme necessity of protecting and maintaining the economy and political philosophy of welfare State.

In 17th century, the concept of mercantilism taught that to maximize State power, State had to grow a healthy population. So the health of the people became a key philosophy of the State[18]. Another most important ideology which influenced health and the political state was the philosophy of democratic citizenship. Apart from this the American and French Revolutions asserted new principles regarding the State and health of its subjects[19].

18 Vivek, Neelakantan. Tracing Human Right in Health. Retrieved from www.cehat.org.

19 According to Thomas Jefferson, sick populations were a product of sick political system. He was of firm belief that democracy was the source of people's health. However it was the French Revolutionaries who added health to the Rights of Man and asserted that health citizenship should be the characteristic of a modern democratic State. Ibid.

The role of State and the responsibilities of State may be analyzed in the backdrop of following events:

(*a*) Ensuring the Standard for Protecting Public Health

The concept of public health germinated in Great Britain and later became practice of other democratic countries. The acceptance of the concept of public health and sanitation to a great extent expanded the role of the State as provider.

The industrial revolution resulted in creation of slums, overcrowding of slums, accumulation of filth in cities and towns, high sickness and death rates etc. It necessitated the State to control the industrial activities and to promote health[20]. It ended in the enactment of the Public Health Act 1848.

By the enactment of the Public Health Act 1848, in Britain, State for the first time became the guarantor of the standards of health and environmental quality and provided resource to local units of Government to achieve the minimum quality of public health standards[21]. The process of State control continued through enacting various other legislations like Public Health Act,1857, The Sanitary Act 1866 etc. This was the first stage of State interference in health care activities.

(*b*) Organizing and Financing Health Care Systems

The new role of State stems from Germany where an organized health care system for the first time came in to existence. With the ultimate goal of universal coverage, States tried to finance the health care services and to organize public health care systems.

State sponsored health care services developed in all western countries for those who could not afford the cost of health care. In addition to this, insurance schemes were introduced in Europe and United States to protect workers against financial losses. Other European countries also saw the development and expansion of compulsory financial arrangements for

---

20 Afzal Wani, (1998) M. State Responsibility for Health: An Onerous Facing of the Tempest, CULR 22, 45-60.

21 Elizabeth., an & Theodore, Brown. (2005) The Public Health Act of 184, B WHO 83(11) 866-867.

health service, whether through the extension of insurance arrangements for medical care (Bismark Model)[22] or through general taxation (Beveridge Model). After World War II almost all countries including India introduced several social security reforms encompassing medical services. But in most of these countries in addition to pubic health care system, private health care system also plays a vital role in delivering health care services.

(c) Recognizing the Right to Health

By the end of 19th century the international community took up the issue of protecting the public health and the character of health turned global. The first move was started when the International Congresses was inaugurated in Paris in the 1870's[23]. The constant effort of US during the period of 1918 – 1920 in establishing health organization finally ended in the League of Nations Health Organization. Article 23 of the Charter of the Health Organization, clearly provided that the State members of the League shall endeavour to take steps in matters of prevention and control of disease[24].

Later the UN conference held in 1945 at San Francisco explored the possibility of setting up an International Health Organization. Finally World Health Organization came into reality and it ultimately turned the role of State in health care activities. Today it is the solemn duty of state to provide and to ensure equity, efficiency and quality in health care services.

HEALTH AND HUMAN RIGHTS

Human rights are those essential minimum rights that are universal, indivisible, and inherent in every human being. Individuals are entitled to enjoy human rights merely because he is a human being without any kind of discrimination based on caste, sex, place of residence etc.

A right based approach to health is the result of efforts made by the international community in the beginning of 20th century. A right –based approach to health refers to the process of[25]:

---

22 Mersonn, H. , Black, C. & Mills, J. (2001) .International Public Health Disease, Programs, Systems and Policies. U.S.A: Jones and Bartlett Learning.

23 Supra n. 18.

24 *Ibid.*

25 25 questions and Answers on Health and Human Rights.(2002) Retrieved from http://www.who.int/hhr/information/25%20Questions%20and%20Answers%20on%20Health%20and%20Human%20Rights.pdf

- Using human rights as a framework for health development
- Assessing and addressing the human rights implications of any health policy, programme or legislation
- Making human rights an integral dimension of the design, implementation, monitoring and evaluation of health – related policies and programmes in all spheres, including political, economic and social.

LINKAGE BETWEEN HEALTH AND HUMAN RIGHTS

Human rights are generally interdependent and interrelated. Any violation of human right may cause adverse effect on health of people and health is one of the basic qualities necessary for enjoying other human rights. The co–relation between health and human rights may be summed up in the following way[26]:

- Violation or lack of attention to human rights can have serious health consequences (e.g. harmful traditional practices, slavery, torture and inhuman and degrading treatment, violence against women and children).
- Health policies and programmes can promote or violate human rights in their design or implementation (e.g. freedom from discrimination, individual autonomy, rights to participation, privacy and information).
- Vulnerability to ill – health can be reduced by taking steps to respect, protect, and fulfill human rights (e.g. freedom from discrimination on account of race, sex and gender roles, and right to health, food, nutrition, education and housing). The figure give below will give a better understanding as to the interrelation between human rights and right to health.

26 *Ibid.*

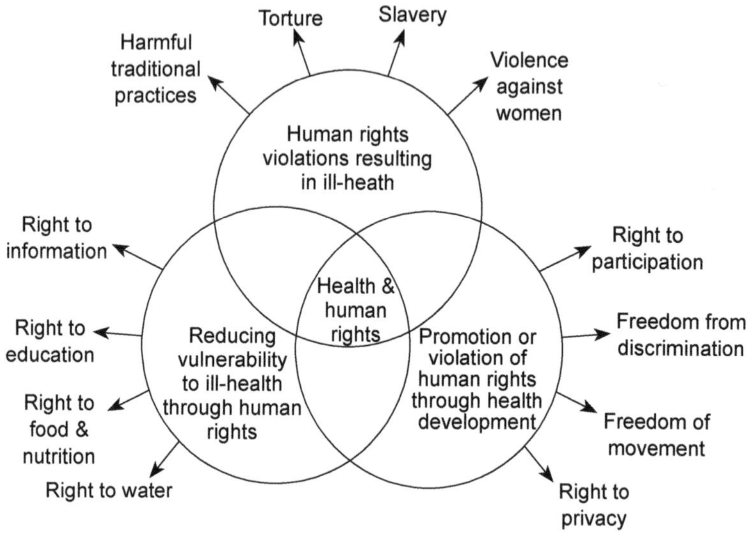

Fig. 1: Linkage between Human Rights and Right to Health

Source*: www.who.int/entity/hhr/HHR%20linkages.pdf*

Even though it gives necessary connection between health and human rights what actually is right to health, its nature and content, whether right to health implies right to be healthy, what is the role of State in ensuring the right to health, all these questions can be answered only by analyzing various international instruments, treaties and declarations.

HUMAN RIGHT TO HEALTH

Though there is no precise definition for right to health, to the minimum it may imply that it is the right of a person to get adequate health care. The earliest attempt to define health was the definition developed by the WHO in its constitution and it observed health in a very positive way[27]. But this has not made any significant contribution in defining right to health beyond what is positive health. But today it is well accepted that it is the right to enjoy the highest attainable standard of health without any discrimination. The right to the highest attainable standard of health in international human rights law is a claim to set social arrangements,

27 Supra n.4.

norms, institutions, laws, and enabling environment that can best secure the enjoyment of this right[28].

Right to health thus means that Governments must generate basic conditions for ensuring the health of people. Such conditions range from ensuring the availability of health services, healthy and safe working conditions, adequate housing and nutritious food etc.

RIGHT TO HEALTH UNDER INTERNATIONAL INSTRUMENTS

Right to health has already formed an important part of various international instruments. The earliest of this was the Universal Declaration of Human Rights, which enshrined the right to a standard of living adequate for health and well – being of every person is a basic human right[29].

The most important interpretation is given by the International Covenant on Economic, Social and Cultural Rights by going a step further by directing the State parties to recognize the right of people to enjoy the highest attainable standard of physical and mental health. It also gives direction to State parties as to the steps to be taken for realizing right to health[30].

Article 5(*e*)(*iv*) of International Convention on the Elimination of All Forms of Discrimination Against Women, 1965 also obligates the State parties to guarantee the right to public health and medical care without any kind of discrimination[31].

Again the Convention on Elimination of All Forms of Discrimination Against Women of 1979 (CEDAW) also direct the State parties to protect the right to health of women and to eliminate the discrimination in health care.[32]

---

28 Supra n.25.

29 Article 25 (1) of the Universal Declaration of Human Rights, 1948.

30 Article 12(1) of International Covenant of Economic, Social and Cultural Rights, 1966.

31 Article 5 (e) of the International Convention on the Elimination of All Forms of Racial Discrimination, 1965.

32 Article 11 (1), 12 & 14(2) of the Convention on Elimination of Discrimination Against Women, 1979.

The Convention on Rights of Child also encapsulates the right to enjoy the highest attainable standard of health and to provide facilities for the treatment of illness and rehabilitation of children[33].

Similarly the Vienna Declaration and Programme of Action 1993 also contain relevant provisions with regard to the protection of health and well–being[34].

The international attempts to realize the goal of human right to health extends over a number other international Conventions[35], Declarations[36] and Conferences including the International Conference on Primary Health Care[37], the United Nations Millennium Declaration and Millennium Development Goals[38].

In addition to these international instruments some regional instruments are also guaranteeing the right to health. It includes the American Declaration of the Rights and Duties of Men, 1948[39] European Social Charter 1961[40], the African Charter on Human and Peoples' Rights of 1981[41], and Additional Protocol to the American Convention on Human Rights in the area of Economic, Social and Cultural Rights etc[42].

In addition to all these instruments, Governments have already made commitments at several forums, for ensuring right to health, including the

---

33 Article 24(1) of the Convention on Right of Child, 1989.

34 Para 31 of the Vienna Declaration and Programme of Action 1993.

35 Article 28, 43 (c) & 45 (c) of the International convention on the Protection of the Rights of all Migrant Workers and Members of their families, 1990.

Article 25 of the Convention on the Rights of Persons with Disabilities, 2006.

36 Declaration on the Rights of Disabled Persons (1975), Declaration on the Right to Development (1986), Universal Declaration on the Human Genome and Human Rights (1997).

37 Declaration of Alma – Ata – International Conference on Primary Health Care, 1978.

38 The UN Millennium Development Goals (MDGs), 2000.

39 Article 11 of the American Declaration the Rights and Duties of Men, 1948.

40 Art.11 of the European Social Charter, 1961.

41 Article 16 of the African Charter on Human and Peoples' Rights, 1981.

42 Article 10 of the Additional Protocol to the American Convention on Human Rights in the area of Economic, Social and Cultural Rights, 1988.

Earth Summit in Rio[43], the International Conference on Population and Development in Cairo[44], the World Summit for Social Development in Copenhagen[45], the Habitat II conference in Istanbul[46].

The right to health has already been recognized by the most of the State parties and others have recognized it either by ratifying the regional arrangements or by incorporating it in their respective Constitutions.

NATURE AND LEGAL CONTENT OF RIGHT TO HEALTH

The most authoritative interpretation as to the nature and legal content of right to health is given by the Committee on Economic, Social and Cultural Rights in its General Comment No. 14. It gives the following ideals with regard to right to health.

(*a*) Right to health is an inclusive right

Right to health is an inclusive right extending not only to timely and appropriate health care but also to the underlying determinants of health, such as access to safe and potable water and adequate sanitation, adequate supply of safe food, nutrition, housing, healthy occupational and environmental conditions, and access to health related education and information[47].

(*b*) The right to health contains freedoms

These freedoms include the right to control one's health and body, and the right to be free from interference, such as the right to be free from torture, non–consensual medical treatment and experiment[48].

43 The United Nations Conference on Environment and Development, 1992.

44 The International conference on Population and Development, 1994.

45 The World Summit for Social Development Copenhagen, 1995.

46 The Habitat Agenda Goals and Principles, Commitments and the Global Plan of Action, 1996.

47 Para 11 of General Comment No.14, UN Committee on Economic, Social and Cultural Rights, 2000.

48 Para 8 of General Comment No.14, UN Committee on Economic, Social and Cultural Rights, 2000

(*c*) The right to health contains entitlements

The entitlements include the right to a system of health protection which provides equality of opportunity for people to enjoy the highest attainable level of health[49].

ESSENTIAL ELEMENTS OF RIGHT TO HEALTH

Right to health in all forms and at all level encompasses the following interrelated and essential elements[50].

(*a*) **Availability**: Public health and health care facilities, goods and services, as well as programmes, have to be available in sufficient quantity within the State party.

(*b*) **Accessibility**: Health facilities, goods and services have to be accessible to everyone without any discrimination and it should be within the safe reach of every one. Accessibility has four overlapping dimensions such as;

- Non–discrimination[51]
- Physical accessibility[52]
- Economic accessibility[53]

---

49 *Ibid.*

50 Para 12 of General Comment No.14, UN Committee on Economic, Social and Cultural Rights, 2000

51 Non–discrimination: Health facilities, goods and services must be accessible to all, especially the most vulnerable or marginalized sections of the population, without discrimination.

52 Physical accessibility: Health facilities, goods and services must be within the safe and physical reach for all sections of the population, especially vulnerable or marginalized groups, such as ethnic minorities and indigenous population, women, children, adolescents, older persons, persons with disability and persons with HIV/AIDS.

53 Economic accessibility: Health facilities, goods and services must be affordable to all. Payment for health care services, as well as services related to the underlying determinants of health, has to be based on the principle of equity, ensuring that these services, whether privately or publicly provided, are affordable to all, including the socially disadvantaged groups. Equity demands that poorer households should not be disproportionately burdened with health expenses as compared to richer households.

- Information accessibility[54]

(*c*) **Acceptability**: All health facilities, goods and services should respect medical ethics, and be gender – sensitive and culturally appropriate and it should also be designed to respect confidentiality and improve the health status of those concerned.

(*d*) **Quality**: Health facilities, goods and services should also be scientifically and medically appropriate and of good quality. So it requires skilled medical personnel, scientifically approved and unexpired drugs and hospitals equipments, safe and potable water and adequate sanitation.

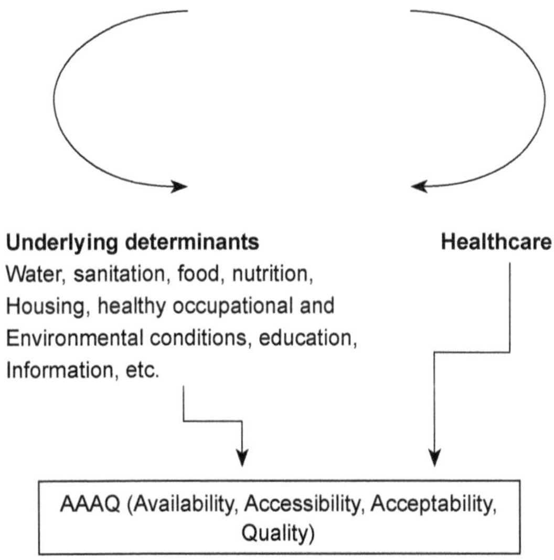

Fig. 2: Elements of Right to Health

Source: http://www.who.int/mediacentre/factsheets/fs323_en.pdf

ROLE OF STATE–GENERAL AND SPECIFIC LEGAL OBLIGATIONS

The Committee on Economic, Social and Cultural Rights has also chalked out the general and specific legal obligation of State parties.

54 Information Accessibility: It includes the right to seek, receive and impart information and ideas concerning health issues. However, accessibility of information should not impair the right to have personal health data treated with confidentiality.

(*a*) General Legal Obligation

The general legal obligation of State parties is clearly enshrined in the ICESCR that to progressively achieve the full realization of right to health and to guarantee the right without any discrimination[55]. This is an implicit recognition that States have resource constraints and that it necessarily takes times to implement the treaty provisions[56].

Here again the General Comment is relevant because it clearly provides that the progressive realization of right to health should not be interpreted as depriving State parties' obligation of all meaningful content. Rather, progressive realization means that State parties have a specific and continuing obligation to move as expeditiously and effectively as possible towards the full realization of Article 12[57].

In addition to that the Committee on Economic, Social and Cultural Right had also prescribed certain core minimum obligation to ensure the satisfaction of minimum essential levels of right health. So the State parties must ensure[58];

(*a*) The right of access to health facilities, goods and services on a non–discriminatory basis, especially for vulnerable or marginalized groups,

(*b*) Access to the minimum essential food which is nutritionally adequate and safe,

(*c*) Access to shelter, housing and sanitation and an adequate supply of safe drinking water,

(*d*) The provision of essential drugs,

(*e*) Equitable distribution of all health facilities, goods and services.

---

55 Article 2 (1) of the International Covenant of Economic, Social and Cultural Rights.

56 The Right to Health, *Fact Sheet No.31*, World Health Organization. Retrieved from http://www.ohchr.org/Documents/Publications/Factsheet31.pdf.

57 *Para 31 of General Comment No.14,* UN Committee on Economic, Social and Cultural Rights, 2000.

58 *Para 43 of General Comment No.14,* UN Committee on Economic, Social and Cultural Rights, 2000.

(*b*) Specific Legal Obligations

The obligation to respect, protect and fulfill are the three specific legal obligations of the State.

- **Obligation to respect**: requires the State to refrain from carrying out, or tolerating any violation of the right to health either directly or indirectly[59].
- **Obligation to protect**: requires the State parties to take legislative and other measures to ensure the equal access to health care and to ensure that the non – state actors are not violating the basic premises of right to health. [60]. So here the role of State is that of a protector and regulator of non – state actors.
- **Obligation to fulfill**: requires the State parties to give sufficient recognition to the right to health in the national political and legal systems, provision for health care, and to ensure equal access to underlying determinants of health[61]. Here the State's role is much larger and is bound to act as provider, promoter and facilitator of health to all people[62].

(*c*) Violation of Right to Health

The violation of right to health may occur in various ways and are given below[63]:

59 *Para 34* of *General Comment No. 14,* UN Committee on Economic, Social and Cultural Rights, 2000.

60 *Para 35* of *General comment No. 14,* UN Committee on Economic, Social and Cultural Rights, 2000.

61 Para 36 of General Comment No. 14 UN Committee on Economic, Social and Cultural Rights, 2000.

62 The obligation to fulfill necessarily involves:

Obligation to facilitate: State must take measures that enable and assist individuals and communities to enjoy the right to health.

Obligation to provide: State parties are obliged to a specific right contained in the covenant when individuals or a group are unable to realize that right.

Obligation to promote: State must undertake actions that create, maintain and restore the health of the population. See, *Para 37 of General Comment No.14,* UN Committee on Economic, Social and Cultural Rights, 2000.

63 *Para 46 – 52 of General Comment. No.14,* UN Committee on Economic, Social and Cultural Rights, 2000.

- Unwillingness to use the maximum of its available resources for the realization of right to health amounts to violation of its obligation under Art. 12 of ICESCR. If the State is having any resource constraints it has to prove that every effort has been made to use all available resources to at its disposal in order to satisfy, as a matter of priority the obligations. But the State parties cannot under any circumstances justify its non-compliance with the core obligations, which are non-derogable.
- Direct action of States or other entities insufficiently regulated by States.
- Adopting any retrogressive measures incompatible with the core obligation under the right to health, outlined in the General Comments.
- Violation through act of commission include the formal repeal or suspension of legislation necessary for the continued enjoyment of the right to health or the adoption of legislation or policies which are manifestly incompatible with pre-existing domestic or international legal obligations in relation to the right to health.
- Violation through act of omission include the failure to take appropriate steps towards the full realization of everyone's right to the enjoyment of the highest attainable standard of physical and mental health.
- Violation of the obligation to respect, protect and fulfill[64] also amounts to the violation of right to health.

---

64 Violation of the obligation to respect are those State actions, policies or laws that contravene the standards set out in Article 12 of the Covenant and are likely to result in bodily harm, unnecessary morbidity and preventable mortality.

Violation of the obligation to protect follow from the failure of a State to take all necessary measures to safeguard person within their jurisdiction from infringements of the right to health by third parties.

Violation of the obligation to fulfill occurs through the failure of State parties to take all necessary steps to ensure the realization of the right to health.

See, *Para.50, 51&52 of General Comment No.14,* UN Committee on Economic, Social and Cultural Rights, 2000.

RIGHT TO HEALTH IN INDIA

Right to health is a judicially recognized fundamental right in India[65]. The part IV of the Indian Constitution gives directives to the State to take necessary measures to protect the health of women, children, infants etc, and it also makes the State responsible for improving the public health of people[66]. Since the principles incorporated in Part IV of the Constitution are directive in nature, a provision was included in the Draft National Health Policy 2015 for recognizing right to health as a fundamental right by enacting the National Health Rights Act. However the National Health Policy, 2017 has not proposed health as fundamental right.

Though the Central and Sate Government have taken many steps to implement the Directive Principles of Sate Policy incorporated in the Indian Constitution, through various disease control programmes, health care provisioning through Government medical institutions, health insurance schemes etc, thousands of people are being denied of their basic health care services. The draft National Health Policy 2015 stated that all the disease conditions for which national programmes provide universal coverage account for less than 10% of all mortalities and only for about 15% of all morbidities. Over 75% of communicable diseases are not part of existing national programmes[67]. In India there occurred a large scale growth of private health care sector. The private health care industry is valued at $40 billion and is projected to grow to $280 billion by 2020[68]. On the other side, the public spending on health is very less as compared

---

65 *Vincent Panikurlangara* v. *Union of India (*1987) 2 SCC 165, *Consumer Education and Research Centre* v. *Union of India* (1995) 3 SCC 42, *Paschim banga Khet Mazdoor Samiti* v. *State of W.B* A.I.R 1996 SC 2426, *State of Punjab* v. *Ram Lubhaya Bagga* A.I.R (1998) 4 SCC 117, *Common Cause* v. *Union of India* A.I.R 1999 SC 925, *Confederation of Ex.serviceman Association and Ors* v. *Union of India & Ors* A.I.R 2006 SC 2945, *R.D Upadhyay* v. *State of Andhra Pradesh & ors* A.I.R 2006 SC 1946, Pratap Kumar Nayak v. State of Orissa &Ors. A.I.R 2012 Ori. 53.

66 Articles 38, 39 (e), 41, 42, 47 48A of the Constitution of India.

67 Para 2.8 of the Draft National Health Policy 2015

68 Para 2.12 of the Draft National Health Policy 2015

to other countries and it is reported that 1.4% of GDP. It also a sad state of fact that about 63 million people are in debt due to health expenditure and nearly a third of population is driven below the property line due to health expenses[69]. When we compare health care service the shocking fact is India is having the lowest number of beds and physicians compared with the population. About 75% of dispensaries and 60% of hospitals are in urban area and 85% of doctors are in urban area treating 28% of population. In rural India, Only 37% people have access to In-Patient Department within a five kilometres distance[70]. These critical issues reaffirm the need of maintaining a right based approach in preparing and implementing the Government policies. But unfortunately in India, though a signatory to many of International Conventions, a right based approach to ensure the right to health in its full spirit is lacking.

CONCLUSION

While perusing the international instruments, it becomes clear that the right to health depends upon the realization of various determinants of health along with the provision for health care. However by the end of 20th century, the neo – liberal ideals to a great extend circumscribed the welfare activities of the State. In developing countries including India, people are denied of their basic essentials such as adequate and safe drinking water, food, sanitation, housing etc. All these essentials are the key determinants of good health. As far as health care is concerned, millions of people are denied of quality health care. In middle and high – Income countries, health care system struggle with widening disparities in health and health care consumption; uncontrolled rises in health care costs; profit – driven inefficiencies, and a deterioration in trust between citizens and providers[71].

69 Report on Healthcare Access Initiative, OPPI- KPMP, 2016.

70 *Ibid.*

71 The *Global Health Watch 2005 – 2006 – An alternative World Health Report 55*(First published in 2005) (Zen Books Ltd.).

Health care systems are now moving towards passive privatization mainly because of uncontrolled growth of private health care sector, public sector downsizing, migration of public health professionals to the private sector etc. The ascendance of neoliberalism added an ideological impetus to the privatization of health care. More recently, the World Trade Organization, together with a number of bilateral and regional trade agreements, have influenced the design of health care systems by reducing the capacity of Governments to regulate health care markets, encouraging cross border 'trade' in health care, and facilitating the entry of corporate health business to operate more freely within health care systems of other countries[72].

Thus State are violating the basic right to health of people in two ways that the failure of State both as provider and as a regulator of private health care sector that ultimately lead to the gross violation of essential elements of right to health. The availability, accessibility, affordability and quality of health care services deserve immediate attention in wake of growing private sector participation.

---

72 *Ibid.*

Right To Health: Human Right, Constitutional Right & International Perspective

Dr. Bhavana Sharma

Abstract

The right to health care is an age-old phenomenon. It is said that 'Health is Wealth' and a healthy body is the very foundation of all human activities. Life of individual is a nature's gift to whole mankind, which is to be preserved, protected and prospered. Although, right to health has not been directly given as a separate fundamental right under the Indian Constitution. But the Preamble and other Provisions of the Constitution of India establishes India as socialistic and welfare state. The basic frame work of socialism is to provide a. decent standard of life to the working people and especially provide security from cradle to grave. Recently Right to Health has been interpreted and incorporated a fundamental right under Right to Life and Personal Liberty of the Indian Constitution and hence this right having now acquired a constitutional status through judicial activism, can be judicially enforced[1]*. Right to Life is, in fact, dependent upon the health of an individual. In other words, right to health is a prerequisite of right to life and live with human dignity. Universal achievement of 'Health for All' has gained importance among nations of the world, as health is declared to be an essential part of right to life.*

This Chapter is divided into parts:-

(1) Concept of Health,

(2) Meaning Of Right to Health,

(3) Right to Health As A Human Right,

1 Right to Health : Limits of Recognition, http://www.nliu.com/anl.htm

(4) Right to health As A Constitutional Right

(5) Right to health As A Fundamental Right

(6) National Health Policy

CONCEPT OF HEALTH

The right to health care is an age-old phenomenon. It is said that 'Health is Wealth' and a healthy body is the very foundation of all human activities. Life of individual is a nature's gift to whole mankind, which is to be preserved, protected and prospered. Although, right to health has not been directly given as a separate fundamental right under the Indian Constitution. But the Preamble and other Provisions of the Constitution of India establishes India as socialistic and welfare state. The basic frame work of socialism is to provide a. decent standard of life to the working people and especially provide security from cradle to grave.[2]

Recently Right to Health has been interpreted and incorporated a fundamental right under Right to Life and Personal Liberty of the Indian Constitution and hence this right having now acquired a constitutional status through judicial activism, can be judicially enforced.[3] Right to Life is, in fact, dependent upon the health of an individual. In other words, right to health is a prerequisite of right to life and lives with human dignity. Universal achievement of 'Health for All' has gained importance among nations of the world, as health is declared to be an essential part of right to life. The Constitution of India not only provides for the health care of the people but also directs the State to take measures to improve the condition of health care rights of the people.[4] . These Directives Principles of State Policy direct the government to promote health of all people in general and vulnerable sections of the society in particular.

---

2 D.S. Nakara V Union of India 1983AIR130.

3 Right to Health : Limits of Recognition, http://www.nliu.com/anl.htm

4 Articles 39 and 47.

MEANING OF RIGHT TO HEALTH

Right to health includes a wide range of factors that can help us lead a healthy life. The Committee on Economic, Social and Cultural Rights, the body responsible for monitoring the International Covenant on Economic, Social and Cultural Rights[5], calls these the "underlying determinants of health". They include:

- Safe drinking water and adequate sanitation
- Safe food
- Adequate nutrition and housing
- Healthy working and environmental conditions
- Health-related education and information
- The right to health contains freedoms from non-consensual medical treatment and torture, other cruel, inhuman, degrading treatment or punishment.
- The right to health contains the right to a system of health protection providing equality of opportunity for everyone to enjoy the highest attainable level of health which includes access to essential medicines.
- Maternal, child and reproductive health
- Equal and timely access to basic health services
- Health services, goods and facilities must be provided to all without any discrimination.
- The facilities, goods and services should also respect medical ethics, and be gender-sensitive and culturally appropriate. In other words, they should be medically and culturally acceptable.
- Finally, they must be scientifically and medically appropriate

5 The Covenant was adopted by the United Nations General Assembly in its resolution 2200A (XXI) of 16 December 1966. It entered into force in 1976 and by 1 December 2007 had been ratified by 157 States.

and of good quality. This requires, in particular, trained health professionals, scientifically approved and unexpired drugs and hospital equipment, adequate sanitation and safe drinking water

RIGHT TO HEALTH AS A HUMAN RIGHT

The right to the highest attainable standard of health is a human right recognized in international human rights law. The International Covenant on Economic, Social and Cultural Rights, widely considered as the central instrument of protection for the right to health, recognizes "the right of everyone to the enjoyment of the highest attainable standard of physical and mental health." It is important to note that the Covenant gives both mental health (which has often been neglected), and physical health equal consideration.

International Covenant on Economic, Social and Cultural Rights (Article 12)

1. The States Parties to the present Covenant recognize the right of everyone to the enjoyment of the highest attainable standard of physical and mental health.
2. The steps to be taken by the States Parties to the present Covenant to achieve the full realization of this right shall include those necessary for:
   - (*a*) The provision for the reduction of the birth rate and of infant mortality and for the healthy development of the child
   - (*b*) The improvement of all aspects of environmental and industrial hygiene
   - (*c*) The prevention, treatment and control of epidemic, endemic, occupational and other diseases
   - (*d*) The creation of conditions which would assure to all medical service and medical attention in the event of sickness.

Subsequent international and regional human rights instruments address the right to health in various ways. Some are of general application while others address the human rights of groups, such as women or children. Motherhood and childhood are entitled to special care and assistances.[6]

Article 25 of the Universal Declaration of Human Rights, 1948 provides that "everyone has the right to a standard of living adequate for the health and well-being of himself and of his family, including food, clothing, housing and medical care and necessary social services and the right to security in the event of unemployment, sickness, disability, widowhood, old age or other lack of livelihood in circumstances beyond his control."

Similarly, Article 11 of the International Covenant on Economic, Social and Cultural Rights stipulates that "the States parties to the present covenant recognize the right of everyone to an adequate standard of living for himself and his family, including adequate food, clothing and housing, and to the continuous improvement of living conditions. And that recognizing the fundamental right to everyone to be free from hunger, they shall take the measures, for securing these rights."

International human rights treaties recognizing the right to health

- The 1965 International Convention on the Elimination of All Forms of Racial Discrimination: Article 5 (*e*) (*iv*)
- The 1966 International Covenant on Economic, Social and Cultural Rights[7]
- The 1979 Convention on the Elimination of All Forms of Discrimination against Women[8]
- The 1989 Convention on the Rights of the Child[9]
- The 1990 International Convention on the Protection of the Rights of All Migrant Workers and Members of their families[10]

6 See Article 25 of Universal Declaration of Human Rights, 1948.

7 Article 12.

8 Articles 11 (1) (f), 12 and 14 (2) (b).

9 Article 24.

10 Articles 28, 43 (e) and 45 (c).

- The 2006 Convention on the Rights of Persons with Disabilities[11]

In addition, the treaty bodies that monitor the International Covenant on Economic, Social and Cultural Rights, the Convention on the Elimination of All Forms of Discrimination against Women and the Convention on the Rights of the Child have adopted general comments or general recommendations on the right to health and health-related issues. These provide an authoritative and detailed interpretation of the provisions found in the treaties. Numerous conferences and declarations, such as the International Conference on Primary Health Care (resulting in the Declaration of Alma-Ata)[12], the United Nations Millennium Declaration and Millennium Development Goals[13], and the Declaration of Commitment on HIV/AIDS[14] , have also helped clarify various aspects of public health relevant to the right to health and have reaffirmed commitments to its realization.

RIGHT TO HEALTH AS A CONSTITUTIONAL RIGHT

Constitutional law is the Supreme law of a nation which prescribes fundamental principles to regulate the relations of government and its citizens, and also prescribed procedure according to which the public affairs of the nation are to be administered. The Constitution also provides certain rights and freedoms, which could also be enjoyed within the reasonable limits of the Constitution.

11 Article 25.

12 Declaration of Alma-Ata, International Conference on Primary Health Care, Alma-Ata, USSR, September 1978.

13 See http://www.un.org/millenniumgoals.

14 General Assembly resolution S-26/2 of 27 July 2001.

RIGHT TO HEALTH AND INDIAN CONSTITUTION

Articles 38[15], 39(a)[16] (d)[17] (e)[18] & (f)[19], 41[20], 42[21], 47[22] and 48 A[23] of the Constitution of India cast the obligation on the State to ensure the creation and the sustaining of conditions congenial to good health. Though the Constitution of India does not confer an enforceable fundamental right to medical assistance to have better health on its citizens but under Part IV, Article 47 imposes a primary duty upon the State to raise the level of nutrition and the standard of living and to improve public health. The mode of Improving public health has also not been explicitly mentioned in the Constitution, the Court by the harmonious construction of fundamental rights and the Directive Principles has prescribed the modality of access to medical treatment.[24]

Article 243 G falls under Part IX of the Constitution labeled, "The Panchayats". Part IX was inserted by "The Constitution (73rd Amendment) Act, 1992 and became effective on April 24, 1993. Article 243 G states that the legislature of a State may endow the Panchayats with necessary

15 social order to promote the welfare of the people.

16 that the citizens, men and women equally, have the right to an adequate means to livelihood.

17 that there is equal pay for equal work for both men and women.

18 that the health and strength of workers, even men and women and the tender age of children are not abused and that citizens are not forced by economic necessity to enter avocations unsuited to their age or strength.

19 children are given opportunities and facilities to develop in a healthy manner and in conditions of freedom and dignity and that youth are protected against exploitation and against moral and material abandonment.

20 The state shall, within the limits of its economic capacity and development, make effective provisions for securing the right to work, to education and to public assistance in case of undeserved want".

21 the State shall make provision for securing just and humane conditions of work and for maternity relief."

22 State shall regard the raising of the level of nutrition and the standard of living of its people and the improvement of public health.

23 the State's duty to protect the environment as inserted by 42nd Amendment Act 1976.

24 C. Manickam & S. Sajith, "Right to Health and Access to Medical Treatment under the Indian Constitution", AIR (1997), Journal Section, p. 104.

power and authority in relation to matters listed in the Seventh Schedule. Under entry six of the State list of Seventh Schedule the State legislature is empowered to make laws with respect to public health and sanitation, hospitals and dispensaries. Entry fifty-two of Union list of the Seventh Schedule to the Constitution allows Parliament to make laws relating to industries in the public interest.

The entries in this Schedule having direct connection to health are as follows:

1. Drinking water (entry 11)
2. Health and Sanitation, including hospitals, primary health centers and dispensaries (entry 23)
3. Family Welfare (entry 24)
4. Women and Child Development (entry 25)
5. Social Welfare, including Welfare of the handicapped and mentally retarded (entry 26)

Article 243-W finds place in Part IX A of the Constitution titled "The Municipalities". It was inserted by the Constitution (74" Amendment) Act, 1992. Article 243-W provides the power, authority and responsibilities of municipalities. Article 243 W provides that the legislature of a State, subject to the provisions of the Constitution, may by law endow -

(*a*) the Municipalities with such power and authority as may be necessary to enable them to Function as institutions of self-government and such law may contain provision for the devolution of powers and responsibilities upon Municipalities, subject to such conditions as may be specified therein, with respect to -

(*i*) the preparation of plans for economic development and social justice;

(*ii*) the performance of functions and the implementation of schemes as may be entrusted to them including those in relation to the matters listed in the Twelfth Schedule.

(*b*) the committees with such powers and authority as may be necessary to enable them to carry out the responsibilities conferred upon them including those in relation to the matters listed in Twelfth Schedule

The entries in this Schedule having direct relevance to health are listed below:

1. Water supply for domestic, industrial and commercial purposes (entry 5)
2. Public health, sanitation conservancy and solid waste management (entry 6)
3. Safeguarding the interests of weaker sections of society, including the handicapped and mentally retarded (entry 9)
4. Vital statistics including registration of births and deaths (entry 16)
5. Regulation of slaughter-houses and tanneries (entry 18)

RIGHT TO HEALTH AS A FUNDAMENTAL RIGHT

Regarding 'Right to Health' many have argued that the phrase, it is inaccurate and misleading, because everyone cannot be assured good or perfect health.[25] However, as health is the optimum state of body and mind, the right to health can be interpreted to mean a right to the highest attainable standards of physical and mental health, and equal access of every human being to medical care facilities as well as to living conditions conductive to the maintenance of good health. The right to health has been defined as "Every woman, man, youth and child has the human right to the highest attainable standards of physical and mental health, without discrimination of any kind. Enjoyment of the human right to health is vital to all aspects of a person's life and well being and is crucial to the realization of many other fundamental human rights and freedoms.[26]

In India, the right to health and protection has been recognized since early times. India is a founder member of the United Nations and it ratified various international conventions[27] promising to secure health rights of individuals in society. In this context, Article 51A of the Constitution of India provides for promotion of international peace and security.

---

25 Malika Ramachandran, "The Right to Health and the Indian Constitution" 1 *DLR (S)*. 2004.

26 Vernellia Randall, http://www.academic.udavton.edu/health/07 Human Rights/ health/health.htm.

27 M.C. Gupta, Health and Law, (2002), p.vii

According to Article 21 of Indian Constitution "No person shall be deprived of his right to life and personal liberty except according to procedure established by law." Though it does not expressly contain the right to health, it has now been well settled through a series of cases that Right to life also includes the right to health.

The Courts in India have played a significant role in realization of the right to health by recognizing it as a part of the fundamental right to life and issued suitable directions to the State authorities for fulfillment of their duties. They have also provided redressal by meaningful and just interpretation to the right to life and commanding enforcement of the duties of a welfare state.

A new facet was given in *Maneka Gandhi v. Union of India*[28] when, by its interpretation, the Supreme Court changed the scenario from one that calls for procedural rights to one that provides for substantial rights. While constitutional zing these substantive rights with the aid of Article 21, the Supreme Court has drawn support from the International Convention on Human Rights. Now the State is mandated to provide to a person ail rights essential for the enjoyment of the right to life in Its various perspectives. Of late, the right to health and access to medical treatment has been Included In the plethora of rights brought under the ambit of Article 21.

The Supreme Court In its path-breaking judgment in *Bandhua Mukti Morcha v. Union of India,*[29] has recognized the rights of the workers and their right to basic health facilities under the Constitution. The right to basic health facilities is also enshrined under the International Conventions to which India is a party.

In *Vincent Panikurlangara v. Union of India*[30] held that a healthy body is the very foundation for all human activities, in a welfare state, therefore, it is the obligation of the State to ensure the creation and the sustaining of conditions congenial to good health. The Court also observed that the maintenance and improvement of public health have to rank high as these

---

28 AIR 1978 SC 597.

29 AIR 1984 SC 802.

30 AIR 1987 SC 990.

are indispensable to the very physical existence of the community, and on the betterment of these, depends the building of society of which the Constitution makers envisaged.

In this case, the petitioner had sought directions from the Supreme Court for banning the import, manufacture, sale and distribution of drugs recommended for a ban by the Drugs Consultative Committee, and for cancellation of all licenses authorizing all such drugs. The Court observed: "The branch of health care of citizens involves an ever changing challenge. The problem is a shifting one and one cannot have a fixed process to deal with such situations that would arise from time to time."

The Supreme Court has also brought occupational health hazards to workers within the coverage of Article 21. The right to health and medical care to protect the health and vigor of a worker while in service or post-retirement has been held to be fundamental right under Article 21 read with the directive principles contained in Articles 39(e), 41, 43, and 47 and all fundamental human rights to make the life of workers meaningful and purposeful, with dignity of person. The Court in Vincent has directed the Central Government to compensate and reimburse the petitioner for the expenses of his recognition of his services for asking directions for maintenance of approved standard of drugs and banning of injurious and harmful drugs. The Court further observed that attending to public health is of high priority-perhaps the one at the top.

In *A.S. Mittal & Ors. v State of Uttar Pradesh & Ors.*[31] the Supreme Court, while dealing with a public interest litigation under Article 32 of the Constitution, alleging negligence on the part of the doctors in providing services at an eye camp organized by the Lions Club, observed that the whole programme at Khurja, however laudable the intentions with which it might have been launched, proved a disastrous medical misadventure for the patients. The operated eyes of the patients were irreversibly damaged owing to a post-operative infection of the intraocular cavities. It is now undisputed that this terrible medical mishap was due to a common contaminating source.

The Court held that a mistake by a medical practitioner, which no reasonably competent and careful practitioner, would have committed, is a negligent

31 AIR 1989 SC 1570.

one. The Indian Medical Council constituted a subcommittee after the above proceedings, and submitted its recommendations before the Court. The Court gave suggestions to the ministry to incorporate these guidelines under the revised guidelines "The operations in the camps should only be performed by qualified experienced ophthalmic Surgeons registered with Medical Council of India or any State Medical Council. There should be a pathologist to examine urine, blood sugar, etc. All medicines to be used should be of standard quality duly verified by the doctor in-charge of the camp.

The Court held that the State government should afford the victims some monetary relief, in addition to the sum of Rs. 5,000 already paid by way of interim relief. The State government was directed to pay a further sum of Rs. 12,500 to each of the victims.

In *Parmananda Katara v. Union of India*[32] Supreme Court extended the scope of Article 21 and held that "It is a professional obligation of all doctors whether government or private to extend medical aid to the injured immediately to preserve life without waiting legal formalities under Cr.P.C.

The Court directed that the decision of the court must be published in all journals and adequate publicity of this aspect should be given by National Media.

In *M/s. Cosmopolitan Hospitals & Anr. v. Smt. Vasantha P. Nair & Ors.*,[33] the Supreme Court reiterated its stand towards the Constitutional Right of an employee, to health and medical aid, and safety from occupational health hazards. It ruled that the employer is obliged to provide protective measures to workmen. Asbestos industries are bound by the directions issued by the International Labour Organization (ILO) in "All Safety in the Use of Asbestos'. It is, therefore, necessary to issue appropriate directions in the light of the rules issued by the ILO and the same shall be binding on all the industries.[34]

It was held that Constitution is the basic law of land from which all other laws derive their authority. The Courts can declare any law or part of law, which violates the Constitution, as ultra vires the Constitution and.

32 (1989) 4 SCC 286.

33 (1992) 1 CPJ 302 (NC).

34 Butterworths, Legal Framework for Health Care in India 24 (2002).

hence, invalid. A very important feature of the Indian Constitution is the fundamental rights guaranteed to every citizen which are listed in Part III of the Constitution. Any citizen whose fundamental rights have been violated can move the Supreme Court or the High Court, praying that the Court may issue a writ to appropriate authority against such violation. The Constitution of India under Articles 32,136, 226, and 227, provides the right to move the Supreme Court or High Courts by appropriate proceedings for the enforcement of the rights conferred and guaranteed under the Constitution.

Any person whose fundamental rights have been infringed can move the Supreme Court under Article 32 of the Constitution. The Court in the recent past has liberalized the traditional private law rule that ' only a person who has suffered injury by reason of violation of his legal right or interest is entitled to seek judicial redress'. The Supreme Court has enlarged the rights of the citizens under this Article, for the purposes of dealing with public law.

In *Nilabati Behera Alias lalit v State of Orissa & ors* [35]Court entertained a letter as a petition and awarded compensation under clause (2) of Article 32 of the Constitution. The Supreme Court shall have the power to issue directions or orders or writs, including writs in the nature of habeas corpus, mandamus, prohibition, quo warranto and certiorari. whichever may be appropriate, for the enforcement of any of the rights conferred by this part.

The Constitution of India under Article 226 provides the right to move the High Court by appropriate proceedings for the enforcement of the rights conferred and guaranteed under the Constitution and other laws.

The Supreme Court of India in a series of cases played a significant role and has awarded compensation to the victims and their families for the violation of right to health and even right to life guaranteed under the Constitution. The Court in realization of the right to health by recognizing it as a part of the fundamental right to life and issued suitable directions to the State authorities for the fulfillment of their duties. Though, the Court in a series of judgments has declared the right to health as a fundamental right .

---

35 1993 AIR 1960.

In *Consumer Education and Research Centre & Ors. v. Union of India*[36] it has been held that right to health and medical care, to protect health and vigor while in service or post-retirement, is a fundamental right of a worker under Right to Life.

This case dealt with the occupational health hazards faced by workers in the asbestos industry. Reading Article 21 with the relevant Directive Principles guaranteed in read Articles 39(e) 41, 43 and 48-A the Supreme Court held that the right to health and medical care is a fundamental right and it makes the life of the workman meaningful and purposeful with the dignity of person. This recognition established a framework for addressing health concerns within the republic of public interest litigation and in a series of subsequent cases, the Court held that it is the obligation of the State not only to provide emergency medical services but also to ensure the creation of conditions necessary for good health, including provisions for basic curative and preventive health services and the assurance of healthy living and working conditions.

The Supreme Court in *Paschim Banga Khet Mazdoor Samity & Ors. V. State of West Bengal & Ors*[37] while widening the scope of Article 21 and the government's responsibility to provide medical aid to every person in the country, held that in a welfare state, the primary duty of the government is to secure the welfare of the people.

It was also held that "The right to health, i.e. the right to the highest attainable standards of physical and mental health and access to health care facilities being an integral part of the right to life, it can be said that the State is under an obligation to safeguard the heath of persons.

The State is bound to provide medical aid and treatment to persons suffering from sickness, injury or disease and if it, through the hospitals and health centers established by it, fails to provide such care, it would be considered as a violation of Article 21. It was also held that denial of medical aid by the government hospital to an injured person on the ground of non – availability of beds amounted to violation of right to life under Article 21.

---

36 1995 AIR 922.

37 1996 AIR SC 2426.

In *Kirloskar Brothers Ltd. v. Employees' State Insurance Corporation*[38] a three judge Bench of the Supreme Court consisting of K. Ramaswamy, S. Saghir Ahmad and G.B. Patnaik, JJ. held that health is a state of complete physical, mental and social well-being and right to health, therefore is a fundamental right of the workmen.

In *State of Punjab and ors. v. Mohinder Singh Chawla etc.*,[39] the respondent, a state employee, had heart ailment. Since the facility of the treatment was not available in the State Hospital of Punjab, permission was given by the Director, with the approval of Medical Board to get treatment outside the State. He was sent for treatment in All India Institute of Medical Sciences (AIIMS) at New Delhi. He submitted his medical bill for reimbursement. While granting reimbursement for the actual expenses incurred, the government rejected his bill for room rent paid to the hospital as inadmissible.

The Supreme Court directed the State Government to pay not only medical expenses incurred by the employee, but also room rent of the hospital.

It was held that it is now well settled that the right to health is integral to the right to life. Government has the constitutional obligation to provide facilities. If a government servant has suffered an ailment which requires treatment therein, it is the duty of the State to bear the expenses incurred by the government servant. Courts have recognized that it may not be possible for the government to provide for sophisticated hospitals in every village in the country. However, the Government has to assist persons to get treatment and at least, primary health centers can be established in villages.

The question of reimbursement of medical treatment of the employees was dealt by the Supreme Court in *State of Punjab v. Ram Lubhaya Bagga* etc[40]. it was held that "Where according to new government policy the employee was given free choice to get treatment in any private hospital in India, but due to financial constraints, the reimbursement was allowed to the level of expenditure as per the rate fixed by the Director, Health and Family Welfare, for a similar treatment package or actual expenditure

---

38 (1996) 2 SCC 682.

39 AIR 1997 SC 1225.

40 1998 AIR SC 1703.

whichever is less, a committee of technical experts was constituted by the Director, Health and Family Welfare to finalize the roles of various treatment packages. No State of any country can have unlimited resources to spend on any of its project. That is why provision of health facilities cannot be unlimited. It has to be the extent finance permit. The principle of fixation of rate and scale under this new policy was justified and cannot be held to be violative of Article 21 or Article 47 of the Constitution of India. The Court also stated that the treatment of a disease in a country abroad would be permitted in extremely rare cases where satisfactory treatment is not available in the country. Prior approval of the State Medical Board shall be a pre-requisite in such cases.

The Supreme Court in *State of Karnataka v. Manjanna*[41]The Court observed: We wish to put on record our disapproval of the refusal of some government doctors, particularly in rural areas, where hospitals are few and far between to conduct any medical examination of a rape victim unless the case of rape is referred to them by the police.

The Court added that such a refusal to conduct the medical examination, necessarily results in a delay in the ultimate examination of victim, by which the evidence of rape may have been washed away by the complainant herself or be otherwise lost. The Court, therefore, directed that the State must ensure that such a situation does not reoccur in future.

In *Murli S. Deora v. Union of India*[42] which was a public interest litigation, the Supreme Court prohibited smoking in public places in the entire country on the grounds that smoking is injurious to the health of passive smokers and issued directions to the Union of India, State Governments as well as the Union Territories to take effective steps to ensure prohibiting smoking in all public places.

In *D.K. Joshi v. Chief Secretary State of Uttar Pradesh and Ors*[43]The Supreme Court had taken notice of the distressing situation of public health in the state of Uttar Pradesh and inaction of the State Government to stop the menace of the unqualified and unregistered medical practitioners proliferating all over the State.

---

41 2000 (6) SCC 188.

42 (2001) 8 SCC 765.

43 AIR 2000 SC 384.

The District Magistrates and District Medical Officer did not take effective steps to stop this menace which is hazardous to human life. The Court directed the Secretary, Health and Family Welfare Department, State of U.P. to take all necessary steps to stop the unqualified and unregistered medical practitioners in carrying on the medical profession, and also directed to the District Magistrates and the Chief Medical Officers to identify such persons within a time limit to fixed by the Secretary, Health and Family Welfare Department. All the District Magistrates and Chief Medical Officers were required to monitor the action taken against such persons. It was also directed that the Secretary, Health and Family Welfare Department should give due publicity to the names of such unqualified/ unregistered medical practitioners so that people do not approach such persons for medical treatment, also issue necessary directions from time to time to these officer so that such unauthorized persons could not pursue their medical profession in the State.

In *Poonam Sharma v. Union of India and Ors*[44] The Delhi High Court held that a citizen of India is entitled to preservation of life not only at the hands of public authorities it will also include hospital authorities.

In *N.D. Jayal & ors. v Union of India*[45], Rajindra Babu, J. of the Supreme Court stated that right to health is a fundamental right under Article 21. Protection to this is inextricably linked with clean and healthy environment itself is a fundamental right.

In *Rajesh Kumar Srivastava v. A.P. Verma*[46] Mr. Sunil Ambwani, J. of the Allahabad High Court held that the fundamental right to profess, practice and propagate religion gets controlled and is subservient to the powers of the State to regulate such practice. No person has a right to make a claim of curing the aliments and to improve health on the basis of his right to freedom of religion. Every form and method of curing and healing must have established procedures, which must be proved by known and accepted methods, and verified and approved by experts in the field of medicines. It is only when a particular form, method or path is accepted by the experts in the field of medicine that It can be permitted

44 AIR 2003 Del. 50

45 2003 Supp (3) SCR 152

46 AIR 2005 All. 175

to be plasticized in public. The right to health included in Article 21 does not come in conflict on overlap with the right to propagate and profess religion. These two are separate and distinct rights. Where the right to health is regulated by validly enacted legislation the right to cure the ailment through religious practices including 'Faith-Healing', cannot be claimed as a fundamental right. The freedom of conscience supplemented by freedom of unhampered expression of free conviction to practice rituals and ceremonies are part of religion or subject to public order, morality and health. There is no conflict between the two. The faith in any religion to practice rituals and observance of such religion is not to be confused with right to conscience and to practice and propagate the religion. The claim to cure ailments falls in the domain of right to health. A person has no right to induce others to believe in his faith in religion to cure others from ailments. The Court held that the propagation, practice and profession of 'faith healing' in public on charging consideration is violative to the Constitutional and Legislative scheme, and that such 'faith healing' based on a person's faith in the religious practices, in public for consideration is not permitted and is violative of the legislations. In the instant case the Lai Mahendra Sewa Shakti Samiti, Kotwa , Allahabad through its members Sri Ajay Pratap Singh had no right to hold congregation in public parks, charge consideration and to profess and practice in public that the chanting of 'Om Namoh Shivai' was cure to all ailments. Such a practice is illegal and violative of law as well as the right of citizen including those innocent persons suffering from various ailments, who participated in such congregation guaranteed under Article 21 of the Constitution of India and which the State and the Court are obliged to protect.

Thus, the learned Judge expressly held that the right to health is regulated by validity enacted legislation. Right to cure ailments through religious practices including 'health healing' could not be claimed as a fundamental right. Professing of 'health healing' in public on charging consideration was violative of constitutional and legislative scheme. The claim to cure ailments falls in the domain of right to health. A person has no right to induce others to believe in his faith in religion to cure others from ailments.

In case of *Confederation of Ex-servicemen Association v. Union of India*[47] a five Judges bench of the Supreme Court held that to get free and full medical care/medical aid is not a fundamental right of ex-servicemen.

The present petition under Article 32 of the Constitution was filed by the confederation of ex-servicemen associations seeking direction to the respondent union of India to recognize the right of full and free medi-care of ex-servicemen, their families and dependents treating such right as one of the fundamental rights guaranteed under the Constitution of India.

Another prayer was made to direct the respondents to take necessary steps to ensure that full and free medi-care was provided to ex-servicemen, their families and dependants on a par with in-service defense personnel. Speaking on behalf of the Court C.K. Thakkar, J. partly allowed the writ petition, and held that to get free and full medical aid/facilities is not a part of the fundamental right of ex-servicemen.

The learned Judge laid down principles regarding medi-care/medical aid to ex-servicemen. The five Judges Bench settled the principles and held that to get free and full medical care is not a fundamental right of ex-servicemen. The learned Judge followed the principles laid down by the apex Court and stated that the right to medical aid is a fundamental right to life and personal liberty under Article 21 of the Constitution, framing of scheme for ex-servicemen and asking them to pay one time contribution is not violative of Part III and Part IV of the Constitution[48].

In case of *Reliance infocom Ltd. v. Chemanchery Grama Panchayat & Ors.*[49] a Division Bench of the Kerala High Court stated that use of mobile phone is a common phenomenon throughout the country and has made drastic changes in the people's life style. Users range from a common man to a multimillionaire and this tiny instrument has revolutionized the medium of communication throughout the world. Constant use of mobile phone, it is reported, may have its own adverse ill effects on human health as well. The question that was posed for consideration in this case was not with regard to ill effects of the use of mobile phones but was not with regard to ill effects of the use of mobile phones but whether installation of

47 (2006) supp (4) SCR 872.

48 The National Human Rights Commission, Annual Report 2001-2002 at pp.58-62

49 AIR 2007 Kerala 33.

mobile base station and its functioning would cause any health hazards to the people who are residing nearby, apprehension- had also been voice that radiation emanating from large telecommunication towers would expose human beings living within the magnetic field to fate deceases like cancer, embryo distribution and changes in DNA structure.

Delivering the judgment of the Court K.S. Radhakrishnan, J. held that RF exposures from mobile base stations are much less than from radio, FM radio and television transmissions and that the consensus of scientific community is that the radiation from Mobile Phone Base Stations is far too low to produce health hazards if people are kept away from direct access to the antenna and the overall evidence indicates that they are unlikely to pose a risk to health. Therefore, it could be concluded that the permission granted for IS installation of Mobile Base Station by the Panchayat would not cause as such any health hazards nor will it affect the fundamental rights guaranteed to citizens under Article 21 of the Constitution. Cancellation of license by the Panchayat based on an apprehension that the radiation may cause health hazards to the people of the locality was therefore not proper. However, court gave a general direction to the TRAI to make periodical inspection to ascertain whether radiation emanated from the. Mobile Base station would cause any health hazards to the people of the locality. It is submitted that the approach of the learned Judge was proper and justified. He made the correct interpretation of the Section 4 of the Telegraph Act (1885) and Article 21 of the Constitution. He stated that installation of Base stations of Mobile Telephone service provider did not cause health hazards to people residing nearby nor infringe fundamental right to life enshrined in Article 21. It can be concluded that permission granted for installation of Mobile Base station by the Panchayat would not cause as such any health hazards nor will it affect the fundamental rights guaranteed to citizens under Article 21 of the Constitution. The Supreme Court, while examining the issue of constitutional right to health care under Article 21, observed that in Article 21 "No person shall be deprived of his life or personal liberty except according to procedure established by law". Thus, right to life is fundamental right guaranteed by the Constitution. But what is the meaning and scope of life and right to life? The Courts have held that "Right to live means something more than 'mere animal existence' and includes the right to live with human dignity and decency"[50]

NATIONAL HEALTH POLICY

The National Health Policy of 1983 and the National Health Policy of 2002 have served well in guiding the approach for the health sector in the Five-Year Plans. Now 14 years after the last health policy, the context has changed in four major ways. First, the health priorities are changing. Although maternal and child mortality have rapidly declined, there is growing burden on account of non communicable diseases and some infectious diseases. The second important change is the emergence of a robust health care industry estimated to be growing at double digit. The third change is the growing incidences of catastrophic expenditure due to health care costs, which are presently estimated to be one of the major contributors to poverty. Fourth, a rising economic growth enables enhanced fiscal capacity. Therefore, a new health policy responsive to these contextual changes is required.

The primary aim of the National Health Policy, 2017, is to inform, clarify, strengthen and prioritize the role of the Government in shaping health systems in all its dimensions- investments in health, organization of healthcare services, prevention of diseases and promotion of good health through cross sectoral actions, access to technologies, developing human resources, encouraging medical pluralism, building knowledge base, developing better financial protection strategies, strengthening regulation and health assurance. NHP 2017 builds on the progress made since the last NHP 2002. The developments have been captured in the document "Backdrop to National Health Policy 2017- Situation Analyses", Ministry of Health & Family Welfare, Government of India.

The Policy recommends prioritizing the role of the Government in shaping health systems in all its dimensions. The roadmap of this new policy is predicated on public spending and provisioning of a public healthcare system that is comprehensive, integrated and accessible to all.

---

50 *Sunil Batra v. Delhi Admn.* AIR 1978 SC 1675

The NHP, 2017 advocates a positive and proactive engagement with the private sector for critical gap filling towards achieving national goals. It envisages private sector collaboration for strategic purchasing, capacity building, skill development programmes, awareness generation, developing sustainable networks for community to strengthen mental health services, and disaster management. The policy also advocates financial and non-incentives for encouraging the private sector participation.

The policy proposes raising public health expenditure to 2.5% of the GDP in a time bound manner. Policy envisages providing larger package of assured comprehensive primary health care through the Health and Wellness Centers'. This policy denotes important change from very selective to comprehensive primary health care package which includes geriatric health care, palliative care and rehabilitative care services. The policy advocates allocating major proportion (upto two-thirds or more) of resources to primary care followed by secondary and tertiary care. The policy aspires to provide at the district level most of the secondary care which is currently provided at a medical college hospital.

The policy assigns specific quantitative targets aimed at reduction of disease prevalence/incidence, for health status and programme impact, health system performance and system strengthening. It seeks to strengthen the health, surveillance system and establish registries for diseases of public health importance, by 2020. It also seeks to align other policies for medical devices and equipment with public health goals.

The broad principles of the policy is centered on Professionalism, Integrity and Ethics, Equity, Affordability, Universality, Patient Centered & Quality of Care, Accountability and pluralism. It seeks to ensure improved access and affordability of quality secondary and tertiary care services through a combination of public hospitals and strategic purchasing in healthcare deficit areas from accredited non-governmental healthcare providers, achieve significant reduction in out of pocket expenditure due to healthcare costs, reinforce trust in public healthcare system and influence operation and growth of private healthcare industry as well as medical technologies in alignment with public health goals.

The policy affirms commitment to pre-emptive care (aimed at pre-empting the occurrence of diseases) to achieve optimum levels of child and adolescent health. The policy envisages school health programmes as a major focus area as also health and hygiene being made a part of the school curriculum.

In order to leverage the pluralistic health care legacy, the policy recommends mainstreaming the different health systems. Towards mainstreaming the potential of AYUSH the policy envisages better access to AYUSH remedies through co-location in public facilities. Yoga would also be introduced much more widely in school and work places as part of promotion of good health. The policy supports voluntary service in rural and under-served areas on pro-bono basis by recognized healthcare professionals under a 'giving back to society' initiative.

The policy advocates extensive deployment of digital tools for improving the efficiency and outcome of the healthcare system and proposes establishment of National Digital Health Authority (NDHA) to regulate, develop and deploy digital health across the continuum of care.

Right To Health and Emergency Health Care

Samuel Molsom

Abstract

Health is a fundamental aspect of every one's life. However, In India, there is no law that deals specifically with the duties of health facilities and personnel to provide medical treatment in emergency cases. The Fundamental Rights and Article 21(Right to Life with Dignity) forms the basis of Right to Health. Fundamental right of the Indian Constitution doesn't directly incorporate the right to health. It is only the Provisions of the directive principles of state policy which somehow shows the relation with public health. In the absence of any specific laws this paper seeks to analyze the constitutional provisions under which the scope of right to health has been extended. It also seeks to provide the Supreme Court judgements where the apex court has time and again by way of judicial interpretation concluded right to health as one of the fundamental rights falling under Article 21 of the Indian Constitution.

INTRODUCTION

The Indian constitution provides a framework for a welfare/socialist pattern of development. While civil and political rights are enshrined as Fundamental Rights that are justiciable, social and economic rights like health, education, and livelihoods etc., are provided for as Directive Principles for the State and hence not justiciable. The latter comes under the domain of planned development which the state steers through the Five years plans and other development policy initiatives.

In India, there is no law that deals specifically with the duties of health facilities and personnel to provide medical treatment in emergency cases.

Emergency health care, like public health facilities falls under the shadow of Article 21 of the constitution of India. In the other words, where there is a refusal to treat an emergency case, the patient may approach the court to claim compensation for violation of his/her right to life. The Supreme to me Court has held that the failure to provide timely medical care amounts to violation of the fundamental right to life.

The state has the obligation to provide medical facilities in such circumstances and financial inability or lack of infrastructure is no justification to avoid this obligation. Whenever the state fails to discharge its constitutional obligations, the patient or immediate kin may approach either the Supreme Court or the High Court under Articles 32 or 226[1] of the constitution as a legal remedy. Court may also be approached by a public-spirited person or organization as the Supreme Court, in a number of landmark judgments has held that the traditional concept of '*locus standi*' does not strictly apply to such cases[2]. The Supreme Court and the High Courts also have the power to convert a letter concerning any issue of public importance into a Public Interest Litigation (PIL) *suo moto* (at its own initiative).

In the ordinary course of practice private medical practitioners and private hospitals have the right to decide whether to undertake a case or not[3].

1 Art 32 is the right to move the Supreme Court by appropriate proceedings for the enforcement of the rights and Art 226 is the power of the courts to issue any person or authority including in appropriate cases, any government, within those territories directions, orders on a case brought before them.

2 One of the basic principles of law is that only such a person can approach the court that is directly affected by the chain of events which gives rise to the legal proceedings. Thus, at the admission stage the aggrieved party must establish its *locus standi*. If such a party fails then the matter is held not maintainable, i.e., the court has the jurisdiction to try the matter but will not do so because the party claiming relief does not have the right to claim such relief.

3 "When a patient consults a doctor, the doctor owes him certain duty viz., a duty of care in deciding whether to undertake the case and a duty of care in deciding what treatment to give. A breach of any of these duties gives a right of action for negligence to the patient". *Dr. Laxman Balkrishna Joshi v. Trimbak Bapu Godbole*, AIR 1969 SC 128.

However, the Supreme Court, while deciding upon delay in treatment of medico-legal cases by government hospitals, has held that neither government nor even private hospitals can refuse treatment in a medico-legal emergency. But, if a private hospital refuses treatment then which forum is to be approached? Article 21 of the Constitution dealing with the right to life is normally not available against private parties. Consumer courts and civil courts deal with tortuous liability[4] of doctor or hospital i.e., negligence in treatment. If the hospital refuses to treat a patient in emergency cases this amount to negligence in the performance of its duty towards the patient and consumer court or civil courts can be approached.

THE INDIAN CONSTITUTION AND RIGHT TO HEALTH AND EMERGENCY HEALTH CARE

The Fundamental Rights and Article 21(Right to Life with Dignity) forms the basis of Right to Health. Article 21 of the Indian Constitution reads as, "No person shall be deprived of his life or personal liberty except through procedure established by law". Till the 1970s, the Supreme Courts, by and large had interpreted 'life' literally i.e., right to exist- right not to be killed. In late 1970s, began to give an expanding meaning to the term 'life' appearing in Article 21. Over the years it has come to be accepted that life does not only mean animal existence but the life of a dignified human being with all its concomitant attributes. This would include a healthy environment and effective health care facilities. Today, therefore the Fundamental Right to Life is seen in a broad context.

The "Right to Health" inseparable from "Right to Life" and the "Right to Medical Facilities" as a concomitant of "Right to Health" is also part and parcel of Right to Life. In a welfare state, the corresponding duty to the right to health and medical facility lies with the state.

---

4 Tortuous liability arises from the breach of a duty primarily fixed by law. In the case of doctors it is negligence in treatment.

Part-III of the constitution prescribes the Fundamental Rights of the citizens. These rights are enforceable against the state in a court of law. However, it does not prescribe that right to health or health care as fundamental right. It is an expanded meaning given to this term that has allowed the courts to prescribe that right to health and health care is a fundamental right.

Part- IV of the constitution lists the Directive Principles of State Policy. These are the principles which should be followed by the state as the guiding principles while enacting laws and policies. The obligation of the state to provide health care facilities is set out in the "Directive Principles of State Policy". These relevant provisions which cast a duty on State to ensure good health for its citizen are:

1. **Article 38:** State to ensure a social order for the promotion of welfare of people-

   State shall strive to promote the welfare of people by securing and protecting as effectively as it may a social order in which justice, social, economic and political shall inform all the institutions of the national life.

   State shall, in particular, strive to minimize the inequalities in income and endeavour to eliminate inequalities in status, facilities and opportunities, not only amongst individuals but also amongst groups of people residing in different areas or engaged in different vocation.

   In other words, no person will be deprived of a healthy life because he cannot afford it. The state must provide facilities that an economically better off person can afford out of his own pocket.

2. **Article 39:** Certain Principles of Policy to be followed by State. The state shall, in particular, direct its policy towards securing-

   (*a*) That health and strength of workers, men and women and the tender age of children are not abused and that citizen are not forced by economic necessity to enter avocations unsuited to their age or strength; and

(*b*) Those children are given opportunities and facilities to develop in a healthy manner and in conditions of freedom and dignity and that childhood and youth are protected against exploitation and against moral and material abandonment.

3. **Article 47:** Duty of State to raise level of nutrition and the standard of living and to improve public health-

   The State shall regard the raising of the level of nutrition and the standard of living of its people and the improvement of public health as among its primary duties and in particular, the state shall endeavour to bring out prohibition of the consumption except for medical purposes of intoxicating drinks and of drugs which are injurious to health.

JUDICIAL INTERVENTION ON RIGHT TO HEALTH AND EMERGENCY HEALTH CARE

To begin with the right to health as a Fundamental right grew as an offshoot of environmental litigation initiated by environmental activists regarding the environment issues. Undoubtedly, the right to environment was crucial because a polluted environment affects public health. A pollution free environment as a fundamental right presupposes right to health as a fundamental right. Logically, the explicit recognition of the fundamental right to health should be preceded the fundamental right to good government. The right to unpolluted environment was recognized as a right in the first instance and from that followed the right to public health, health and health care.

Secondly, the right to health care has been debated by the courts in the context of rights of Government employees to receive health care. A number of observations of the court concerning the importance of these rights are to be found in cases dealing with denial or restriction of health care facilities for Government employees and not to the general masses.

While dealing with the issues of fundamental right to health and health care the courts have also dealt with specific categories such as under trials, convicts and mental ill persons. The courts have recognized that imprisonment does not deprive a person of right to health and health care.

In *Municipal Council, Ratlam v. Vardhichand others*[5], The Municipal Corporation was prosecuted by some citizens for not clearing up the garbage. The corporation took the plea that it did not have money. While rejecting the plea, the Supreme Court through Justice Krishna Iyer observed that: "The State will realize that Article 47 makes it a paramount principle of governance that steps are taken for the improvement of public health as amongst its primary duties.

In *CESC Ltd. v. Subash Chandra Bose*[6], the Supreme Court relied on international instruments and concluded that right to health is a fundamental right. Further, it observed that health is not merely absence of sickness:

"The term health implies more than an absence of sickness. Medicine care and health facilities not only protect against sickness but it ensure stable manpower for economic development. Facilities of health and medical care generate devotion and dedication to give the workers best physically as well as mentally, in productivity. It enables the worker to enjoy the fruit of his labour, to keep him physically fit and mentally alert for leading a successful economic, social and cultural life. The medical facilities are therefore, part of social security and like gift edged security. Right to emergency health care is thus a state of complete physical, mental and social wellbeing and not merely the absence of disease or infirmity. In the light of Article 22 to 25 of the Universal Declaration of Human Rights, International Convention on Economic, Social and Cultural Rights and in the light of socio-economic justice assured in our constitution, right to health is a fundamental human right to workmen. The maintenance of health is a most imperative constitutional goal whose realization requires interaction by many social and economic factors".

In *Mahendra Pratap Singh v. State of Orissa*[7], the petitioner, an Ex-Sarpanch of Pachhikote Gram Panchayat approached the court for issuance of appropriate writ commanding the opposite parties to take effective measures to run Primary Health Centre at Pachhikote within the Korei

5 1980 Cri LJ 1075.

6 AIR 1992 SC 573, 585.

7 AIR 1997 Ori 37.

block in the district of Jaipur by providing all amenities and facilities for proper running of the said health centre. The Government of Orissa decided to open certain primary health centres in different areas in 1991-92 subject to fulfilment of certain conditions on basis of demands of the local people and public at large. The court observed that:

"Great achievements and accomplishments in life are possible if one is permitted to lead an acceptably healthy life. Health is life's grace and efforts are to be made to sustain the same. In our country like ours, it may not be possible. To have sophisticated hospitals but definitely villagers of this country within their limitation can aspire to have a Primary Health Centre. The Government is required to assist people and its endeavour should be to see that the people get treatment and lead a healthy life. Primary concern should be the PHC and technical fetters cannot be introduced as subterfuges to cause hindrances in the establishment of health centre".

The judgment stated that the gram Panchayat was agreeable to offer of the gram Panchayat building for running of the health centre. If the building was still available, the same could be utilized for the purpose of running of the PHC, till the new building was completed. Thus, this is perhaps the only judgment commending the right to health for a general population.

In *CERC v. Union of India*[8], the Supreme Court while dealing with the rights of workers in asbestos manufacturing and health hazards related to it. The court noted that the right to health and health care of a worker is a component of the fundamental right to life guaranteed under Article 21 of the constitution of India. Further, the court observed that:

Article 38 (1) lays down the foundation for human rights and enjoins the state to promote the welfare of the people by securing and protecting, as effectively as it may, a social order in which justice, social, economic and political shall inform all the institutions of the normal life. Art. 46 directs the State to protect the poor from social injustice and all forms of exploitation. Article 39(e) charges that the policy of the State shall be to secure "the health and strength of the workers". Article 42 mandates that the States shall make provision, statutory or executive "to secure just and humane conditions of work". Article 43 directs that the State shall "endeavour to secure to all workers, by suitable legislation or economic

8 (1995) 3 SCC 42.

organisation or any other way to ensure decent standard of life and full enjoyment of leisure and cultural opportunities to the workers".

The right to health to a worker is an integral facet of meaningful right to life to have not only a meaningful existence but also robust health and vigour without which worker would lead life of misery. Lack of health denudes his livelihood. Therefore, it must held that the right to health and medical care is a fundamental right under Article 21 read with Article 39(c), 41 and 43 of the Indian Constitution and make the life of the workman meaningful and purposeful with dignity of person. Right to life includes protection of the health and strength of the worker is a minimum requirement to enable a person to live with human dignity. Thus, the State, be it Union or State Government or an industry, public or private, is enjoined to take all such action which will promote health, strength and vigour of the workman during the period of employment and leisure an health even after retirement as basic essential to live with health and happiness.

ENVIRONMENT POLLUTION IS LINKED TO HEALTH AND IS VIOLATION OF RIGHT TO LIFE WITH DIGNITY

In *T. Ramakrishna Rao v. Hyderabad Development Authority*[9], the Andhra Pradesh High court observed that:

"Protection of the environment is not only the duty of the citizens but also the obligation of the State and it's all other organs including the courts. The enjoyments of life and its attainment and fulfillment guaranteed by Article 21 of the Indian Constitution embraces the protection and preservation of nature's gift without which life cannot be enjoyed fruitfully. The slow poisoning of the atmosphere caused by the environmental pollution and spoliation should be regarded as amounting to violation of Article 21 of the Indian Constitution.

In *T. Damodarand others v. Special Officer, Municipal Corporation of Hyderabad,*[10] the court through P.A Choudary, J., held that the legitimate duty of the courts as the enforcing organs of the constitutional objectives to

---

9 Writ Petition 36929/1998 *T. Ramakrishna Rao v. Hyderabad Urban Development Authority* decided on 20.07.2001.

10 AIR 1987 AP 171.

forbid all actions of the State and the citizens from upsetting the ecological and environmental balance.

In *Virendra Gaur v. State of Haryana,*[11] the Supreme Court held that environmental, ecological, air and water pollution, etc., should be regarded as amounting to violation of right to health guaranteed by Article 21 of the constitution. It is right to state that hygienic environment is an integral facet of the right to healthy life and it would not be possible to live with human dignity without a humane and healthy environment.

In *Consumer Education and Research Centre v. Union of India*[12]& In *Kirloskar Brorthers Ltd. v. Employees' State Insurance Corporation*[13], the Supreme Court held that right to health and medical care is a fundamental right under Article 21 read with Article 39 (e), 41 and 43 of the Constitution of India.

In *Unnikrishnan, JP v. State of A.P*[14], the maintenance and improvement of public health is the duty of the State to fulfill its constitutional obligations casts on it under Article 21 of the Constitution of India.

OBLIGATION TO PROVIDE EMERGENCY HEALTH CARE

In Paschim Banga Kheta Mazdoor Samiti v. State of W.B[15], the issue before the Supreme Court was the legal obligation of the Government to provide facilities in government hospitals attention. The petitioner who had suffered brain haemorrhage in a fall from the train was denied treatment at various government hospitals because of non-availability of beds.

The patient was given first aid in a PHC and referred to a .specialized state hospital for better treatment. At the specialized hospital, the patient was examined and X-rays of his skull were taken which showed his condition to be serious. Immediate admission for further treatment was recommended. However, he was not admitted in that hospital as there was no vacant beds and was referred to another specialized hospital. There too, he was refused admission as there were no vacant beds. After doing the rounds of three

11 1995 (2) SCC 577.

12 (1993) 3 SCC 42.

13 (1996) 2 SCC 682, AIR 1996 SC 3261.

14 AIR 1993 SC 2178.

15 (1996) 4 SCC 37.

more state run specialized hospitals, the patient was admitted to a private hospital and the final bill came to much more than he could afford. He has to spend ₹ 17000 for his treatment.

The Supreme Court observed that while financial resources would be required for the implementation of the directions, the constitutional obligation of state to provide adequate medical services to the people cannot be ignored. Further, the Court also observed that: "In the context of the constitutional obligation to provide free legal aid to the poor accused this court has held that the state cannot avoid its constitutional obligation in that regard on account of financial constraints. (*Khatri II v. State of Bihar*). These observations will apply with equal, if not greater, force in the matter of discharge of constitutional obligations of the state to provide medical aid to preserve human life. In the matter of allocation of funds for medical services the said constitutional obligation of the state has to be kept in view".

The court held that it was necessary that a time-bound plan for providing these services should be chalked out keeping in view the recommendations of the committee as well as the requirements for ensuring availability of proper medical services in this regard as indicate d and steps should be taken to implement the same. The court also observed that:

Providing adequate medical facilities is an essential part of the obligation undertaken by the state in a welfare state. The Government discharges this obligation b running hospitals and health centres. Article 21 imposes an obligation on the state to safeguard right to life of every person. Preservation of human life is thus of paramount importance. Government hospitals run by the state and the medical officers employed therein are duty-bound to extend medical assistance for preserving human life. Failure, on the part of a government hospital to provide timely medical treatment to a person in need of such treatment results in violation of his right to life guaranteed under Article 21 of the Indian Constitution.

RIGHT TO EMERGENCY CARE DURING ACCIDENTS

In *Parmanand Katara v. Union of India*[16], was a petition filed by a human rights activist seeking direction against the union of India that every injured

16 AIR 1989 SC 2039.

citizen brought for treatment should be instantaneously given medical aid to preserve life and thereafter the procedural criminal law should be allowed to operate in order to avoid negligent death. The petition also demanded that in the event of breach of such direction, apart from any action that may be taken for negligence, appropriate compensation should be admissible.

The Supreme Court agreeing with this held that, "There is no legal impediment for a medical professional when he is called upon or requested to attend to an injured person needing his medical assistance immediately. The effort to save the person should be the top priority not only of the medical professional but even of the police or any other citizen who happens to be connected with the matter or who happens to notice an incident or a situation".

Preservation of human life is of paramount importance. That is so on account of the fact that once life is lost, the status quo ante cannot be restored as resurrection is beyond the capacity of man. The patient whether he is innocent person or liable to be punished under the laws of the society, it is the obligation of those who are in charge of the health of the community to preserve life so that innocent n may be protected and the guilty may be punished. Social laws do not contemplate death due negligence to tantamount to legal punishment. A doctor at the government hospital positioned to meet the state obligation is, therefore, duty bound to extend medical assistance for preserving life. Every doctor whether at a Government hospital or otherwise has the professional obligation to extend his service with due expertise for protecting life. No law or state action can intervene to avoid delay the discharge of the paramount obligation case upon the members of the medical profession. The obligation being total, absolute and paramount, laws of procedure whether in statutes or otherwise which would interfere with discharge of this obligation cannot be sustained and must, therefore, give way....Zonal regulations and classification cannot operate as fetters in the process of discharge of the obligation and irrespective of the fact whether under instructions or rules, the victim has to be sent elsewhere or how the police shall be contacted, the guidelines indicated in the 1985 decision of the committee on Forensic Medicine (set up by the Ministry of Home Affair of the Government of India) are to be operative.

Significantly, in this case the Supreme Court observed that every doctor whether in a government establishment or a private individual has the duty to extend immediate medical treatment in consonance with his skill to save life.

ROLE OF POLICE IN EMERGENCY CASES

In *Supreme Court Legal Aid Committee v. State of Bihar*[17], the Supreme Court held that the responsibility to provide immediate medical treatment to an injured person in a medico-legal case extends even to the police. Thus, where the deceased who was lynched by the mob for attempting to rob passengers of train, died because of negligence of the police in taking him to a hospital on time and also for the inhuman manner in which he was bound up and dumped in the vehicle, the court held that this amounted to a violation of right to life and the state was bound to pay Rs 20,000 as compensation for the loss of life. It is altogether another matter that the compensation awarded was a pittance.

In *Poonam Sharma v. Union of India*[18], is another case pertaining to the liability of police and government hospitals in medico-legal case, the petitioner's husband met with an accident while driving in an alleged drunken state. The police took him to a government hospital for a check-up where the doctor on duty stitched up an inch long cut on his scalp and gave him Brufen tablets. Later, the deceased was taken into custody and charged for drunken driving under the Motor Vehicles Act, 1988. In the night the deceased complained of severe headache and the police took him to the same doctor who again prescribed Brufen tablets. During the night the condition of the deceased deteriorated. The next day his family bailed him out and took him to another hospital where he succumbed to brain haemorrhage.

The High Court observed that in a case of head injury, it is elementary knowledge that extra care is required to be taken, particularly in medico-legal cases. In medico-legal cases, the doctor as also the police authorities are under statutory obligation not only to see that injuries suffered by a person who has been brought to the hospital are properly taken care of

17 (1991) 3 SCC 482.
18 AIR 2003 Delhi 50.

but also, every doctor at the government hospital having regard to the paramount importance of preservation of human life is statutorily obliged to extend his service with due expertise.

Thus, in light of the facts and circumstances of the case and the deceased was only 30 years old drawing a salary of ₹ 3000 per month, the High Court ordered ₹ 2 lakh as compensation to the petitioner.

CONCLUSION

The courts have now been recognizing that the state and state-run medical institutions have the obligation to provide medical care in cases of emergency. This cannot be dependent upon adequate infrastructure, etc., In *Paschim Banga Case*[19], the court ordered central bed bureaus as also upgraded facilities in district and sub district hospitals to be set up. These have not been widely implemented. But group's workings on health can definitely file public Interest Litigations in high courts for implementation of these orders in their respective states.

Although the responsibility of the State and government hospitals is well provided by a radical interpretation of the Constitution, there is no definite corresponding legal duty imposed on private hospitals and practitioners to treat emergency cases except for the observation which is excerpted above. The above judgements focus on the duty of State and government hospitals. In this regards, in *Paschim Banga Khet Mazdoor Samiti* case made a few interesting suggestions drawing from the legal position in the US. It was urged that the denial of treatment should be specifically made a cognizable offence and further that it should be made actionable as a tort[20].

Indian Courts have held that in emergencies neither government nor even private doctors can insist on payment of money before dealing with the patient. In *Pravat Kumar Mukherjee v. Ruby General Hospital*[21],

19 1996, 4 SCC 37.

20 In civil law, the liability of doctor arises when there is a duty of care, a breach of such duty and consequential injury. The duty is not absolute, which implies that a doctor need not treat all those who approach him. He has the right to refuse. He is liable for harm caused only to those whom he undertakes to treat.

21 Original Petition No. 90 of 2002 decided by the National Commission on 25.4.2005.

the National Consumer Commission was concerned with the case of a young student whose motorcycle was dashed by a bus in Calcutta. He was brought to the respondent hospital but the treatment was not continued as ₹ 15,000 as demanded by the hospital were not immediately paid. The boy died. The National Commission held that though a doctor was not bound to treat each and every patient, in emergencies the doctor was bound to treat the patient and could not insist on delaying treatment until the fees were paid. The petitioner was awarded a compensation of ₹ 10 lakh.

Thus, in conclusion all doctor and hospitals, whether private or government, have treat emergency patients. If they do not so, the patient or immediate kin can approach the court for compensation for violating their right to life (Article 21). The excuse of having no beds does not hold in the case of government hospitals and detailed recommendations are given in this regard. The obligation is the same for government hospitals and private hospitals. The courts have clearly held that no legal procedures can take priority over providing life-saving treatment for the patient. If such procedures are required by the law, then that law must be amended.

Human Rights Perspectives Of Clinical Trials In India – A Critical Study

Sajal Sharma

Abstract

Clinical trials of new medicines are an essential evil in the development of approved chemicals for human treatment. Given the inherently dangerous nature of such trials for the participants, it is essential for the law to deal with the rights of such participants. It is important to analyze the rights of the subjects given their weaker bargaining position vis-à-vis the pharmaceutical companies. This research article makes a comprehensive assessment of the human rights of the subjects of clinical trials in all its forms and manifestations. It comes to a conclusion that there is a need to fix the loopholes in the regulatory framework, enactment of law to monitor clinical research and drug trials of the country thereby making it more safer and to ensure that trial subjects who undergo such trials are well informed about risk of participation and are not exploited especially the vulnerable subjects participating in such trials. Enactment of law is not meant to restrict the clinical trials but to regulate and to enhance conducting of clinical trials in a more rational and scientifically sound manner thereby developing capacity building. Thus a two pronged approach is needed firstly a concrete enumeration of the human rights of the trial subjects and secondly a robust enforcement mechanism in case of adverse events.

INTRODUCTION

The forward march of science particularly in the realm of chemistry has had an un-precedented impact on the preservation of human health.

This can be visibly seen from the development of the drug penicillin by Alexander Fleming in 1928. Thereafter many a new chemical compounds have either been created or isolated to treat various ailments either as a cure post contracting of the disease or as a preventive mechanism in the form of vaccine.

The use of any chemical substance as a drug or medicine is fraught with risk of an unknown nature. Unless these chemicals are previously tested it is not possible to know as to how they would react in the human body. The human body is a unique bio-chemical engine, thus any chemical entering the body either orally or intravenously produces its own set of actions and reactions in the body. Given this reality of the human body, drug developers have to pass the acid test of human drug trials before a new drug can be legally sold in the market to deal with a particular type or types of ailment.

These drug trials on human beings also known as clinical trials are research studies that aim to improve different aspects of patient care. They aim to test whether different treatments or drugs are safe and how well they work. Some trials involve healthy members of the public while others involve patients who may be offered the option of taking part in a trial during their care and treatment. Clinical trials cover a broad range of different types of research. For example, trials are often used to test new medicines or vaccines but can also be used to look at new combinations of existing medicines. They can also be used to test whether giving a treatment in a different way will make it more effective or reduce any side effects. Some trials are designed to try out ways to prevent a particular disease in people who have never had a disease, or to prevent a disease from returning.

Human rights form the basis of any society and it is important to protect the human rights of individuals who are subjected to clinical trials. The purpose of the study is to identify and analyze the various human rights issues that arise as a result of clinical trials being conducted on human beings. On the one hand, there is a need to conduct the clinical trials to test the efficacy of a drug before it is introduced in the markets and on the other hand there is a need to protect the human rights of individuals who are being subjected to clinical trials. There is a need to strike a balance between the two.

Clinical trials are a systematic study of new drugs in human subjects to generate data for discovering and/or verifying the clinical, pharmacological (including the pharmocodynamic and pharmacokinetic) and/or adverse effect with the objective of determining safety and/or efficacy of the new drug.[1] It is no secret that a spate of new drugs and molecules are coming in the market and these new drugs have been mostly tried on individuals from outside the country, predominantly on Caucasian race. The genetic back ground, and the physical belt of Indians is different from the westerners. Therefore, it becomes imperative that any medicine which doctors plan to use on patients of Indian ethnicity should be tried on patients from within the country so that they know the effective dosage level, and the side effects which may occur as a consequence of these medications.

Increasingly a number of multinational pharmaceutical companies are conducting their clinical drug trials in India. This is due to the fact that our norms relating to clinical trials are less stringent and not properly monitored. This puts the subjects of clinical trials at a grave danger more so because such participants are not properly informed and the lure of earning money under cash strapped circumstances forces them to undergo such trials. At the same time it is vital that we conduct research and try the new preparations in clinical setting on day to day basis in India before the doctor's start recommending these medicines in the country based on western studies.

HUMAN RIGHTS PERSPECTIVES OF CLINICAL TRIALS–ISSUES AND CONCERNS

The development in Science and technology has increased the amount of clinical and scientific research being undertaken. Such research may lead

1 Rule 122 DAA of Drugs and Cosmetic Rules, 1945.

to incredible discoveries and 'miracle' cures but at the same time this is an area dogged with controversy. The abuses which occurred in Germany during the Second World War have cast a long shadow. This has raised a concern at the international level to ensure that in the future, research practices will be ethical and in accordance with the legal principles. This idea has led to the Nuremberg Code in 1949 and the Declaration of Helsinki which was initially produced in 1964. In the European context statements which have been influential at least at a rhetorical level include the Council of Europe Convention on Human Rights and Bio-medicine. The Council of Europe has now issued a Draft Additional Protocol to the Convention on Human rights and Bio medicine. The European Convention on Human rights is also of utmost importance in the context of human rights. Nevertheless, despite the promulgation of such statements internationally scientific research is still dogged with controversy.

In countries such as India ambiguity and uncertainty to provide for a minimum standard of protection for clinical trial test subjects is prejudiced given the wide disparity in access to health care, without such adherence contract research organizations are far from doing good as the fundamental responsibility to secure the rights of trial subjects are not secured in turn being heavily guilty of violating human rights by exploiting the bodies of poor and vulnerable trial subjects for economic gains. In August 2013, a Parliamentary committee severely criticized Program for Appropriate Technology in Health (PATH) when it said "its sole aim has been to promote the commercial interests of Human Papillomavirus (HPV) vaccine manufacturers who would have benefited windfall profits had PATH been successful in getting the HPV vaccine included in the universal immunization program of the Country". To date, International human bodies' human rights framework is utilized to call for protective standards of minimum care while experimenting a new clinical trial in a developing country. The International Covenant on Economic, Social, and Cultural Rights (ICESCR) lays down rights to life, freedom from non-consensual medical experimentation, and non-discrimination as three relevant non-derogable rights and also provisions relevant to the standard of care in clinical trials is laid down by the International Covenant on Civil and Political Rights (ICCPR). In addition, implementation of a right to the "highest attainable standard of health," subject to progressive realization and core obligations is emphasized by the ICESR. An authoritative interpretation of the right to health is enumerated in General Comment 14, the Committee on Economic, Social, and Cultural Rights (CESCR) as "core obligations" and elucidates that "a State party cannot, under any circumstances whatsoever, justify its non-compliance with the core obligations which are non-derogable".[2] Furthermore "State parties have to respect the enjoyment of the right to health in other countries and to prevent third parties from violating the right to health in other countries, if they are able to influence these third parties by way of legal or political means".[3] Striking aspect of right to health is that the core obligation of the right to health is non-derogable and it prioritizes certain aspects that is they reflect minimum core content of the right to health, non-negotiable foundation of the right to which all individuals are entitled regardless of the economic situation in a country but CESCR does not always describe the core obligation of a right as non-derogable.[4] The concept of minimum core obligation of the right to health that is non-derogable provides a direction in setting a minimum standard of care for clinical trials. However the proposal of emphasizing responsibilities of developed countries to provide assistance and regulate corporations counters criticism that focusing more on minimum care obligations ignores the violations of affluent countries. The standards that developed countries adopt must be consistent with the core obligations of the right to health. The most important issue that arises

2 Committee on Economic, Social and Cultural Rights, General Comment No. 14, The Right to the Highest Attainable Standard of Health, UN Doc. No. E/C.12/2000/4 (2000), paras. 9, 47. Available at http://www1.umn.edu/humanrts/gencomm/escgencom14.htm [hereinafter "General Comment No. 14"].

3 General Comment No. 14 (see note 2).

4 K. Frank, "The minimum core of economic and social rights: A concept in search of content," Yale Journal of International Law 33 (2008), pp. 154-156.

is that what if a non-state actor is a sponsor of a clinical trial? However relevancy of minimum core obligations remains undisputed as economical and social approach is taken by the tribunal[5] "Violations of the right to health can occur through the direct action of States or other entities insufficiently regulated by States."[6]

General Comment 14 describes "the failure to regulate the activities of . . . corporations so as to prevent them from violating the right to health of others", clearly states the responsibility on States while approving experimentation of drug trial and marketing of drugs based on foreign clinical trial protecting the human rights and by not violating the obligation to protect.[7] International perspective provides limited guidance on applicability of human rights norms relating to clinical research trials, one of the major guidelines with regard to human right perspective by the Special Rapporteur on right to health considered as one of the major report issued in the year 2009, this report emphasizes on the basic essentiality of clinical research trials that is informed consent[8]. It includes a single sentence flagging the standard of care as an area of concern but the important question remains whether ethical standard can be maintained by developing countries while conducting clinical research trials, in spite of opting for appropriate non-placebo interventions, placebo interventions are conducted[9] .The Special Rapporteur called for most protective standards if the research board adopts the required changes for informed consent by eliminating double standards applied to developing countries recognizing

5 M. Hall and D. Weiss, "Human rights and remedial equilibration: Equilibrating socio-economic rights," Brooklyn Journal of International Law 36 (2011), p. 469.

6 *Ibid.*

7 *Ibid.*

8 Anand Grover, UN Special Rapporteur on the right of everyone to the enjoyment of the highest attainable standard of physical and mental health, Report of the Special Rapporteur on the Right of Everyone to the Enjoyment of the Highest Attainable Standard of Physical and Mental Health, UN. Doc. No. A/64/272 (2009). Available at http:// www.un.org/en/ga/third/64/documentslist.shtml.

9 *Ibid.*

the need for ethics review board.[10] Emphasis on a close scrutiny by independent ethics committees that apply standards in a transparent and diligent manner designed mainly to uphold these rights should be proposed by developing countries.

Clinical Trials-Human Rights Perspective

Amidst the technicalities surrounding the debate, there is a compelling need to revisit the issue from a human rights perspective. The ‘patient perspective’ is particularly relevant for the focus of this discourse on clinical/drug trial as the primary target group in India are sick poor patients rather than healthy volunteers. It is important to reiterate that the concept of patient rights globally evolved keeping the 1948 Universal Declaration of Human Rights which recognizes “the inherent dignity” and the “equal and unalienable rights of all members of the human family” as the primary reference. Any discourse on patient rights should imbibe this larger and fundamental spirit of inalienable human rights. Also, “the Universal Declaration of Human Rights has been instrumental in enshrining the notion of human dignity in international law, providing a legal and moral grounding for improved standards of care on the basis of our basic responsibilities towards each other as members of the “human family”, and giving important guidance on critical social, legal and ethical issues”

THE RIGHTS OF A SUBJECT OF A CLINICAL TRIAL

1. Right to Autonomy and Bodily Integrity

In the Introduction to the book, Experimentation with Human beings, Jay Katz writes, that when human beings become the subjects of experimentation….tensions arise between two values basic to western society: freedom of scientific inquiry and protection of individual inviolablilty. At the heart of this conflict lies an age-old question: when may a society, actively or by acquiescence, expose some of its members to harm in order to seek benefits for them, for other, or for society as a whole?

10 *Ibid.*

Sir Isaiah Berlin speaks of the importance of safeguarding the principle of autonomy.[11]

John Locke encompassed both rights when he wrote that, "every man has property in his own person. This nobody has any right but to himself.[12]

The Universal Declaration of Human rights, 1948, declares bodily integrity central to both human rights and human dignity, providing in Art. 5, that No one shall be subjected to torture or to cruel, inhuman or degrading treatment or punishment. Most physicians do not view human experimentation as torture, but the treaty that followed the declaration, the International Covenant on civil and political rights made the link unmistakable by adding that, "No one shall be subjected to torture or to cruel, inhuman or degrading treatment or punishment. In particular no one shall be subjected without his free consent to medical or scientific experimentation. This is now fundamental precept of international human rights law. Moreover, under the treaty, this right is non derogable even in times of public emergency which threatens the live of the nation."

The United Nations International Covenant on Civil and Political Rights in Art. 7 juxtaposes the rights to autonomy and bodily integrity: "No one shall be subjected to torture or to cruel, inhuman, or degrading treatment or punishment. In particular, no one shall be subjected without his free consent to medical or scientific experimentation. The drafter of the Covenant wished to convey that human experimentation, without his or her free consent constitutes inhuman and degrading treatment akin to 'torture', no matter what the motives of the investigator.

Article 1 of the UNESCO Universal Declaration on Bioethics and Human Rights (2005) (hereafter "the Declaration") states that it seeks to address the "ethical issues related to medicine, life sciences and associated technologies as applied to human beings, taking into account their social, legal and environmental dimensions" (the full text of the Declaration is given in Annex I). Article 8 reinforces this commitment by linking it to respect for personal integrity and the need to protect vulnerable individuals and groups: In applying and advancing scientific knowledge, medical

11 Isaiah Berlin, Two concepts of Liberty, in Four Essays on Liberty, 136-37 (1969).

12 John Locke, Two treatises on Government, 305 (Peter Laslett ed., 1960).

practice and associated technologies, human vulnerability should be taken into account. Individuals and groups of special vulnerability should be protected and the personal integrity of such individuals respected.

2. Right to Life

Art. 21 of the Constitution of India, reads: "No person shall be deprived of his life or personal liberty except according to procedure established by law". Thus right to life is fundamental right guaranteed by the Constitution. The expression 'life' has been interpreted by the Supreme Court rather liberally and broadly. In *Munn v. Illinois*[13] Field J. observed that the term, 'life' means something more than mere animal existence. In *Francis Coralie v. Delhi*,[14] Bhagwati J. observed that the right to life includes the right to live with human dignity and all that goes along with it, the bare necessaries of life such as adequate nutrition, clothing and shelter over the head and facilities for reading, writing and expressing oneself in diverse forms, freely moving about and mixing and commingling with fellow human beings. In *P. Rathinam v. Union of India*, the Supreme Court has defined life as follows: The right to live with human dignity and the same does not connote continued drudgery. It takes within its fold some of the fine graces of civilization which make life worth living and that the expanded concept of life would mean the tradition, culture and heritage of the person concerned.

Despite clinical trials coming under scrutiny in various courts, little has changed on the ground. In 2011, the industry experienced its first jolts, when reports of increasing number of deaths during trials emerged. During the period of 2005-12, over 2,868 deaths were reported in India, all of which resulted from clinical trials.

At least 370 deaths have been reported during clinical trials in India since February 2013, [15]

13 94 U.S. 113 (1876).

14 AIR 1981 SC 746.

15 Sushmi Dey | TNN | Dec 15, 2014.

3. Right to Health of Human Subjects

Right to health is central to all human rights and denial of health right would mean denial of all human rights. Generally, the context in which an individual lives is of great importance to health and quality of life. Health is the level of functional or metabolic efficiency of a living being. It is the general condition of a person's mind, body and spirit, usually meaning to be free from illness, injury or pain. Law is an important public health tool that plays a critical role in protecting the health of general public. The framers of the constitution incorporated right to health in the Directive Principles of State policy (DPSP) which enjoins the state to provide comprehensive, creative, preventive, promotional and rehabilitative health services and proper nutrition to all the people of India. Ultimately, it is the effort of the Indian judiciary who treat health as a right to life which is fundamental to all human beings under Article 21 of the constitution. Therefore, entitlement to healthcare must be ensured by developing specific statutes, programs and services. The right to health is one of the economic, social and cultural Human right that requires affirmative government action to create better conditions for people rather than just governmental restraint vis-à-vis citizens. The first expression of the right to health is an international legal instrument came in the Constitution of the WHO in 1946.[16] Right to health is embodied in various International Instruments like Article 25 of the UDHR; Art. 12 of the ICESCR, Declaration of Alma-Ata (1978), and World Health Declaration (1998) adopted by the World Health Assembly.

The General Assembly of the United Nations has adopted various resolutions to safeguard the interest of patients. Art. 25 of the Universal Declaration of Human Rights states that: everyone has the right to a standard of living adequate for the health and well-being of himself and his family, including food, clothing, housing and medical care, and necessary social services and the right to security in the event of unemployment, sickness, disability, widowhood, old age or other lack of livelihood in circumstances beyond his control.

16 WHO: Basic Documents, Forth third edition. (Geneva: World Health Organization 2001). The Constitution was adopted by the International Health Conference in 1946.

Article 12 of the International Covenant on Economic, Social and Cultural Rights, 1966, interalia, states that:

The State Parties to the present Covenant recognize the right of everyone to the enjoyment of the highest attainable standard of physical and mental health.

The International Covenant on Civil and Political Rights 1966, the UN Declaration on Elimination of All Forms of Discrimination Against Women 1967, the Convention on the Elimination of All forms of Discrimination against women 1979, and the Convention on the rights of the child provide for the protection of health care rights of persons including women, children and other disadvantaged sections of society.

The preamble to the World Health Organization Constitution, inter alia provides:

1. The enjoyment of the highest standards of health is one of the fundamental rights of every human being without distinction of race, religion, political belief, economic and social condition.
2. The health of all peoples is fundamental to the attainment of peace and security and is dependent upon the fullest co-operation of individuals and states.
3. The achievement of any state in the promotion and protection of health is of value to all.
4. Unequal development in different countries in the promotion of health and control of diseases, especially communicable diseases, is a common danger.
5. Healthy development of the child is of basic importance, the ability to live harmoniously in a totaling changing environment is essential to such development.
6. The extension to all people of the benefits of medical, psychological and related knowledge is essential to the fullest attainment of health.
7. Informed opinion and active co-operation on the part of the public are of the utmost importance in the improvement of health of the people.

8. Governments have responsibility for the health of their people, which can be fulfilled only the provision of adequate health and social measures.

4. Right to Informed Consent

Few principles are as often identified with bioethics as informed consent. In clinical practice, the doctrine of informed consent rose to dominance during the course of the 20th century. It replaced a medical ethos founded on trust in physicians' decisions—often on the assumption that "doctor knows best"—with an ethos that sought to put patients in charge of their own care. In medical research on human subjects, informed consent requirements gained prominence in reaction to abuses. One influential response to the cruelty of Nazi experiments was the Nuremberg Code of research ethics, which stipulated, "The voluntary consent of the human subject is absolutely essential". But why should we require informed consent when it comes at a cost to the individual's health? What is the content, the scope, and the status of that requirement? How does informed consent in bioethics, the focus of the present entry, relate to consent in sexual ethics, business ethics, and political philosophy. Person needs to give consent before any type of medical treatment. The main arguments for informed consent revolve around:

1. protection,
2. autonomy,
3. prevention of abusive conduct,
4. trust,
5. self-ownership,
6. non-domination, and
7. personal integrity

The simplest rationale for the informed consent requirement is that it protects patients' and participants' health and welfare. It protects potential research participants from investigators' overzealous attempts to promote science and their careers, even on participants' backs, and it also protects regular patients from physicians' overconfident, but often incorrect, paternalistic judgments on what is good for them. This pragmatic and instrumental rationale is often considered utilitarian, although many moral doctrines endorse duties to protect patients and research participants.

The existing national (ICMR) and international guidelines on clinical drug trials make it mandatory that participants should be recruited for trials only after securing their informed consent. Our findings reveal that none of the participants were informed that they are being recruited into a drug trial. Further, the details of drug trials, risks and possible side effects of the trials were not communicated to the participants. One of the strange justifications put forward by a principal investigator of a clinical drug trial was that "if everything is communicated to the patients as required, they (patients) won't agree to participate in the trial". He further elaborated that due to their low level of understanding in this area the patients will misinterpret the information and will hesitate to participate! The patients were not given the copy of the signed informed consent form thus depriving them of any documentary evidence to prove their participation in a given trial. It was also found that doctors are recruiting their own patients without any monitoring by an independent doctor who is supposed to check the conflict of interests involved in such cases

1.1 The informed consent of the participant/patient in the presence of a third party is a prerequisite for the conduct of any drug/clinical trial. 1.2 Such trials should not be carried out on those who are unable to express their will, unless the consent of a legal representative has been obtained and the trials would likely be in the interest of the patient/participant. 9 Some elements have been adopted from

(*a*) A Declaration on the Promotion of Patient Rights in Europe, WHO 1994.

(*b*) Patient Bill of Rights[17] A participant/patient has the right to refuse or to halt a medical intervention. The implications of refusing or halting such an intervention must be carefully explained to the patient. In all other situations where the patient is unable to give informed consent and where there is no legal representative

17 accessed at http://www.cc.nih.gov/participate/patientinfo/legal/bill_of_rights.shtml 13 | P a g e 1.3

or representative designated by the patient for this purpose, appropriate measures should be taken to provide for a substitute decision making process, taking into account what is known and, to the greatest extent possible, what may be presumed about the wishes of the patient. The participant/patient has a right to refuse to participate in research, to refuse treatment to the extent permitted by law, and to be informed of the medical consequences of these actions, including possible dismissal from the study and discharge from the health facility. If discharge would jeopardize their health, they have the right to remain in the medical facility until discharge or transfer is medically advisable

In general, four international covenants/codes are evoked:

1. Nuremberg Code (articulated in 1947 by U.S. judges): "The voluntary consent of the human subject is absolutely essential . . . [and includes] legal capacity . . . free power of choice . . . sufficient knowledge and comprehension of the [nature, duration, and purpose of the experiment] . . . to make an understanding and enlightened decision."
2. International Covenant on Civil and Political Rights (international treaty became effective in 1976): "No one shall be subjected to torture or to cruel, inhuman or degrading treatment or punishment. In particular, no one shall be subjected without his free consent to medical or scientific experimentation."
3. Declaration of Helsinki of the World Medical Association (promulgated in 1964 and revised eight times since): "The physician should obtain the subject's freely given informed consent, preferably in writing. . . . [But in clinical research] if the physician considers it essential not to obtain informed consent, the specific reasons for this proposal should be stated in the experimental protocol for transmission to [an] independent committee."
4. International Ethical Guidelines for Biomedical Research Involving Human Subjects (published in 1993, and since revised, by the Council for International Organizations of Medical Science): "The investigator must obtain the voluntary, informed consent of the prospective subject [or legally authorized representative]. . . .

Waiver of informed consent is to be regarded as uncommon and exceptional, and must in all cases be approved by an ethical review committee.

During 1976-88, 1158 women with varying degrees of cervical dysplasia were recruited for long term follow-up in an attempt to study rates of progression to malignancy.[30] The investigators from the Institute of Cytology and Preventive Oncology in New Delhi did not obtain written consent on the grounds that most of the women in the study were illiterate and that written consent was not mandatory when the study was launched.[31]

5. Right to Privacy and Confidentiality

All information about a patient's health status, medical condition, diagnosis, prognosis and treatment and all other information of a personal kind must be kept confidential. Confidential information can only be disclosed if the patient gives explicit consent or if the law expressly provides for this. All identifiable data must be protected. The protection of the data must be appropriate to the manner of their storage. Human substances from which identifiable data can be derived must be likewise protected. Patients/participants have the right of access to their medical files and technical records and to any other files and records pertaining to their diagnosis, treatment and care and to receive a copy of their own files and records or parts thereof. Patients/participants have the right to demand the correction, completion, deletion, clarification and/or updating of personal and medical data concerning them which are inaccurate, incomplete, ambiguous or outdated, or which are not relevant to the purposes of diagnosis, treatment and care.

6. Right to Compensation

Absence of insurance coverage and compensation to the participants. The existing guidelines require ensuring proper insurance coverage or adequate compensation scheme for the trial participants. However, our findings show that in reality there is no insurance coverage or a compensation package for the participants. Ironically (thought not surprisingly) insurance coverage is available only to the doctor who conducts the trial in order to meet any liability that may occur due to any serious adverse event during the conduct of clinical drug trial. It was also revealed that the poor patients are denied a compensation for their opportunity costs, including daily wages and travel expense.

During clinical trial, a patient can die because of several reasons: life threatening diseases like cancer, cardio-vascular diseases like heart failure/ stroke and other serious diseases that the participant may have be suffering from in the past. Death can also occur due to adverse effects of the trials. However, there is no standard protocol for post-mortem mechanism to investigate it (Biswas, 2013). The pharmaceutical companies conduct investigations only to ascertain the cause of death: whether it was the result of a clinical trial or simply because of a pre-existing disease. Compensation is to be given only if a death is said to have been caused due to clinical trial. Also, the amount of compensation varies across different companies. But now, the government is in the process of fixing a minimum compensation amount in case of death or injuries sustained during the course of the trials. The Ministry of Health and Family Welfare has authorized DGCI to determine the amount of compensation to be given in case of death or injuries sustained during trials (The Tribune, 2013). Another unethical practice is the simultaneous conduct of Phase II and Phase III trials by CROs. Clinical trial laws were amended in 2005 to help familiarize India with international clinical research activities as well as allow for Phase II and Phase III trials to be conducted concurrently. Before 2005, Phase II and Phase III trials were allowed with a phase lag—that is, after their gross safety aspects were somewhat known abroad (Srinivasan, 2013). These concurrent clinical trials may have a serious adverse effect on the trial participants, for instance, causing disability or permanent damage or death.

7. Right to Information

One of the most disturbing findings is the deliberate and willful denial of any information with regard to the drug trials. The area of drug trials remains totally opaque; not even the names of Ethics Committee Members are disclosed! The much touted Right to Information (RTI) Act failed to elicit any response. Interestingly enough, most of our requests were turned down by the authorities raising the 'patient confidentiality' clause. We honestly believe that the confidentiality clause, meant to protect the best interests of trial participants in reality is being grossly and deliberately misinterpreted and misused to work against the interests of participants and hence needs a substantive review

CONCLUSION

Need for Law and Balance in India

As of today there is a need to fix the loopholes in the regulatory framework, enactment of law to monitor clinical research and drug trial of the country thereby making it more safer and to ensure that trial subjects who undergo such trials are well informed about risk of participation and are not exploited especially the vulnerable subjects participating in such trials. Enactment of law is not meant to restrict the clinical trials but to regulate and to enhance conducting of clinical trials in a more rational and scientifically sound manner thereby developing capacity building. Further a strong requirement for liberalizing the regulatory atmosphere of the scientific research and development in India is felt in favour of the sponsors conducting trial by bringing lot of clarity in regulations and by striking a balance between the trial subjects and the sponsors. Further clarity in approval regulations needs to be more time efficient, transparent and speed in licensing procedures or delay in approval process must be quashed to match global standards. India being a developing economy with suitable conditions for favourable clinical trials like multinational corporations willing to act as sponsors and trained investigators, developed infrastructure facility, reputed pharmaceutical companies, large diverse population, cost efficiency and availability of resources it is necessary to promote, appreciate and develop research culture and sound scientific development in the health sector in a more rational way by implementing existing laws with utmost transparency and diligence for which identifying the loopholes in the regulatory framework is required and not by restricting the growth of clinical trials in India. Indian Chapter of Association of Clinical Research Professionals (ACRP) is enacted which aims at bringing more professionalism. Issues and concerns voiced by the Human right activists and NGOs are indisputable, but setting a thumbs rule of rejecting or delaying the applications for conducting clinical trial is not providing a solution to the problem. Law and ethics are far from coterminous hence regulators must acknowledge other elements like social utility, economic growth etc. While framing laws as it is believed law often embodies ethical principles and law would always forbid as what is considered as unethical. In today's booming business environment no company or institution would touch upon a negative revelation for any reason whatsoever especially in matters related to violation of human rights, unprofessionalism, unethical treatment of trial subjects in a diverse competitive atmosphere. It is unfortunate to end up losing the prospects of growth of clinical research activities and scientific research development as in long run clinical trials not only contributes to better care of trail subjects than normal clinical practice and development in the research activities but can be foreseen as boon to the society eventually leading to development of new generic drugs or specific medications. Hence the Government of India has realized prospects of clinical research activities to a certain level but uncertainty in regulatory framework and approval mechanism would certainly cause huge losses to our health care sector therefore there is an urgent need to strike a balance between need for strict regulatory regime and need for clinical trials in India.

❑❑❑

2

Medical Profession, Patient and The Law

Consent – Informed Consent and Requirements of Consent

Dr. Nirmala Kumari K

Abstract

In the medical treatment, the relationship between the doctor and the patient has been in terms of benevolent paternalism. In ancient times, the obligation of the physician was solely in terms of promoting the welfare of the patient, diagnosing the ailment, and prescribing medicine or surgery, but seldom had they thought about patient's right. But nowadays this locus of the authority in decision making has been shifted from the physician to the patient. A patient will receive all the information that he or she needs in order to make decision as to take treatment or not or a particular operation. There involves the consent of the patient. Consent to treatment is the principle that a person must give permission before they receive any type of medical treatment, test or examination. This must be done on the basis of an explanation by a clinician. Consent from a patient is needed regardless of the procedure, whether it's a physical examination, organ donation or something else. The principle of consent is an important part of medical ethics and the international human rights law.

The earliest expression of this fundamental principle, based on autonomy, is found in the Nuremberg Code of 1947. The code makes it mandatory to obtain voluntary and informed consent of human subjects. Similarly, the Declaration of Helsinki adopted by the World Medical Association in 1964 emphasizes the importance of obtaining freely given informed consent for medical research by adequately informing the subjects of the aims, methods, anticipated benefits, potential hazards, and discomforts that the study may entail. Several international conventions and declarations have similarly ratified the importance of obtaining consent from patients before testing and treatment.

In India the principle of autonomy is enshrined within Art. 21 of the Indian Constitution, which deals with the right to life and personal liberty. Sec 88 of IPC, provides- Nothing which is not intended to cause death, is an offence to any person for whose benefit it is done in good faith, and who has given a consent. When a tort is committed, meaning that a defendant's actions interfered with the plaintiff's person or property, a plaintiff's consent will excuse the defendant of the wrongdoing.

In the view of the above background, the present chapter proposes to deal briefly with the aspects of laws concerning consent in medical cases, and their implications. The chapter discusses about the capacity to give consent, 'Real' consent in the United Kingdom (UK) and as 'Informed' consent in the United States (US). To account for the Indian position, unlike in the West, the courts have assigned immense significance to the requirement of informed consent. The Honorable Court has in different cases summarized principles relating to consent and the necessity to enact full-fledged laws so as to adjust to the need of the day.

Keywords: *Consent, Indian law, real consent, informed consent, requirements of consent*

INTRODUCTION

In common speech, consent occurs when one person voluntarily agrees to the proposal or desires of another.[1] The concept of consent has been relevantly used in several major contexts, including in law, medicine and intellectual property rights. Consent to treatment is the principle that a person must give permission before they receive any type of medical treatment, test or examination. This must be done on the basis of an explanation by a clinician. Consent from a patient is needed regardless of the procedure, whether it's a physical examination, organ donation or something else. The principle of consent is an important part of medical ethics and the international human rights law.

TYPES OF CONSENT

1. Implied consent is granted by a person's actions and the facts and circumstances of a particular situation or in some other cases by a person's silence or inaction.
2. Express consent is clearly and unmistakably stated, it may be given orally or by speech, or by non-verbally or by clear gesture such as a nod.
3. Informed consent in medicine is consent given by a person who has a clear appreciation and understanding of the facts, implications, and future consequences of an action. The term is also used in other contexts.
4. Unanimous consent, or general consent, by a group of several parties (e.g., an association) is consent given by all parties.

The element of consent is one of the critical issues in the area of medical treatment today. It is the prerogative of the patient to refuse to treatment even if the said treatment will save his or her life. No doubt this raises many ethical debates and falls at the heart of medical law today.

In the view of the above background, the present chapter proposes to deal briefly with the aspects of laws concerning consent in medical cases, their implications, and the necessity to enact a full-fledged law so as to adjust

1 Oxford English dictionary.

to the need of the day. This Chapter also highlights the ethical and legal dilemmas faced by doctors due to absence of legislation regarding age for giving valid consent for medical examination and procedures in India.

The earliest expression of this fundamental principle, based on autonomy, is found in the Nuremberg Code of 1947[2]. The code makes it mandatory to obtain voluntary and informed consent of human subjects. Similarly, the Declaration of Helsinki adopted by the World Medical Association in 1964[3] emphasizes the importance of obtaining freely given informed consent for medical research by adequately informing the subjects of the aims, methods, anticipated benefits, potential hazards, and discomforts that the study may entail. Several international conventions and declarations have similarly ratified the importance of obtaining consent from patients before testing and treatment.

The Chapter 7 of the Medical Council of India (MCI) Code of Ethics Regulation, 2002 defines consent as follows: Before performing an operation the physician should obtain in writing the consent from the husband or wife, parent or guardian in the case of minor, or the patient himself as the case may be. In an operation, which may result in sterility the consent of both husband and wife is needed.

CONSENT IN INDIAN LAW

The principle of autonomy is enshrined within Art. 21 of the Indian Constitution, which deals with the right to life and personal liberty. The

2 BRITISH MEDICAL JOURNAL No 7070 Volume 313: Page 1448, 7 December 1996. http://www.cirp.org/library/ethics/nuremberg/ visited on November 5, 2017 The judgment by the war crimes tribunal at Nuremberg laid down 10 standards to which physicians must conform when carrying out experiments on human subjects in a new code that is now accepted worldwide. This judgment established a new standard of ethical medical behavior for the post World War II human rights era. Amongst other requirements, this document enunciates the requirement of voluntary informed consent of the human subject. The principle of voluntary informed consent protects the right of the individual to control his own body.

3 https://www.wma.net/policies-post/wma-declaration-of-helsinki-ethical-principles-for-medical-research-involving-human-subjects/ visited on November 5, 2017 .The World Medical Association (WMA) has developed the Declaration of Helsinki as a statement of ethical principles for medical research involving human subjects, including research on identifiable human material and data.

expression personal liberty under Art. 21 is of the widest amplitude and covers a wide variety of rights, including the right to live with human dignity and all that goes along with it, and any act which damages, injures, or interferes with the use of any limb or faculty of a person, either permanently or temporarily.[4]

Indian Penal code is a comprehensive code intended to cover all the substantive aspects of criminal law. Sec 88 of IPC, provides – Nothing which is not intended to cause death, is an offence by reason of any harm which it may cause, or be intended by the doer to cause, or be known by the doer to be likely to cause, to any person for whose benefit it is done in good faith, and who has given a consent, whether express or implied, to suffer that harm, or to take the risk of that harm.

Sec. 89. Act done in good faith for benefit of child or insane person, by or by consent of guardian – Nothing which is done in good faith for the benefit of a person under twelve years of age, or of unsound mind, by or by consent, either express or implied, of the guardian or other person having lawful charge of that person, is an offence by reason of any harm which it may cause, or be intended by the doer to cause or be known by the doer to be likely to cause to that person

Sec 90 – Consent known to be given under fear or misconception – A consent is not such a consent as it intended by any section of this Code, if the consent is given by a person under fear of injury, or under a misconception of fact, and if the person doing the act knows, or has reason to believe, that the consent was given in consequence of such fear or misconception; or Consent of insane person.—if the consent is given by a person who, from unsoundness of mind, or intoxication, is unable to understand the nature and consequence of that to which he gives his consent; or Consent of child.—unless the contrary appears from the context, if the consent is given by a person who is under twelve years of age.

Thus Section 89 and Section 90 of the IPC suggest that the age for giving valid consent for any medical procedure is twelve years. Hence a doctor taking consent for medical or surgical treatment from a person aged twelve years or more can be legally said to have taken a valid consent and cannot be held criminally liable on this account.

4 *Maneka Gandhi v. Union of India*. AIR 1978 SC 597.

However Sections 87[5] IPC mentions eighteen years as the age for giving consent for acts not intended and not known to be likely to cause death or grievous hurt. These acts are not necessarily for the benefit of the person. Hence Section 87 IPC is not applicable to the medical profession as here, the acts are NOT done for the person's benefit. However valid consent can only be given at or above eighteen years of age.

Consent is a contract between two parties and as the Indian Contract Act states that to enter into a contract both parties must be at least eighteen years of age, this should be the age for giving valid consent in medicine. Under Indian Contract Act, consent[6] is said to be free when it is not caused by coercion, undue influence, fraud, misinterpretation or mistake. The consent must be to do a lawful act and it must not disobey any provision of the law.

The relationship between a medical professional and his patient is a contract by parties competent to contract giving rise to contractual obligations. Parties are generally competent (in accordance with the Indian Majority Act) (*i*) if they have attained the age of 18, (*ii*) are of sound mind, and (*iii*) are not disqualified by any law to which they are subject to. Furthermore, there is a stipulation in the contract law stating that consent of any party

---

5 87. Act not intended and not known to be likely to cause death or grievous hurt, done by consent.—Nothing which is not intended to cause death, or grievous hurt, and which is not known by the doer to be likely to cause death or grievous hurt, is an offence by reason of any harm which it may cause, or be intended by the doer to cause, to any person, above eighteen years of age, who has given consent, whether express or implied, to suffer that harm; or by reason of any harm which it may be known by the doer to be likely to cause to any such person who has consented to take the risk of that harm.

6 Consent is said to be free when it is not caused by—Consent is said to be free when it is not caused by—"

1. coercion, as defined in section 15, or
2. undue influence, as defined in section 16, or
3. fraud, as defined in section 17, or
4. misrepresentation, as defined in section 18, or
5. mistake, subject to the provisions of sections 20, 21 and 22. Consent is said to be so caused when it would not have been given but for the existence of such coercion, undue influence, fraud, misrepresentation or mistake.

(in our case it is the patient) that is obtained by coercion, undue-influence, mistake, misrepresentation or fraud, will render the agreement invalid.

However it should be noted that the Indian Contract Act is for conditions like marriages, financial agreements etc. and is not specific for the medical profession.

Tort is a civil wrong for which the aggrieved party may seek compensation from the wrong doer. The consequences would be payment of compensation (in civil) and imprisonment (in criminal). To commence, the patient may sue the medical practitioner in tort for trespass to person. When a tort is committed, meaning that a defendant's actions interfered with the plaintiff's person or property, a plaintiff's consent will excuse the defendant of the wrongdoing. Although a defendant's conduct may be considered immoral, or harmful, if the plaintiff allows these interferences to occur, then the defendant is not considered to have committed a tort. Consent occurs when a plaintiff displays a willingness to participate in the defendant's conduct. This consent can be express or implied.

In tort law, usage of force against any human body, without proper justification, is actionable irrespective of the quantum of force. If the medical practitioner attempts to treat a patient without obtaining proper consent, he will be held guilty under tort law. Consent for treatment may be expressed or implied. The patient entering the consultation chambers by his own volition may be considered to have given consent for a clinical diagnosis to be carried out. Consent may be inferred from the general submission by a patient to orders given by a doctor during clinical diagnosis. This is an excellent example of implied consent.

CAPACITY AND INFORMATION WHILE SEEKING CONSENT

There are two more additional aspects to be borne in mind: first, valid consent can be obtained only from a patient who is competent to consent and secondly, such consent must also be informed consent.[7]

7 https://www.ncbi.nlm.nih.gov/pmc/articles/PMC2779959/ Consent and medical treatment: The legal paradigm in India by *Om prakash v. Nandimath* visited on 9-Nov-17.

To be competent to give a legally effective consent, the patient must be endowed with the ability to weigh the risks and benefits of the treatment that is being proposed to him. The law presumes that such an ability is generally acquired with the attainment of the age of maturity. A person who has attained the competent age and who has sound mind can give valid consent to the medical practitioner for any treatment. The law thus presumes capacity, rationality, autonomy, and freedom if the person has attained the age of so called maturity. On the other hand, where there is reason to believe that a patient is unable to understand the nature of the treatment and its benefits or side effects before making the decision, it is necessary to consider whether an adult presumption of capacity is rebutted in that particular case. If the patient is incompetent to give consent, then the consent may be obtained from the attendant of the patient.

The law also presumes that the medical practitioner is in a dominating position vis-à-vis the patient; hence, it is his duty to obtain proper consent by providing all the necessary information. Consent without necessary information is no consent at all. Unfortunately, the expression 'informed consent' is often used without precision.[8]

There is a difference in the nature of express consent of the patient, known as 'Real' consent in the United Kingdom (UK) and as 'Informed' consent in the United States (US).[9]

The "informed consent" doctrine is American in origin and relates to the amount of information that a patient should be provided with to avoid any probable action in negligence. Rarely, a medical practitioner or a hospital administrator can rely upon the consent form signed by the patient, when the contention is that he was made to sign on the dotted lines of such format without proving necessary information. This practice is also developed by the practice of treating the consent form as a one of standard forms of contracts and eliminating all such unfair and sweeping clauses, which will only benefit the medical practitioner. However, the nature of the information that a patient must have in order to give informed consent is a

8 *Ibid.*

9 mediLAW- Real Consent and not Informed Consent Applicable in India-By KK Aggarwal-Available in http://medind.nic.in/iaa/t14/i9/iaat14i9p392.pdf visited on 29-10-2017.

debatable question, as the American and English viewpoints differ to some extent. In contrast to this, the English approach is doctor centric, which is also popularly narrated as the prudent doctor test of disclosure. Here, the doctor is taken as a professional-man endowed with greater prudence to protect the right interest of the patient and bestowed with the final right to decide what information shall be divulged to the patient considering the circumstances and how much information is to be divulged.

Finally, whatever might be the difference of approach it is evident that a medical practitioner is obligated to provide the necessary information before obtaining consent from a patient. To account for the Indian position, unlike in the West, it may be concluded that the courts have assigned immense significance to the requirement of informed consent.

A medical practitioner in India has a duty to provide all the necessary information to the patient in a language that is understandable to him. Regarding the quantum of information, there are no clear parameters laid down by the courts. Therefore, it is reasonable information which a doctor deems fit considering best practices. Considering the knowledge gap in this regard, the professional regulatory body for medicine can play an important role in establishing standards. Importance of written consent has also not been given its due. As far as court cases are concerned written consent is of paramount importance in legal matters as verbal consent can be denied and is difficult to prove in court.[10]. Oral consent is legally valid when taken for some specific procedures like injecting medication, drawing blood for pathological examination, gynaecological examinations etc. Oral consent can be proved in court if it was taken in the presence of witnesses or if the doctor records in the case record of the patient that oral consent was taken. For major procedures and surgery, written consent should be taken but if for some reason only oral consent is possible then the doctor should enter it into the case record of the patient.[11]

10 Medical consent in India - Ethical and legal issues-by Anil Kohli -Department of Forensic Medicine, University College of Medical Sciences, Delhi-110095 accessed from http://www.anilaggrawal.com/ ij/vol_008_no_002/papers/paper004.html on 2-11-2017.

11 *Ibid.*

The value of signed written consent is important for those cases that go to court as a written consent will be of great value for the doctor when he defends himself. According to the Indian Medical Council (Professional Conduct and Ethics) Regulations 2002, before performing an operation written consent should be obtained. Those doctors who take consent to be legal contracts between two parties feel that both the doctor and patient should sign the consent form as this is the basic requirement of a contract, otherwise it becomes null and void. Two witnesses who are uninterested third parties should preferably also sign it.[12] The Consent form used in All India Institute of Medical Sciences, New Delhi (our country's premier medical institute) also requires the form to be countersigned by the treating doctor who certifies that informed consent has been taken.[13]

Regarding this, the apex court gave an impacting judgment in the area. Wherein the court observed that "where a surgeon is consulted by a patient and consent of the patient is taken for diagnostic procedure/surgery, such consent can't be considered as authorization or permission to perform therapeutic surgery either conservative or radical (except in a life-threatening emergent situation)"[14].

For the first time in India, the court ruled that however broad consent might be for diagnostic procedure, it cannot be used for therapeutic surgery. Furthermore, the court observed that "where the consent by the patient is for a particular operative surgery it can't be treated as consent for an unauthorized additional procedure involving removal of an organ only on the ground that it is beneficial to the patient or is likely to prevent some danger developing in the future, where there is no imminent danger to the life or health of the patient". This proposition puts fetter upon the role of a "paternal doctor" in the Indian scenario. In this[15] case, a 44-year-old unmarried female consulted her doctor and was advised to undergo a laparoscopy. A few consent forms were taken from her of which one was for admission and another one was for the surgery. The relevant one among

12 Bastia BK, Kuruvilla A, Saralaya KM. Validity of consent- A review of statutes. Indian J Med Sci. 2005 Feb; 59(2): 74-8.

13 Sharma RK. Concise Textbook of Forensic Medicine and Toxicology.1st ed. India: Elsevier; 2005. p. 161-2.

14 *Samera Kohli v Dr. Prabha Manchanda and Another*. 2008;(1) SCALE 442.

15 *Ibid.*

such consent forms gave the doctor an allowance to carry out a "diagnostic and operative laparoscopy" and there was an additional endorsement that a "laparotomy may be needed". When the patient was in the operation theatre (and was unconscious), another proxy consent was taken from her attending mother for a hysterectomy. Her uterus, ovaries, and fallopian tubes were removed. Subsequently, when an action was brought, it was held that the operation was conducted without real consent and the doctors were held liable.

This decision is of very far reaching consequences, pushing the development of consent law to new heights. It is contended that it is not only informed consent which is imperative now, but the same shall be "prior informed consent" unless there is imminent threat to the patient's life. In addition, this decision curtails the scope of proxy consent from the person having parental authority or an attendant.

The Honourable Court summarized principles relating to consent as follows:

(*i*) A doctor has to seek and secure the consent of the patient before commencing a 'treatment' (the term 'treatment' includes surgery also). The consent so obtained should be real and valid, which means that the patient should have the capacity and competence to consent; his consent should be voluntary; and his consent should be on the basis of adequate information concerning the nature of the treatment procedure, so that he knows what is consenting to.

(*ii*) The 'adequate information' to be furnished by the doctor (or a member of his team) who treats the patient, should enable the patient to make a balanced judgment as to whether he should submit himself to the particular treatment as to whether he should submit himself to the particular treatment or not. This means that the Doctor should disclose (*a*) nature and procedure of the treatment and its purpose, benefits and effect; (*b*) alternatives if any available; (*c*) an outline of the substantial risks; and (*d*) adverse consequences of refusing treatment. But there is no need to explain remote or theoretical risks involved, which may frighten or confuse a patient and result in refusal of consent for the necessary treatment. Similarly, there is no need to explain the remote or theoretical risks of refusal to take treatment which may persuade a patient to undergo a fanciful or unnecessary treatment. A balance should be achieved between the need for disclosing necessary and adequate information and at the same time avoid the possibility of the patient being deterred from agreeing to a necessary treatment or offering to undergo an unnecessary treatment.

(*iii*) Consent given only for a diagnostic procedure, cannot be considered as consent for therapeutic treatment. Consent given for a specific treatment procedure will not be valid for conducting some other treatment procedure. The fact that the unauthorized additional surgery is beneficial to the patient, or that it would save considerable time and expense to the patient, or would relieve the patient from pain and suffering in future, are not grounds of defence in an action in tort for negligence or assault and battery. The only exception to this rule is where the additional procedure though unauthorized, is necessary in order to save the life or preserve the health of the patient and it would be unreasonable to delay such unauthorized procedure until patient regains consciousness and takes a decision.

(*iv*) There can be a common consent for diagnostic and operative procedures where they are contemplated. There can also be a common consent for a particular surgical procedure and an additional or further procedure that may become necessary during the course of surgery.

(*v*) The nature and extent of information to be furnished by the doctor to the patient to secure the consent need not be of the stringent and high degree mentioned in Canterbury but should be of the extent which is accepted as normal and proper by a body of medical men skilled and experienced in the particular field. It will depend upon the physical and mental condition of the patient, the nature of treatment, and the risk and consequences attached to the treatment.

EMERGENCY SITUATION AND THE CONSENT

Interestingly, in India, the entire gamut of laws on consent turns into complex propositions if an emergency medical situation arises. In, *Paschim*

Banga Khet Mazdoor Samity and Ors v State of West Bengal[16] and Another the apex court ruled that a medical practitioner has a duty to treat a patient in an emergency. Emphasizing the paramount duty of any "welfare state", the Supreme Court stated that Art. 21 imposes an obligation on the State to safeguard the right to life of every person. Preservation of human life is thus of paramount importance. The government hospitals run by the state are bound by duty to extend medical assistance for preserving human life. Failure on the part of a government hospital to provide timely medical treatment to a person in need of such treatment results in the violation of his right to life guaranteed under Art. 21.

Proceeding in the same direction, the court emphasized further that every doctor whether at a Government hospital or otherwise has the professional obligation to extend his services with due expertise for protecting life. No law or state action can intervene to avoid or delay the discharge of the paramount obligation cast upon members of the medical profession. The obligation of a doctor is total, absolute, and paramount. Laws of procedure whether in statutes or otherwise that would interfere with the discharge of this obligation cannot be sustained and must, therefore, give way.[17]

In *Pt. Parmanand Katara v Union of India*,[18] the apex court laid down some important guidelines such as (i) The doctor when approached by an injured person, shall render all such help which is possible for him at that time, including referring him to the proper experts, (ii) the doctor treating such persons shall be protected by law, as they are not contravening any procedural laws of the land (regarding jurisdictions etc.), and (iii) all legal bars (either real or perceived by the doctors) are deemed to have been eliminated by the verdict. This is in consonance with the hypocratic oath, which a doctor takes when entering the profession. Hence, a doctor is duty-bound to treat a patient in the case of an emergency, without waiting for any formalities. There are several statutes (like medical institutions regulation acts in various states) imposing this duty upon medical establishments to treat emergency patients, especially accident victims.

---

16 *Paschim Banga Khet Mazdoor Samity and Ors v State of West Bengal and Another*. 1996. 4 SCC 37.

17 *Pt. Parmanand Katara v Union of India*, AIR 1989 SC 2039.

18 *Ibid.*

The initial proposition (and the attempt of the Supreme Court) is quiet understandable as the doctor has to do his best to save life in emergency situations. This is irrespective of complying with any of the formalities, including consent. Hypothetically, if a patient in an emergency resists taking treatment, what shall be the way out? Indian courts are not very clear on that. The above decisions are delivered keeping in mind the accident victims who were denied medical treatment by doctors, terming them as medico-legal cases. Moreover, in the above instances, the patient would go himself, or be taken by someone (due to an unconscious state) to the doctor to seek medical treatment.

In *Dr. T.T. Thomas v. Elisa,*[19] the patient was admitted into the hospital on March 11, 1974. Upon admission, the patient was diagnosed as a case of perforated appendix with peritonitis requiring an operation. But, unfortunately no operation was done until his death on March 13, 1974. The contention of the doctor was that no surgery could be adhered to, albeit the suggestion, because the patient did not consent for the surgery. Therefore, other measures were taken to ameliorate the condition of the patient, which grew worse by the next day. Although the patient was then willing to undergo the operation, his condition did not permit it. On the other hand, the version of the respondent (i.e., the Plaintiff) was that the doctor demanded money for performing the surgery. Furthermore, the doctor was attending to some chores in an outside private nursing home to conduct operations on the other patients and that the appellant doctor came back only after the death of the patient. The two versions before the court were: 1) the plaintiff (the deceased patient's wife) said that the doctors concerned demanded a bribe, hence the operation was delayed until it proved fatal and 2) the version of denial for consent. Finally, the court delivered a verdict in favour of the plaintiffs stating that consent under such an emergent situation is not mandatory.[20] It is interesting to note the following observations:

"The consent factor may be important very often in cases of selective operations, which may not be imminently necessary to save the patient's life. But there can be instances where a surgeon is not expected to say that

19 *15. TT Thomas (Dr.) v. Elisa*. AIR 1987 Ker. 52.

20 *Ibid.*

'I did not operate on him because, I did not get his consent'. Such cases very often include emergency operations where a doctor cannot wait for the consent of his patient or where the patient is not in a fit state of mind to give or not to give a conscious answer regarding consent. Even if he is in a fit condition to give a voluntary answer, the surgeon has a duty to inform him of the dangers ahead of the risks involved by going without an operation at the earliest time possible".

"When a surgeon or medical man advances a plea that the patient did not give his consent for the surgery or the course of treatment advised by him, the burden is on him to prove that the non-performance of the surgery or the non-administration of the treatment was on account of the refusal of the patient to give consent thereto. This is especially so in a case where the patient is not alive to give evidence. Consent is implicit in the case of a patient who submits to the doctor and the absence of consent must be made out by the patient alleging it".

Finally, as stated above, before holding the doctor liable, the court said that "we also hold that the failure to perform an emergency operation on the deceased on 11-3-1974 amounts to negligence and the death of the deceased was on account of that failure". This decision makes the entire discussion of consent law more complex. Although this case law can't be given more accent (because it is a High Court decision), the viewpoint is an interesting one to note. In light of all these developments, it may be concluded that there are many grey areas in this field of consent law in India, which can be eliminated by pro-active intervention by the concerned professional regulatory body.

As a result of the confusion and panic on informed consent, doctors are scurrying to prepare various 'legally foolproof' consent forms. A signed consent form of any nature neither guarantees a doctor protection against legal action nor ensures patient satisfaction. It merely demonstrates that some process to exchange information was followed. Wrangling about consent forms does little to advance the debate about the ethical aspect of informed consent.[21]

---

21 http://ijme.in/articles/informed-consent-legal-and-ethical-aspects/?galley=html – Indian Journal of Medical Ethics-Medicine and the Law-Informed consent — legal and ethical aspects by Arun Bal visited on 20-10-2017.

Requirements of a Valid Consent

1. A doctor must take the consent of the patient before commencing a treatment/procedure. Except in emergencies, informed consent should be obtained sometime prior to the procedure so that the patient does not feel pressurized or rushed to sign. On the day of surgery, the patient may be under extreme mental stress or under influence of pre-medicant drugs which may hamper his decision-making ability. Consent remains valid for an indefinite period, provided there is no change in patient condition or proposed intervention. It should be confirmed at the time of surgery.

2. Consent must be taken from the patient himself: The doctor before performing any procedure must obtain patient's consent.[22] No one can consent on behalf of a competent adult. In *Dr. Ramcharan Thiagarajan Facs v. Medical Council of India*[23] case, disciplinary action was awarded to the surgeon for not taking a proper informed consent for the entire procedure of kidney and pancreas transplant surgery from the patient.

   In some situations, beside patient consent, it is desirable to take additional consent of spouse. In sterilization procedures, according to the Ministry of Health and Family Welfare, Government of India guidelines, consent of spouse is not required. The Medical Council of India (clause 7.16) however states that in case an operation carries the risk of sterility, the consent of both husband and wife is needed. [24] It is advisable to take consent of spouse when the treatment or procedure may adversely affect or limit sex functions, or result in death of an unborn child[25]. In case of minor, consent of person with parental responsibility should be taken. In an emergency, the person in charge of the child at that time can

22 *Samira Kohli v. Dr. Prabha Manchanda and Anr* on 16 January, 2008. Civil Appeal No. 1949 of 2004. (2008) 2 SCC 1; AIR 2008 SC 1385.

23 Karnataka High Court. Writ Petition No. 11207/2013 (GM-RES). Available from: http://www.indiankanoon.com /doc/10293098/ visited on 29-10-2017.

24 Supra note 4.

25 Reddy KS, Murty OP. Medical law and ethics. In: The Essentials of Forensic Medicine and Toxicology. 32 nd ed. Hyderabad: K Suguna Devi; 2013. p. 22-55. Back to cited text no. 9.

consent in absence of parents or guardians (loco parentis). In a medical emergency, life-saving treatment can be given even in absence of consent.

3. The patient should have the capacity and competence to consent

   A person is competent to contract if (*i*) he has attained the age of majority, (*ii*) is of sound mind and (*iii*) is not disqualified from contracting by any law to which he is subject.

4. Consent should be free and voluntary.

   Consent is said to be free when it is not caused by coercion, undue influence, fraud, misrepresentation, or mistake.

5. Consent should be informed.

   Consent should be on the basis of adequate information concerning the nature of the treatment procedure. Consent should be informed and based on intelligent understanding. The doctor must disclose information regarding patient condition, prognosis, treatment benefits, adverse effects, available alternatives, risk of refusing treatment and the approximate treatment cost. He should encourage questions and answer all queries. If the possibility of a risk, including the risk of death, due to performance of a procedure or its refusal is remote or only theoretical, it need not be explained. Exceptions to physician's duty to disclose include: (i) Patient refusal to be informed; this should be documented. (ii) If the doctor feels that providing information to a patient who is anxious or disturbed would not be processed rationally by him and is likely to psychologically harm him, the information may be withheld from him (therapeutic privilege); he should then communicate with patient's close relative, family doctor or both.

6. Consent should be procedure specific.

   Consent given only for a diagnostic procedure, cannot be considered as consent for the therapeutic treatment. Consent given for a specific treatment procedure will not be valid for conducting some other procedure. In *Samira Kohli v. Dr. Prabha Manchanda and Anr*[26] case, the doctor was held negligent for performing

26 Supra note 21.

an additional procedure on the patient without taking her prior consent. An additional procedure may be performed without consent only if it is necessary to save the life or preserve the health of the patient and it would be unreasonable to delay, until patient regains consciousness and takes a decision.

7. A common consent for diagnostic and operative procedures may be taken where they are contemplated.
8. Consent obtained during the course of surgery is not acceptable

   In Dr. *Janaki S Kumar and Anr v. Mrs. Sarafunnisa* case[27], in an allegation of performing sterilization without consent, it was contended that consent was obtained during the course of surgery. The commission held that the patient under anaesthesia could neither understand the risk involved nor could she give a valid consent.
9. Consent for examining or observing a patient for educational purpose. Prior to examining or observing patients for educational purpose, their consent must be taken.
10. Blanket consent is not valid. Consent should be procedure specific. An all-encompassing consent to the effect 'I authorize so and so to carry out any test/procedure/surgery in the course of my treatment' is not valid.
11. Fresh consent should be taken for a repeat procedure.

    A fresh written informed consent must be obtained prior to every surgical procedure that includes re-exploration procedure. In *Dr. Shailesh Shah v. Aphraim Jayanand Rathod* case,[28] the surgeon was found deficient in service and was liable for compensation as he had performed a re-exploration surgery without a written consent from the patient.

---

27 *Dr. Janaki S Kumar and Anr v. Mrs. Sarafunnisa* on 21 June, 1999. Kerala State Consumer Disputes Redressal Commission, Thiruvananthapuram. Appeal No. 850 of 1998. (1999) I CPJ 66. Back to cited text no. 25.

28 *Dr Shailesh Shah v. Aphraim Jayanand Rathod.* National Consumer Disputes Redressal Commission New Delhi, FA No. 597 of 1995. From the order dated 8 Nov, 1995 in complaint No. 31/94, State Commission Gujarat. Available from: http://www.ncdrc.nic.in/fa59795.html. [Last accessed on 29-10-2017).

12. Patient has the right to refuse treatment. Competent patients have the legal and moral right to refuse treatment, even in life-threatening emergency situations. In such cases informed refusal must be obtained and documented, over the patient's witnessed signature. To detain an adult patient against his will in a hospital is unlawful. If a patient demands discharge from hospital against medical advice, this should be recorded, and his signature obtained.
13. Unilaterally executed consents are void, Consent signed only by the patient and not by the doctor is not valid.
14. Witnessed consents are legally more dependable. The role of a witness is even more important in instances when the patient is illiterate, and one needs to take his/her thumb impression.
15. Consent should be properly documented. Video-recording of the informed consent process may also be done but with a prior consent for the same. This should be documented. It is commonly done for organ transplant procedures. If consent form is not signed by the patient or is amended without his signed authorization, it can be claimed that the procedure was not consented to.
16. Patient is free to withdraw his consent anytime. When consent is withdrawn during the performance of a procedure, the procedure should be stopped. The doctor may address to patient's concerns and may continue the treatment only if the patient agrees. If stopping a procedure at that point puts patient's life in danger, the doctor may continue with the procedure till such a risk no longer exists.
17. Consent for illegal procedures is invalid. There can be no valid consent for operations or procedures which are illegal. Consent for an illegal act such as criminal abortion is invalid. Consent is no defence in cases of professional negligence.

CONCLUSION

Consent to medical procedures plays an extremely important role in the context of health care provision. The concept of consent operates as a unifying principle running through health care law. It represents the legal and ethical expression of the human right to have one's autonomy and self – determination respected.

The requirement that the patient's consent be obtained thus operates as a constraint on the power of the health care professional. It is particularly important that the law protects this right given that the health professional, particularly the doctor, is in a powerful position vis-à-vis the patient, and that her role frequently involves touching, examining and operating upon patients. Given this power dynamic, control of information becomes a key feature in defining the balance of power between the health professional and the patient.

Medical Negligence

Dr. Suneet Kashyap

Abstract

This paper titled 'medical negligence' basically deals with those aspects of negligence which is committed by a medical professional in the course of his employment. The paper focuses on the nature of medical negligence and the legal framework available under the Indian law. Negligence committed by a medical professional can be generally categorized under three heads which are civil negligence, criminal negligence and negligence under the consumer protection Act. When can a person sue a medical professional under the aforesaid heads is well discussed in this paper. A few suggestions are also recommended keeping in view the difficulties faced by patient and a doctor both.

INTRODUCTION

Medical Profession is one of the oldest noble professions and the most humanitarian one, which is directly related to the life of human beings. That is why the doctors are placed next to God and treated as second God. This profession is built on the concept of the utmost good faith where a patient has a blind faith on the doctor under whom he is given medical treatment for cure of his ailments. This profession demands for, extra care and caution on the part of a medical professional i.e. the Doctor, while he is engaged in medical treatment of a patient. Due to emergence of institutionalization of the medical professional in the present day scenario; the hospitals are equally under obligation for the same duty of care as that of a doctor who is working on its panel for delivery of his service to a patient.

The standard of care from doctors and hospital authority is expected to be more in comparison with other cases of professional services. Therefore, proper care must be taken by the doctors and other authorities of a hospital to avoid negligence in their services which is known as medical negligence in common parlance.

NEGLIGENCE MEANING

It is very difficult to define negligence in specific terms as no generalized definition of it has been provided in any Statute or law. It is one of a most debatable topic in the jurisprudence of Law of Torts. As a general rule, the violation of a public duty, enjoined by a person for the protection of his person or property, under any law is termed as negligence.

The Black law dictionary definition the term negligence as –

" a conduct, whether of action or omission, which may be declared and treated as negligence without any argument or proof as to the particular surrounding circumstances, either because it is in violation of statue or valid municipal ordinance or because it is so palpably opposed to the dictates of common prudence that it can be said without hesitation or doubt that no careful person would have been guilty of it.".

In the case of *Jacob Mathew v. State of Punjab,*[1] the Supreme Court while considering the matter related to the medical negligence has held as under-

"Negligence is the breach of a duty caused by omission to do something which a reasonable man guided by those considerations which ordinarily regulate the conduct of human affairs would do, or doing something which a prudent and reasonable man would not do. The definition of negligence as given in Law of Torts, Ratanlal & Dhirajlal (edited by Justice G.P. Singh), referred to hereinabove, holds good. Negligence becomes actionable on account of injury resulting from the act or omission amounting to negligence attributable to the person sued. The essential components of negligence are three: `duty', `breach' and `resulting damage'.".

Accordingly, it may be observed that the following may be the basic element of the term 'negligence'–

1 2005(3) K.L.T. 965(SC).

1. A legal duty to take care;
2. Breach of the said duty; and
3. Consequential damage that follows.

In order to prove a case of negligence before a court of law, all the aforesaid criteria are required to be satisfied and in cases of medical negligence in India, the ambit of duty of care further increases, as the question of life and death of a person is involved in such situation.

Nature of medical negligence- In the laws of Torts the term negligence is confined in relative terminology, which directly relates to certain category of persons who professes some special type of skill such as architects, doctors, accountants and lawyers. Therefore, the person performing services under any of the afore-mentioned category of profession are required to have the requisite skill to do their work while acting in the capacity of such professional.

It is also observed that in India there is growth in regard to cases of medical negligence and the reasons behind the same may be assigned to the degrading standards of professional competence of the doctors and other related facilities provided by the hospitals as also the faculty therapeutic and diagnostic system and procedures adopted by the medical professional while providing treatment to a patient.

In past, the common people were afraid of suing doctors or hospitals due to non-awareness of related laws and procedures, however, with the passage of time, and emerging technological development; awareness among common people regarding their rights in cases of medical negligence has been emerged with a fast pace. As a result the Indian society has now developed awareness in regard to their rights and duties towards the medical profession vis-à-vis the growing trends of medical negligence. The awareness of legal rights and their remedies may be self-evident from the filing of cases related to the medical negligence seeking of redressal of grievance for and on behalf of the patients as also for claim of damages suffered by them due to the negligence of doctors and hospitals.

LEGAL FRAMEWORK OF MEDICAL NEGLIGENCE IN INDIA

The legal framework , in India, to regulate the medical profession and its working as also to provide for appropriate remedies to a victim in cases of medical negligence is very sound. Although there is no unified law for the aforesaid purposes however, the relevant provisions of different laws in force may be said to be sufficient enough to regulate and prohibit the emerging trends of the medical negligence.

In the context of Indian law, broadly, the medical negligence comes under following three categories, namely:

(*i*) criminal negligence;

(*ii*) civil negligence; and

(*iii*) negligence under the Consumer Protection Act, 1986.

Different provisions regarding the remedies in the form of punishment and compensation are provided under the aforesaid schemes of legal jurisprudence.

(*i*) **Criminal law and medical negligence** – Under the legal frame work of the criminal law in India, the negligence caused by a medical professional is primarily regulated by the provisions of section 304A of the Indian Penal Code, 1860 which provides that –

"whoever causes the death of a person by a rash or negligent act not amounting to culpable homicide shall be punished with imprisonment for a term of two years, or with a fine or with both.".

Accordingly, when a person engaged in the profession of medicines is charged for the commission of an offence within the meaning of aforesaid provisions of the Indian Penal Code, he shall be liable for the punishment of the offence as provided therein.

The Criminal liability liable to be imposed upon a doctor under the aforesaid provisions of the Indian Penal Code directly relates with the specific situations under which a patient suffers any harm or succumbed to death due to the medical administered by the doctor charged under the said provision.

Certain conditions must be satisfied before criminal liability may be considered by the Court. The person who is accused must have committed an act of omission or commission; this act must have been in breach of the person's duty, and this must have caused harm to the injured person. The complainant must prove the allegation against the doctor by citing the best evidence available in medical science and by presenting an expert opinion. The question of degree has always been relevant for distinguishing negligence under the civil and criminal law. In *Kurban Hussein v. the State of Maharashtra*,[2] in the case concerning Section 304 (A) of Indian Penal Code, 1860, it was held that-

"To impose criminal liability under Section 304-A, it is necessary that the death should have been the direct result of rash and negligent act of the accused, without other person's intervention.".

(ii) **Civil law and medical negligence** – The position regarding medical negligence under civil law is very important as it encompasses many elements within itself. In the ambit of the law of torts, the right to sue under the general civil law is available to a patient even if medical professionals has provided medical treatment to him without any consideration.

Under the provisions of the law of torts cases of negligence related to transfusion of blood of incorrect blood groups, leaving a mop in patient's abdomen after the operation, removal of organs without consent and administering wrong medicine resulting in injury etc. may be covered.

In the case of the *State of Haryana v. Smt Santra*,[3] the Supreme Court held that every doctor "has a duty to act with a reasonable degree of care and skill." However, since no human is perfect and even the most renowned specialist can commit a mistake in diagnosing a disease, a doctor can be held liable for negligence only if one can prove that she/ he is guilty of a failure that no doctor with ordinary skills would be guilty of if acting with reasonable care.

2 (1965) 2 SCR 622.

3 AIR 2000 SC 3335.

(*iii*) **Consumer Protection Act and Medical Negligence** – Initially, there was a huge speculation and debate on the issue whether medical services are explicitly or categorically included in the definition of "Services" as enshrined under section 2(1)(o) of the Consumer Protection Act, 1986, as per which the expression deficiency of service means any fault, imperfection, shortcoming, or inadequacy in the quality, nature, or manner of performance that is required to be maintained by or under any law for the time being in force or has been undertaken to be performed by a person in pursuance of a contract or otherwise about any service. However, in the year of 1995, the Supreme Court in the case of *Indian Medical Association v. V.P Shantha,*[4] *by its verdict* brought the medical profession within the ambit of 'service' as defined in the Consumer Protection Act, 1986. The aforesaid landmark judgment of the apex court has paved the ways for bringing in the relationship of patient and medical professional within the ambit of the provisions of the Consumer Protection Act, 1986 and resultantly providing the patient the power to sue doctors under the provisions of the Consumer Protection Act, 1986, if they sustained injuries during the course of treatment for claiming compensation.

VICARIOUS LIABILITY OF HOSPITALS FOR MEDICAL NEGLIGENCE

The principle of vicarious liability is based on a latin maxim "*qui facit per aliumfacit per se*" which describes that the one who acts through another act in his or her own interest.

A doctor or a hospital may also be liable vicariously within the aforesaid provision, if his employee or servant causes the death of a patient due to their reckless behaviour.

In the case of medical negligence, if any of the doctor (including doctor engaged for specific cases) or staff of the hospital is negligent in the performance of their prescribed work, the hospital may be held liable on the negligent conduct of such staff or doctor. This principle was established in the case of *Aparna Dutt .v. Apollo Hospital Enterprises Ltd.*[5]

4 AIR 1996 SC 550 : (1995) 6 SCC 651.

5 *2002 ACJ 954 (Mad. HC).*

CONCLUSION AND SUGGESTIONS

1. Keeping in view the scope and ambit of the Indian laws related to the aspects of medical negligence. The most crucial aspect is related to the principle of 'Burden of Proof'. In the cases of medical negligence, the burden of proof lies on the plaintiff or the victim. Therefore, if a patient alleges malpractice or negligence on the part of the medical professional, the law will require from him to establish a higher standard of evidence to support his claim. Here, for an ordinary human being or a patient, it may be very difficult to determine the exact damage and the causal relation between the injury and the fault of the doctor. Resultantly, the patient may not be able to prove doctor's fault beyond a reasonable doubt, since, the field of medicine is unexpected and unpredictable and anytime anything can happen in a human body and so, it reverts to the plaintiff. Therefore, it is high time that the laws dictating upon the medical negligence get changed so as to suit patients first. And the patients should be sensitized regarding their rights against medical malpractices by civil societies through a proper education channel.
2. Negligence should be regulated *vide* the principles of reasonableness of common prudence and considering the said principles only the negligence should be first established in order to give the compensation in medical negligence cases. Provided that where a doctor performs his duty with the utmost care he should not be held responsible for the consequential harms caused to a patient in the garb of medical negligence.
3. Standard of care in cases of medical professional should be comparatively higher and that higher standard should be taken into account while deciding the issue of negligence and awarding compensation to the victim.
4. Medical professional should not be harassed unreasonably and unwanted apprehension and fear should not be created on the medical fraternity because such unwanted fear may restrict him to apply his best mind and ability in extending treatment to the

patient for the ailment rather they should be given some liberty in certain peculiar situation where they need to make their judgment without any apprehension freely for the benefit of the patient in particular and for the society in general.

Books Referred

1. Medical negligence and the laws in India by tapas Kumar Koley, OUP India Publications.
2. Laws of Medical Negligence and Compensation by RK Baig, Bharat law Publications.
3. Medical Negligence: What doctor, patient and Hospitals should know by PB Shenoy, Sterling Publishers Pvt Ltd.
4. Legal issues in Medical Practices: medico-legal guidelines for safe practice by VP Singh, Jaypee brothers medical publishers.

❑❑❑

3

Medical Jurisprudence

Medical Jurisprudence: An Appraisal on Right to Health in India From Ethical Perspective

C.E. Pratap

Abstract

Medical jurisprudence deals with the legal responsibilities of the medical practitioner those arise from doctor patient relationship. Preservation and saving of life with duty of care are established as absolute and supreme constitutional obligations of the medical profession. Conversely, refusing adequate and emergency care in public and private medical establishments is considered a violation of the fundamental right to life. The issue of emergency medical care, which often includes dealing with life and death situations, brings into sharp focus several intersecting concerns regarding health services, the rights of patients, and the duty of the State and medical profession. The indignity caused by the refusal to treat patients in critical condition, resulting in the loss of life, undue suffering, consequent morbidity and financial loss has been challenged in courts on the ground of moral and ethical principles that form the core of the medical profession. This happens so because of the medico-legal procedure that is involved in certain cases which a doctor is duty bound to follow, but however the physician should respond to any request for his assistance in an emergency.

Keywords: *Right to health, medico-legal cases, ethics, emergency medical care, rights of patient*

INTRODUCTION

Medical service being the most humane of the services to humanity needs constant improvement, enrichment and application of mind. Medical jurisprudence embraces all questions which affect the civil or social rights of individuals, as well as cases of injuries to persons, and brings the medical practitioner in contact with law.[1] Thus medical jurisprudence deals with the legal aspect of medical practice which is guided and guarded by some codes, ethics and legislations.[2] The goals of medicine, as laid down in the Hippocratic Oath, are founded on profound moral and ethical principles, which require healthcare providers to be committed to the mitigation of suffering, to uphold the primacy of life and to recognize their corresponding obligations.[3] A qualified medical practitioner, who is entrusted with the physical and mental well-being of his patient, must realize his obligations to his patient. Medical jurisprudence certainly encompasses within its ambit the ethical aspects to be followed by the doctors while providing medical treatment to the patient, more so particularly in medico-legal cases involving accidents and emergency medical care. The right to health though not expressly provided under the Constitution of India, the same is guaranteed implicitly as fundamental right under Article 21 as part of right to life. The core principle of medical jurisprudence thus expects articulation of positive duty by the medical practitioner in safeguarding the life of an individual who is in need of immediate care and medical treatment at times of emergency without looking in to the medico-legal

1 Jaising Modi, P., (2016). A Textbook of Medical Jurisprudence and Toxicology, LexisNexis, Haryana, India, p.3.

2 Apurba Nandy, (2010). Principles of Forensic Medicine including Toxicology, New Central Book Agency (P) Ltd, Kolkatta, India, p.1.

3 *Parmanand Katara v. Union of India,* AIR 1989 SC 2039.

formalities that are incidental thereto. The right to health thus casts a constitutional obligation and legal responsibilities upon the doctors to provide medical treatment without insisting on the procedural formalities from a patient who is in dire need of medical care.

RIGHT TO HEALTH: A CORE COMPONENT OF MEDICAL JURISPRUDENCE

Medical jurisprudence requires some basic formalities to be complied with by a doctor in treating the patients involving medico-legal cases. These *interalia* include the formal registration of complaint to the police authorities, registering of a case that involves medico-legal nature etc. But a doctor should respond to any request for his assistance in cases of emergency without insisting on the compliance of legal formalities by the police on receipt of information regarding a medico-legal case as mandated under Code of Criminal Procedure. The doctors should only view the patient from the point of providing immediate medical assistance by taking in to consideration of his right to health as it would implicitly affect the fundamental right to life of an individual. Medical jurisprudence must give due importance to right to health and medical care which is a core component of ethics. The ethical dimensions of the medical jurisprudence are founded on and integral to the principle of the right to life and dignity, enshrined in Article 21 of the Constitution.[4] The term Right to health is nowhere mentioned in the Constitution yet the Supreme Court has interpreted it as a fundamental right under Right to life enshrined in Article 21. It is a significant view of the Supreme Court that first it interpreted Right to Health under Part IV. i.e. Directive Principles of State Policy and noted that it is the duty of the state to look after health of the people at large. In its wider interpretation of Article 21 it was held by the Supreme Court that, the right to health is a part and parcel of right to life and therefore is a fundamental right provided under Indian Constitution. Thus the scope of the right to health has also been very broad encompassing several different aspects of health care and services.

4 Pinto E.P., The jurisprudence of emergency medical care in India: an ethics perspective. *Indian J Med Ethics*. Published online on April 25, 2017.

The Supreme Court of India in *Paschim Bang Khet Mazdoor Samiti v. State of West Bengal*[5] held that Article 21 of the Constitution casts an obligation on the state to take every measure to preserve life. Further the Apex Court has laid down guidelines to the doctors in all the hospitals throughout the country to ensure immediate medical attention to people in need. The medical records of the patient attended to in the emergency services should be preserved in the hospital. The issue of protecting doctors from legal hassles in medico-legal cases so that they can provide immediate care to patients in need of emergency life-saving care has also been addressed in the case of *Parmanand Katara v. Union of India*.[6] Medical jurisprudence thus mandates the medical practitioners with a duty of providing medical assistance to those who are in need and to respond with reasonable promptness whenever the patient calls him. The doctors must carry out complete examination and utilize all diagnostic tools that are available and necessary to arrive at a diagnosis. He must give proper and complete instructions for the care of his patient. He cannot ask another practitioner to examine or treat his case without the consent of the patient.[7]

PUBLIC HEALTH CARE IN INDIA *VIS-À-VIS* DUTIES OF DOCTORS

In India the concept of right to health is dynamic in nature. It is not restricted to the pragmatic concept of right to health and emergency medical treatment only but has a broader meaning. The court has played a pivotal role in imposing positive obligations as authorities to maintain and improve public Health. In fact, the Supreme Court of India in *CECS v. Subhash Chandra Bose and other*[8] has interpreted right to health so as to include other related rights like medical care and health facilities not only protect against sickness but also ensure stable manpower. It is pertinent to mention that it is the *sine qua non* duty of a doctor to take special care in

5 (1996) 4 SCC 37.

6 *Supra* note 3.

7 Prof. Dogra, T.D., & Lt. Col. Abhijit Rudra, (2016). Lyon's Medical Jurisprudence and Toxicology, Delhi Law House, Delhi, India, p. 117.

8 AIR 1992 SC 573.

respect of patients who are incapable of looking after themselves. Medical jurisprudence *per se* includes certain voluntary duties of a medical practitioner *interalia* implied contract of continuing to treat the patients, reasonable care and skill, keep professional secrets inviolate except under privileged circumstances, not undertaking procedures beyond skill, special precautions to be taken in case of children and adults not capable of taking care of themselves.[9]

The ethical perspective of medical jurisprudence aims at ensuring right to health to all the patients by fixing responsibility on the doctors. Responsibility towards a patient is undertaken as soon as a doctor agrees to examine the case. The doctor must not then abandon his treatment except under certain circumstances viz., when the patient is well, the patient is under some other responsible caregiver, the doctor has given due notice for discontinuing treatment, the patient has signified his intention of changing the doctor, the patient does not co-operate and follow the doctor's instructions, the patient consults another doctor without the knowledge of the attending doctor, the doctor is convinced that the illness is a feigned one.[10] Similarly while a doctor cannot be forced to treat any person, he has certain responsibilities for whom he accepts. It is an implied contract. A doctor-patient relationship is not established when the doctor renders first aid in emergency, he makes a pre-employment medical examination for a prospective employer, he performs an examination for life insurance purposes, he is appointed by the trial court to examine the accused for any reason. The doctor has to exercise reasonable care in certain special cases when an operation is to be performed on a case in which there has been a criminal assault, in case of pregnancy in which criminal interference has already taken place, in cases when there is a suspicion of poisoning or other criminal act and in medico-legal post-mortems in case of dowry deaths.

---

9 Subrahmanyam B.V., Parikh's Textbook of Medical Jurisprudence, Forensic Medicine and Toxicology, CBS Publishers & Distributors Pvt. Ltd., New Delhi, India, p.26.

10 *Ibid* at p.27.

MEDICO-LEGAL CASES AND EMERGENCY MEDICAL CARE – AN ETHICS PERSPECTIVE

The ethical aspects of a doctor in treating patients during emergency and medico-legal cases are governed by the International Code of Medical Ethics and the Declaration of Geneva. The Constitution of India, to a large extent, embodies the moral-ethical principles of human rights and social rights jurisprudence of the international human rights law in dealing with medico-legal cases. To illustrate the importance of emergency medical care here are two cases, which fall under medico-legal and criminal litigation, that are widespread but under-reported issue of ill treatment, torture and lack of medical care in police custody. An accused, who was thrashed by a mob for an alleged robbery on a train, was tied to a cycle rickshaw by the police and taken to the police station. However, he was not given any medical treatment and consequently died.[11] Another person met with an accident while driving and a criminal case was brought against him for drunken driving. As he was not provided timely medical care, he died in police custody.[12] Further the ethical aspects of medical jurisprudence necessitate the doctor to provide immediate medical treatment to a person who has met with an accident so as to save his life. The doctor should not wait for the completion of legal formalities and denial of emergency medical care to a person suffering from an accident on the ground of medico-legal complications is gross violation of right to life and basic human rights of an individual.

The jurisprudence on emergency medical care, which closely intersected ethical principles, laid the foundation for the evolution of healthcare litigations in India in the 1980s. It served as a bridge for the courts to apply the right to a dignified life and the constitutional obligation of the State to save life in subsequent litigations concerning the medical profession, and private and public healthcare providers. It also facilitated the crafting of healthcare jurisprudence and the declaration of healthcare as a fundamental right. In addition, ethics jurisprudence, an ethical

11 *Supreme Court Legal Aid Committee v. State of Bihar*, (1991) 3 SCC 482.

12 *Poonam Sharma v. Union of India*, AIR 2003 Delhi 50.

reading of the jurisprudence on emergency medical care, opens up avenues to recalibrate the various contours of health rights and the policy framework. The significance of ethics jurisprudence can be gauged by its contribution to the historical evolution of healthcare jurisprudence in India and the potential it holds for guiding various actors in the current policy ecosystem. The duty of a doctor to treat patients in cases of emergency and in particular, when a patient has met with an accident is squarely covered within the ambit of medical jurisprudence. The failure on the part of a doctor to provide necessary treatment including first aid shall constitute professional misconduct rendering him liable for disciplinary action for violation of medical ethics.[13] Ethics jurisprudence provides medical professionals with a historical opportunity to rebuild their commitment to ethics and patients' care, and also, partially salvage their own tainted image. Quite a few of the respondents felt that the courts had played a positive role in ushering in the necessary changes, both in the medical profession and the healthcare system.

The doctor's obligation to provide medical assistance to a patient during emergency is total and absolute and it is dehors the legal formalities prescribed under medico-legal jurisprudence. The legal framework for the duty of care as a binding ethical and constitutional principle was provided by the Supreme Court of India in a judgment which declared the Code of Medical Ethics[14] as the prevailing law for the medical profession.[15] In a sense, this provides medical ethics with the backing of legal authority in India. The core jurisprudential principle thus emanates from the right to life guaranteed under Article 21 underlines that failure to provide medical treatment is a violation of the right to life; preserving life of a person is an absolute and non-negotiable duty of medical professionals under Article 21. The ethics of the medical profession is upheld and in emergencies, doctors cannot delay, refuse or discontinue service if there is delay in payment or non-payment.

13 The Indian Medical Council (Professional conduct, Etiquette and Ethics) Regulations, 2002.

14 Section 33 of the Indian Medical Council Act, 1956.

15 *Supra* note iii at pp.1005-6.

The Supreme Court in *State of Karnataka v. Manjanna*[16] deprecated the tendency of refusal to conduct medical examination of rape victims by doctors in rural government hospitals unless referred by the police. The court observed that the refusal of some government doctors, particularly in rural areas, where hospitals are few and far between to conduct any medical examination of a rape victim unless the case of rape is referred to them by the police. The court added that such a refusal to conduct the medical examination necessary results in a delay in the ultimate examination of the victim by which the evidence of rape may have been washed away by the complainant herself or be otherwise lost, the court, therefore, directed that the state must ensure that such a situation does not recur in future. The duty of doctors to conduct medical examination of rape victims and to assist the police for the purpose of collecting bodily sample from the body of the accused and the victim with the help of medical practitioner is recognized under Code of Criminal Procedure. The doctors have to conduct proper medical examination on the rape victim so as to collect material evidence that may be used for forensic purposes.[17]

POLICY FRAMEWORK ON RIGHT TO HEALTH IN INDIA

Medical jurisprudence underwent a sea change in terms of ensuring right to health to victims of accidents who were not provided with emergency medical assistance due to the refusal of the private hospitals to admit victims even for emergency medical care, on the plea that the cases are medico-legal cases and they direct the victims to go to government hospitals, howsoever far they may be. Some private hospitals refuse purely on monetary grounds, if the victim is either poor or is not immediately in possession of funds. The medical literature on the subject states that the 'Golden Hour' is the first hour immediately after the accident in which 'emergency medical care' is necessary and most victims die if no such care is available or is not given soon after the accident. The purpose of emergency medical care is to 'stabilize' the patient and this, unfortunately, is not done.[18] The Law Commission of India observing the indifference towards victims of accidents and those in emergency medical

16 AIR 2000 SC 2231.

17 Section 53(1), Code of Criminal Procedure, 1973.

18 Law Commission of India 201st Report on "Medical Treatment after Accidents and During Emergency Medical Condition and Women in Labour", August 2006.

conditions and even women under labour who are about to deliver is not peculiar to India but is prevalent in other countries also had compared the legal position in other jurisdictions. In the United States, there is a statute called Emergency Medical Treatment and Labour Act which was enacted by introducing it in 1986 into the Consolidated Omnibus Budget Reconciliation Act, 1985. This Act is also known as the Patient Anti-Dumping Act. It imposed a mandatory duty on hospitals to give medical treatment to patients in emergency medical condition and women under labour, failing which the defaulter can be punished under the criminal law. Under that law, a hospital must screen and stabilize such persons and then provide emergency medical treatment. After screening, if the hospital has no facilities, it must transfer the person to another hospital having necessary facilities. The Law Commission Report, have adopted several provisions of Emergency Medical Treatment and Labour Act, 1986[19] and made suitable changes to suit our conditions.

Though, Indian medical jurisprudence does not have a special law concerning emergency medical care to the victims of accidents akin to that of United States, it is implicitly encapsulated within the constitutional mandate of Article 21. The legal dimensions of right to life *interalia* include within its ambit the salutary provisions of extending emergency medical treatment as part of medical jurisprudence. That apart the existing procedures relating to treatment in medico-legal cases have to be simplified and a comprehensive law is need of the hour so as to preserve life of an individual. There are no provisions in the Indian Penal Code, Criminal Procedure Code, Motor Vehicles Act, etc., which prevent doctors from promptly attending on seriously injured persons and accident cases before the arrival of police and thus taking into cognizance of such cases, preparation of FIR and other formalities by the police. Every injured citizen brought for medical treatment should instantaneously be given medical aid to preserve life and thereafter the procedural criminal law should be allowed to operate in order to avoid negligent death.[20] The doctors should be free from fear that they would be unnecessarily harassed or prosecuted for doing their duty without first complying with the police formalities. It is further submitted that a doctor should not feel himself

19 In 1986, Congress enacted the Emergency Medical Treatment & Labor Act (EMTALA) to ensure public access to emergency services regardless of ability to pay.

20 *Supra* note 3.

handicapped in extending immediate help in such cases fearing that he would be harassed by the police or dragged to court in such a case. It is submitted that Evidence Act should also be so amended as to provide that the doctor's diary maintained in regular course by him in respect of the accident cases would be accepted by the courts in evidence without insisting the doctors being present to prove the same or subject himself to cross examination and harassment for long period of time.[21] One of the integral facets of medical jurisprudence is that besides understanding of the medical knowledge the doctors must also acquaint themselves with the legal aspects and certain provisions of the relevant laws of this country so that they can perform their duty hassle free and without any fear while attending medico-legal cases. Therefore medical jurisprudence should inculcate some basic idea to all the medical practitioners on the ethical concerns of health care issues and providing medical treatment in emergency and the allied legal procedure involved thereon.

The Law Commission of India vide its 201st Report has proposed for a model law to mandate emergency medical treatment by hospitals and medical practitioners to victims of accidents and those in other emergency medical condition including women in labour without raising any objection or objections that the cases are medico-legal cases or any other objection and without demanding any payment as a condition precedent for such treatment and to provide for scheme for reimbursement of emergency medical treatment and for other matters incidental thereto.[22] It is a dismal state of affairs that despite the Law Commission's recommendation for an emergency care law in India, public sector hospitals have made no provision for such emergencies and private sector hospitals have turned a blind eye to the guidelines.

MEDICAL JURISPRUDENCE: A CONCEPTUAL ANALYSIS ON WEB OF JUDGMENTS

The case of *Indian Medical Association v. V.P. Shantha*[23] exemplifies the long standing resistance of the medical profession to any regulation of medical professionals on the pretext of professional self-regulation. In this

---

21 *Supra* note 17 at p.10.

22 Model Law on Medical Treatment after Accidents and During Emergency Medical Condition and Women in Labour Bill.

23 (1995) 6 SCC 65.

case, the definition of service as applicable to healthcare under different conditions was contested to determine the status of the healthcare seeking patient as a consumer. Collectively, the litigations point to the denial of admission in public hospitals, invariably resulting in death or subsequent treatment in private hospitals. They also point to medical malpractices and ethical violations in private hospitals. These include the discontinuation of medical care for not depositing money instantly, negligence in medical care and charging exorbitant amounts for treatment. The complete failure to provide medical care for people in police custody is another aspect that is brought out by the cases.

The National Consumer Disputes Redressal Commission in *Pravat Kumar Mukherjee v. Ruby General Hospital & Others*[24] declared that a hospital is duty bound to accept accident victims and patients who are in critical condition and that it cannot refuse treatment on the ground that the victim is not in a position to pay the fee or meet the expenses or on the ground that there is no close relation of the victim available who can give consent for medical treatment. This duty is casted upon the medical practitioners as part of their professional conduct, etiquette and ethics as mandated by the Indian Medical Council Act, 1956.[25]

However, many progressive judgments, such as those analyzed in this paper, have turned out to be of merely symbolic value or infructuous in the long run due to their vagueness and the lack of specific directives. This has hindered the process of their getting translated into systemic practices or institutional mechanisms.[26] For example, despite the strongly worded judgments, private healthcare establishments routinely deny admission to poor patients, citing moot reasons. Similarly, the policy directive to provide free services to poor and indigent patients applicable

---

24 Original Petition No. 90 of 2002, judgment of National Consumer Disputes Redressal Commission, New Delhi dated 25.04.2005. Available at https://indiankanoon.org/doc/173553/ Last accessed on 17/10/2017, 15.45 hrs IST.

25 Section 20A and Section 33(m) of the Indian Medical Council Act, 1956.

26 Pinto E.P., Decoding the politics of the Supreme Court judgment on sterilization camps. *The Wire*, New Delhi, September 23, 2016 [Internet]. Available from: https://thewire.in/67590/decodingpolitics-sterilisation-judgment/Last accessed on 12/10/2017 10.20 hrs IST.

in private charitable nursing homes in some states is flouted flagrantly though it has been upheld in several court judgments.[27] A major lacuna in these judgments is the failure to specify the consequences that medical professionals and healthcare providers would face in case of breach of the court's directives. For the translation of progressive judgments and ethical principles into entitlements to patients, a comprehensive enabling law that creates systemic mechanisms for the use of ethical protocols in healthcare provision would be a positive step forward.

CONCLUSION

Though the Supreme court of India in a series of judgments has declared the right to health care to be fundamental right, it had not been given due recognition by the state. What is also quite unfortunate is that in a country where poor and marginalized are more in members and these people cannot afford paid services in any government and private hospitals, the state should develop novel health insurance policies at a nominal rate. The changing dimensions of medical jurisprudence should thus focus on the core issues addressed herein above so that emergency health care and medical assistance be afforded to those who are in need without waiting for the intricate medico-legal procedures to be adhered to in all cases thereby making life more complicated. Medical jurisprudence as it would include certain ethical aspects besides the legal formalities in cases of emergency to provide immediate medical care and treatment. The other side of the coin requires the medical practitioners to have some minimal concern for the lives of individuals by giving utmost regard to their right to life as guaranteed under the Constitution. Indian laws governing medical jurisprudence shall be directed towards the betterment of patients and enduring their rights envisaged within the wide spectrum of statutes.

27 Kurian O.C., Charitable hospitals: charity at market place. *Econ Pol Wkly*. 2012;47(39):23–5.

Importance of Medical Jurisprudence in Criminal Trials in India: A Medico-Legal Study

Dr. Meena Ketan Sahu

Abstract

Medical jurisprudence plays prominent role in trial of criminal cases in India. It applies medical knowledge to criminal law especially in anatomy, pathology, and psychiatry. Medical jurisprudence or forensic medicine is nothing but application of medical science to legal problems. "Medico-legal" is the concept which is related to two sister professions i.e. Medicine and Law. Lawyers, those who do not regularly deal with medical issues in their legal practice, know very little about the medical profession and its problems. Similarly, physicians frequently comprehend too little about the law and how it affects them in the practice of their profession. In the present paper, the author has elaborately discussed the conceptual analysis and benefit of medical jurisprudence in the present day context. The author has made an attempt to discuss the statutory provisions prescribed in both substantive and procedural law pertaining to application of medical jurisprudence in trial of criminal cases. An attempt has been made to highlight the difficulties in detecting the medico-legal cases and suggestions has been made for forensic professionals to use their scientific backgrounds to help law enforcement personnel in trial of criminal cases in the courts of law.

Keywords: *Medical Jurisprudence, Criminal Cases, Trials, Judges, Medico-legal etc.*

INTRODUCTION

The Medical jurisprudence deals with the legal aspects of practice of medicine viz. medical negligence, rights & duties of doctor, professional misconduct. The forensic medicine deals with the medical aspects of law viz .death, injuries, sexual offences, infant deaths, poisoning, accidents and homicide. Both Forensic medicine and Medical Jurisprudence are very relevant in the criminal Justice system in India. It is typically involved in cases concerning blood relationship, mental illness, injury, or death resulting from violence. An autopsy is often used to determine the cause of death, particularly in cases where foul play is suspected. Post-mortem examination can determine not only the immediate agent of death but may also yield important contextual information, such as how long the person has been dead, which can help trace the killing. In medico-legal cases, treatment gets priority. Thereafter, the procedural criminal law will operate to avoid negligent death.[1]

CONCEPTUAL ANALYSIS

Medical jurisprudence means legal aspects of practice of medicine. For instance, a physician while prescribing medicines for his patients is guided by certain rules and regulations. If he is negligent towards his patients, he may have to face the law. All the rules and regulations which guide a physician during his practice come under medical jurisprudence.[2]

Medical jurisprudence also deals with the application of medical and paramedical knowledge to aid in the administration of justice. It is used by the legal authorities for the solution of legal problems such as applying the medical knowledge in deciding cases of injuries, murder, suicide, accidents, sexual offences, poisoning, etc. In short, it deals with medical aspects of the law. Medical jurisprudence or legal medicine is the branch of science and medicine involving the study and application of scientific and medical knowledge to legal problems, such as inquests, and in the field of law.[3] As modern medicine is a legal creation, regulated by the state, and

1 Duhan Roshni, "FORENSIC MEDICINE AND INDIAN CRIMINAL LAWS: A STUDY OF RELEVANCY WITH LEGAL PROVISIONs" Innovare Journal of Medical Sciences, Vol. 4, Issue, 2016, p.1.

2 Aggrawal Anil, "Introduction To Forensic Medicine And Legal Procedures Prevalent In India - Part I. Anil Aggrawal's Internet Journal of Forensic Medicine and Toxicology, 2001; Vol. 2, No. 1 (January-June 2001): http://www.anilaggrawal.com/ij/vol_002_no_001/ug002_001_1.html; Published: March 19, 2001.

3 Beck TR, Dunloop W., "Elements of Medical Jrisprudence" 2nd ed. London: Oxford University Press; 1825.

medico-legal cases involving death, rape, paternity, etc., require a medical practitioner to produce evidence and appear as an expert witness, these two fields have traditionally been interdependent. So, we get that forensic medicine is that science which teaches the application of every branch of medical knowledge to the purposes of the law; hence, its limits are, on the one hand, the requirements of the law, and on the other, the whole range of medicine. Anatomy, physiology, medicine, surgery, chemistry, physics, and botany lend their aid as necessity arises; and in some cases, all these branches of science are required to enable a Court of law to arrive at a proper conclusion on a contested question affecting life or property.

The primary tool of forensic medicine has always been the autopsy. Frequently used for identification of the dead, autopsies may also be conducted to determine the cause of death. In cases of death caused by a weapon, for example, the forensic pathologist – by examining the wound – can often provide detailed information about the type of weapon used as well as important contextual information. (In death by gunshot, for example, he can determine with reasonable accuracy the range and angle of fire). Forensic medicine is a major factor in the identification of victims of disaster such as landslide or plane crash. In cause-of death determinations, forensic pathologists can also significantly affect the outcome of trials dealing with insurance and inheritance.[4]

Medical jurisprudence or forensic medicine is the application of medical science to legal problems. It is typically involved in cases concerning blood relationship, mental illness, injury, or death resulting from violence. Forensic medicine has also become increasingly important in cases involving rape. In brief, we can understand that medical jurisprudence or legal medicine is the branch of science and medicine involving the study and application of scientific and medical knowledge to legal problems, such as inquests, and in the field of law. As modern medicine is a legal creation, regulated by the state, and medico-legal cases involving death, rape, paternity, etc., require a medical practitioner to produce evidence and appear as an expert witness, these two fields have traditionally been

4 Available at https://www.britannica.com/topic/forensic-medicine. Accessed on 14/10/2017 at 7.45 p.m.

interdependent.[5] Forensic medicine, which includes forensic pathology, is a narrower field that involves collection and analysis of medical evidence (samples) to produce objective information for use in the legal system.[6]

STATUTORY PROVISIONS

As far as the medico-legal is concerned, there are some relevant provisions of law prescribed in different substantive and procedural aw pertaining to detection, investigation and trial of the case. These provisions of law speak not only with regard to causes, gravity but also determination of guilty with the help of medical science. Following are the various provisions discussed in nutshell.

Indian Penal Code, 1860

(*a*) Insanity

It is impossible to see the working of human mind. So, it will be more difficult to see the working of an abnormal person's mind when he is committing an offence. It is an established principle that a man with an abnormal mind is not responsible for his outward acts.

Section 84 of the code[7] exempts mentally abnormal persons from criminal liability. This section is based on the famous M. Naughten's rules which are mentioned below:

1. Every man is presumed to be sane and to possess a sufficient degree of reason to be responsible for his crimes, until the contrary be proved.
2. To establish a defence on the ground of insanity, it must be clearly proved that at the time of committing the act, the accused was labouring under such a defect of reason, from

---

5 Mohr JC. Doctors and the Law: Medical Jurisprudence in Nineteenth Century America. New York City: Oxford University Press; 1993.

6 Taylor A S, Smith FJ, editors. Taylor's Principles and Practice of Medical Jurisprudence. 7th ed. New York: Taylor & Francis; 1920.

7 Section 84, Indian Penal Code, 1860 says, "Nothing is an offence which is done by a person who at the time of doing it, is by reason of unsoundness of mind, incapable of knowing the nature of the act, or that he is doing what is either wrong or contrary to law.

the disease of the mind, as not to know the nature and quality of the act he was doing, or if he did know it that he did not know he was doing what was wrong.

3. If the accused was conscious that the act was one which he ought not to do and if the act was at the same time contrary to the law of the land, he is punishable. Thus, the test is of the power of distinguishing between right and wrong not in the abstract but with regard to the particular act committed.
4. Where a criminal act is committed by a man under some insane delusion as to the surrounding facts, which conceals from the true nature of the act he is doing, he will be under the same degree of responsibility as if the facts had been as he imagined them to be. He may, for instance, kill under the imagination that he is an executioner, full carrying out a judicial sentence or on the other hand, merely that the person killed had once cheated him at cards.
5. A medical witness who never saw the prisoner to the trail, but who was present during the whole trial and examination of the witness, cannot be asked to give his opinion as to the state of the prisoner's mind at the time of the commission of the offence.

The basis of law of insanity is seen in the series of answers given by the Law Lords after the M. Naughten's case. In this case,[8] a political maniac who wanted to shoot Britain's foreign minister Robert Peel instead killed his private secretary Drumond on 20th January 1843 in daytime. The killer was declared to be mentally insane by the medical experts. The case involved two important issues before the Court. The point raised on the one hand was that an insane person is incapable of distinguishing between right and wrong, while on the other hand, the argument that public safety demanded that this plea should not be readily accepted as a defence to shield the criminal from penal consequences needed proper attention. After a careful consideration their Lordships observed that every man is presumed to be sane and to possess sufficient degree of reason to be held

8 *R. v. Naughten*, (1843) CL & f. 240.

responsible for his crime until the contrary is proved. In order to establish a defence on the ground of insanity, it must be clearly proved that at the time of committing the act the accused was labouring under such a degree of reason from disease of mind as not to know the nature and quality of the act he was doing or if he did know it, as not to know he was doing what was wrong."[9]

Similar issues were raised in a subsequent decision in *Durham v. United States* (1954) where the accused was held not guilty for his criminal act because it was a product of his mental depravity. There is another view about the mentally depraved persons. In certain cases, a person is intellectually capable of distinguishing between right and wrong yet he commits criminal act because of his irresistible impulse. This proposition, however, stands completely discarded after the decision in M. Naghten's case.

Dr. Arnold olds that M. Naghten's test of criminality is irreconcilable with the modern psychiatric insights. Modern trends in medical insight in criminological considerations accept the complexities of human nature and emotions. They regard insane persons as emotionally disturbed individuals incapable of being cured. The practical implications of this view find support in the present criminal law which accepts the basic weakness of an individual as a valid defence against his criminal prosecution or at least a sufficient ground for mitigation of his sentence to a certain extent.[10] In result, it has now been possible to link up mental disease as an explanation for crime. Aggressive personalities have often to face many problems because of their conflicts and overt acts due to their mental unsoundness.

In fact, punishment is intended to act on the kind of the person punished and to alter the direction in which his mind has been working so far. If the mind was not in substance a party to the conduct, then the question of changing the direction of mind cannot arise."[11]

(*b*) Medical insanity and legal insanity

---

9 *Ibid.*

10 Paranjape N.V, "Criminlogy and Penology", Central Law Publications, Allahabad, Eleventh Edition, 2001, (Reprinted) March, 2004, p. 42.

11 Prof. Bakshi P.M, "Limiting the Criminal Liability" 36 JILI (1994) p. 153.

Legal insanity means unsoundness of mind which incapacitates a person from knowing the nature of the act or that he is doing what is either wrong or contrary to law. According to medical science insanity is another name for mental abnormality.[12] Simply for the reason that a person is confined in mental hospital does not exempt him from liability. Emotional imbalance, uncontrollable anger or jealousy, lack of self control etc., are also not relief from liability. In a case,[13] the accused killed his father by hitting him with a grinding stone on his head for refusing to give him money for his wayward expenses. He pleaded unsoundness of mind, that he was incapable of knowing the nature of the act or that he was doing what was either wrong or contrary to law. The Court held that the accused had grudge against his father for his refusal to pay money, and because of that he threatened his father with death and murdered him. He was in full senses and so he was held liable. It was further held that "there is a great difference between medical insanity and legal insanity. The Courts are concerned only with legal and not with medical aspect of the matter. Medical insanity is as much narrower concept and confined to the impairment of the cognitive faculty of the mind which makes the offender incapable of knowing that it was wither wrong or contrary to law. If the accuse is conscious of the nature of his act, he is presumed to have been conscious of its criminality. Abnormality of mind is not by itself sufficient to show that the accused must have acted while of unsound mind. The mere fact that the accused's mind was partially deranged or that he was subject to some uncontrollable impulse due to insanity is not a valid defence in criminal law. The law recognizes nothing but incapacity to realize nature and quality of the act that he was doing or if he did know it, that he did not know he was doing what was either wrong or contrary to law".

What medical science call an insanity, may not amount to legal insanity. Law is not concerned with every type of insanity. The medical man usually puts the question thus, "Is the man insane?"

12 Sahu M.K, Principles of Criminal Law (Cases & Materials), First Edition, 2016, Allahabad Law Agency, Faridabad, p.173.

13 *Velusamy v. State*, 1985 Cr. L.J 1981.

But the lawyer puts the question thus, "Did the insanity cause the act; if it did not, then it is immaterial whether the man is insane." There cannot be any legal insanity unless the cognitive faculty of mind is destroyed as a result of unsoundness of mind to such an extent as to render the accused incapable of knowing the nature of the act of that what he is doing is wrong or contrary to law. Thus, in law, eccentricity or strange behaviour or mere mental upsetting not amounting to legal insanity, does not absolve a person from the consequences of his act.[14]

Code of Criminal Procedure, 1973

As far as Code of Criminal Procedure, 1973 (Cr. P.C) is concerned, it prescribes certain provisions for investigation of an offence pertaining to death which is caused under the suspicious circumstances which are analytically discussed below:

Inquest

The term inquest is derived from Latin word in, into, and quaro, which means to seek or look for. An inquest is an enquiry or investigation into the cause of death where death has occurred under mysterious and suspicious circumstances. Whenever a death occurs, it is necessary to establish the cause of death. If the death is due to natural circumstances, such as a heart attack, no further investigation is required, and the body may be disposed of according to the customs and traditions prevalent in the religion of the deceased. But if death occurs under suspicious circumstances, (say a newly married bride found hanging from a ceiling fan), or if some suspicion and/or mystery is associated with the death of a person (say, a person who left for office in the morning is found dead in a field far away from his office), a detailed enquiry becomes necessary to find out the true nature, cause and manner of death. There are various types of inquest which are discussed below:

(*a*) The Police Inquest

According to Section 174 of Code of Criminal Procedure, 1973, inquest is conducted by a police officer, not below the rank of a

14 Sahu M.K, Principles of Criminal Law (Cases & Materials), First Edition, 2016, Allahabad Law Agency, Faridabad, p.174.

head constable. A police officer conducting an inquest is known as an investigating officer. Whenever a suspicious death occurs anywhere, the information reaches the local police officer first of all. He immediately informs the Executive Magistrate of the area and then proceeds to the place where the body is lying. The idea of informing the Executive Magistrate is that in certain cases, the Magistrate may himself want to conduct the inquest (his inquest being fairer and superior to that of the police inquest). There are certain specific cases in which only the Magistrate shall hold an inquest (as mentioned under the relevant heading), but the Magistrate reserves the right to conduct inquest in any other case which he deems fit. If there is no order from the Magistrate to the contrary, the Police officer conducts an inquiry into the cause of death in the presence of two or more respectable witnesses of the locality. These witnesses are known as panchas, panch witnesses or panchayatdars. He also looks at the body for evidence of any injury, poisoning, etc. Based on his findings after viewing the body, as well as information received from the witnesses, he prepares a report on the probable cause of death, as judged by him. This report is called the panchnama or the inquest report.[15]

(*b*) The Magistrate's inquest

This type of inquest is conducted under Section 176 of Code of Criminal Procedure, 1973 by a Magistrate. This means an inquiry conducted by a magistrate to ascertain certain matters of fact. Section 176 Cr. P.C empowers the Magistrate to hold an inquest in following three types of cases:

1. Death occurring in police custody
2. Suicide of a woman within seven years of marriage
3. Death of a woman within seven years of marriage in any circumstances raising a reasonable suspicion that some other person committed an offence in relation to such woman.

Besides the above mentioned 3 cases in which a magistrate is legally bound to hold an inquest, the magistrate also reserves the

15 Available at ww w.anilaggrawal.com › ... › Undergraduate Section: Index. Last visited on 22/10/2017 at 10.45 p.m.

right to hold an inquest in any other case of death which he deems fit. On receipt of information of death by the police officer, he may choose to hold an inquest himself.

Furthermore, it is found that a magistrate generally holds an inquest in some other type of cases such as, if any death in which the police is involved in any way, such as death of a convict in jail, death in police firing, or death occurring during police investigation. The essence behind this provision is that the suspect culprit (police) himself cannot be the judging authority as to who has committed the offence.

Autopsy

An autopsy is frequently done in cases of sudden death where a doctor is not able to give a death certificate or when death is believed due to an unnatural cause[16] Section 174 and 176 Code of Criminal Procedure (Cr.P.C.) mention the concept of a medico-legal autopsy during the investigations of a sudden, suspicious, unnatural death. The objective of medico-legal post-mortem examination is to establish the identity of a body, when not known; to ascertain the time since death and the cause of death; and whether the death was natural or unnatural and if unnatural, whether it was homicidal, suicidal or accidental.[17]

Section 509 (1) Code of Criminal Procedure further says that if the civil surgeon's evidence is taken before the committing magistrate, and attested by him, that is to say, the committing magistrate must state below the civil surgeon's deposition that it was taken in presence of accused, and explained to him, and that he had an opportunity of cross-examination, the higher court may accept it as evidence without calling the civil surgeon. So, where the attendance of a medical witness cannot be obtained, and his evidence is taken as per the provisions, his depositions can be used at the time of trial and will be considered as relevant.

---

16 Kannan K, Mathiharan K. Ed. In: Modi-A textbook of Medical Jurisprudence and Toxicology. 24th Ed 2012. LexisNexis Butterworth's Nagpur: p. 293, 295,297, 360.

17 The Punjab Medical Manual, 1933, Punjab, Lahore, Chapter X, p. 154, Para 595.

Indian Evidence Act, 1872

Section 3 of Indian Evidence Act speaks regarding documentary evidence. Medical certificate produced by the doctor is considered as documentary evidence. The evidence of eyewitnesses is positive. The evidence of doctor as an expert is only an opinion which is corroborative. It is of three types:

(*a*) **Medical certificates**

They refer to ill-health, insanity, age, death, etc. They are accepted in a Court of law, only when they are issued by a qualified registered medical practitioner. The certificate of ill-health should contain exact nature of the illness and probable period of expected absence. The signature or left thumb impression of the patient should be taken at the bottom or top of the certificate. Two identification marks should be noted. The doctor should retain a duplicate of the certificate issued for 2 years. A medical practitioner is legally bound to give a death certificate, stating the cause of death without charging fee, if a person whom he has been attending during his last illness dies (Registration of Births and Deaths Act, 1970). The death certificate should not be issued by a doctor without inspecting the body and satisfying himself that person is really dead.

(*b*) **Medico-legal reports**

Medico-legal are the reports prepared by a doctor on the request of the investigating officer, usually in criminal cases, e.g. assault, rape, murder, etc. The examination of an injured person or a dead body is made when there is a requisition from a police officer or Magistrate. These reports consist of two parts: (1) The facts observed on examination (all relevant, objective descriptions including important negative finding), (2) the opinion drawn from the facts. These reports will be attached to the file relating to the case, and the file is produced in the Court. The report will be open to the scrutiny of the defense lawyer. It will not be admitted as evidence unless the doctor attends the Court and testifies to the fact under oath. Great care should be taken in writing the reports to avoid any loose wording or careless statement. This gives a chance to the defense lawyer to use them to his own advantage. The report should give the date, time, and place of examination and the name of individual who identified the person or dead body. Exaggerated terms, superlatives, etc., should not be used. The opinion should be based on the facts observed by himself and not on information obtained from other sources. In an injury case, if it is not possible to give an opinion immediately, the person should be kept under observation, and necessary investigations should be done before giving the report. The report should show competence, lack of bias, and offer concrete professional advice. The report should be made soon after the examination. It should be clear, concise, complete, legible, and it should avoid technical terms as far as possible.[18]

(*c*) **Exhibits**

Clothing, weapons, etc., sent for medical examination should be described in detail, sealed, and returned to the police after obtaining a receipt. An outline of the weapon may be drawn on paper, and the measurement noted or a photograph taken.

Dying Declaration

It is a written or oral statement of a person, who is dying as a result of some unlawful act, relating to the material facts of the cause of his death or bearing on the circumstances (S.32, I.E.A.).[19] If there is time, the Executive Magistrate should be called to record the declaration. Before recording the statement, the doctor should certify that the person is conscious, and his mental faculties are normal (compos mentis). If the condition of the victim is serious, and there is no time call a Magistrate, the doctor should take the declaration in the presence of two witnesses. The statement should be recorded in the man's own words, without any alteration of terms or phrases. Leading questions should not be put. The declarant should be permitted to give his statement without any undue influence, outside prompting or assistance.

Statements, written or verbal, made by a person who is dead, as to the cause of his death or as to any of the circum- stances of the transaction which resulted in his death, are admissible in cases where the cause of that person's death comes into question, no matter whether the person making such statement was or was not under expectation of death at the time of making it. [I. E. A., s. 32, and Cr. P. C., s. 164.] If an injured person is

18 Available at http://healthdrip.com/documentary-evidence/ Viewed on 24/10/2017 at 8.45 a.m.

19 Section 32 of Indian Evidence Act, 1872.

likely to succumb, the doctor, failing the police, should arrange for the declaration to be made properly in the presence of a magistrate if possible, failing whom he may record the declaration himself.

The declaration should, if possible, be written by the person making it, otherwise it must be taken down in the identical words uttered by the dying man in his own vernacular, and nothing suggested or added. It should be read over to him and then, if possible, signed by him and attested by the writer, and any witnesses present. It should then be forwarded in a sealed envelope direct to the magistrate who would ordinarily inquire into the case. The state of mind of the declarant at the time when he made his declaration is of great importance.

PROBLEMS OF DETECTION OF CRIME RELATED TO MEDICO-LEGAL ISSUE

Sometimes, it is a stupendous task to detect the crime involving the medico-legal aspect. The reasons may be different such as certificate furnished by the medical officer, destruction of bodies, decomposition of bodies etc which causes hardship for the determination of the cause of death..The following are the various aspects which causes problems for detection of the crime especially where medical as well as legal issue are involved:

1. **Furnishing Medical Certificate** – It is necessary that the police-report accompanying the body should furnish the medical officer with sufficient particulars to indicate the direction in which he should pursue his search into the cause of death. Otherwise when decomposition has fully set in he cannot be expected to throw much light on the cause of death. Certain tissues, such as those of the uterus,' resist decomposition for a long time; certain poisons such as arsenic) may persist for many months, fractures will be evident, though, if decomposition is far advanced, it will be difficult to say whether the fracture occurred during life or not, and some important identification marks may be elicited.[20]

20 Available at https://archive.org/stream/medicaljurispru00waddgoog/medicaljurispru00waddgoog_djvu.txt. Last visited on 12/10/2017 at 6.55 p.m.

2. **Concealment and destruction of bodies** – In India, it is a common practice to cremation of dead body as quick as possible to hide the evidence of death. Even sometimes, it is seen that the body is thrown into the rivers so that the police will be unable to trace the corpse. The sole intention of doing such practice is to conceal the evidence. Moreover, as the common mode of disposing of the ordinary dead from natural causes is to throw the bodies into rivers or ponds or strew them about the outskirts of the villages in shallow graves, whence the bodies are dragged out by dogs and jackals, it is not easy to identify among these' any murdered body when once it is somewhat decomposed or defaced. The commonest way of disposing of a murdered body in the plains is to throw it into a river, or into a disused well — for this purpose it may be trussed up and carried many miles from the scene of murder, or tied to a pole and dragged along if the murderer be single-handed.

CONCLUDING OBSERVATIONS

It is crying need of the hour that every police officers, magistrates, and advocates who are dealing with criminal cases involving medico-legal questions should possess knowledge on medical jurisprudence, forensic medicine and toxicology for better administration of criminal justice system in India. From the lack of elementary medico-legal knowledge amongst those officers, who have to conduct the preliminary investigation of criminal cases, many points of the highest importance frequently escape observation. The diffusion of such information among officials concerned in the investigation of crime must undoubtedly tend towards preventing the miscarriage of justice. The medical officer should ensure that the medical certificate is submitted in the Court of law in time with details. The police officer or the investigating officer should investigate the crime especially the murder to prevent the destruction or concealment. Enactment of law in this context is not sufficient; it is to be properly implemented. The law enforcing agencies are to be properly trained to handle the cases. Training, workshops, seminars, etc are to be conducted regularly for the police officers in the police training schools and in medical colleges to create awareness and for better implementation of the provisions of pertaining to medico-legal cases.

❑❑❑

Medico-Legal Aspects of Injury or Wound – An Appraisal

Dr. Caesar Roy

Abstract

Injury or wound has great importance in medico-legal aspects. The legal and medical meaning of injury or wound is quite different. Legal meaning of injury is any harm caused illegally to a person i.e. to his body, mind, reputation or property. Medically, injury means breach of continuity of any tissue of the body, which means all wounds or all bodily injuries. Every injury recorded by the medical practitioners who has examined the injured, issue medical certificate and reports which are important to start a legal action against the accused persons. But before examination of the injured, the doctor should take consent from the injured person. The detailed and accurate record of the injuries and other relevant particulars of the injured noted during medico-legal examination, from the basis of medico-legal diagnosis is important under criminal justice system. Every injury recorded by the medical practitioner, who has examined the injured, is an expert under section 45 of the Indian Evidence Act, 1872 and examined before the court of law as a witness. Depending upon the nature, severity, time etc injuries are classified. All those classifications are discussed in this writing. Procedures for recording the injury report and the duty of the medical practitioner are also mentioned. Evidentiary value of such reports before the court of law is also explained in this writing.

Keywords: *Medical jurisprudence, Injury, wound, medico-legal, injury report, criminal case*

INTRODUCTION

Medical practitioners very frequently need to examine, treat victims and issue medico-legal reports in pursuit of their profession dealing with wounded persons. Law enforcing officers may send the wounded victims for routine treatment and necessarily for medico-legal reports of the cases. Occasionally the victims from their own selves request the attending medical practitioners to issue medical certificates and reports which will be needed to start a legal action against the accused persons. From the medico legal point of view, every injury recorded by the doctor who has examined the injured, is important and needs to be medico legally diagnosed in the right perspective in the disbursement of justice as a doctor is an "expert witness" in a court of law as per section 45 of Indian Evidence Act, 1872. The detailed and accurate record of the injuries and other relevant particulars of the injured noted during medico legal examination, form the basis of medico legal diagnosis and epidemiological observations are very important under the criminal justice system.

MEANING OF INJURY OR WOUND

The conception of a legal man about the term injury is quite different from what a medical man understands by them. To a medical man, injury means "breach of continuity of any tissue of the body," which means all wounds or all bodily injuries. To a legal man, injury has a much broader meaning which includes "any harm caused illegally to a person, i.e., to his body, mind, reputation or property."[1] Clinically a wound is produced when there is breach of anatomical continuity of the skin or mucous membrane with or without damage of the underlying tissues. Forensically it is wound when there is damage of any tissue or organ irrespective of breach of continuity of the skin or mucous membrane. A wound is produced when the intensity of the applied force to the body exceeds the capability of the tissue to adapt or resist the force. The capability of the tissue to adapt or resist the force depends on mass, velocity, exact area of the weapon pressing the body, structure of the tissue, mode of application of the applied force like compression, traction, torsion, tangent and leverage of the stress. According to the Indian Penal Code, 1860, the word "injury" denotes any harm whatever illegally caused to any person, in body, mind, reputation or property.[2]

1 Nandy, Apurba (1995). *Principles of Forensic Medicine*, 1st Edition, p. 204. Kolkata, New Central Book Agency.

2 Section 44.

DIFFERENT KINDS OF INJURY OR WOUNDS

Injuries or wounds may be classified on the following heads –

1. Depending upon causative factors:
   (*i*) Mechanical or Physical injuries:
      (*a*) Abrasion
      (*b*) Bruise or Contusion
      (*c*) Laceration
      (*d*) Incised wound
      (*e*) Punctured wound
      (*f*) Fracture or dislocation of a bone, tooth or joint
      (*g*) Firearm wound
   (*ii*) Thermal injuries:
      (*a*) Due to cold
      (*b*) Frostbite
      (*c*) Trench foot
      (*d*) Immersion foot
      (*e*) Due to heat
      (*f*) Burns
      (*g*) Scalds
   (*iii*) Chemical injuries:
      (*a*) Corrosive acids
      (*b*) Corrosive alkalis
   (*iv*) Injuries due to electricity, lightening, X-rays, radioactive substances etc.
2. Depending upon severity of the injury:
   (*i*) Simple
   (*ii*) Grievous
3. Medico-legal classification:
   (*i*) Self-inflicted or Suicidal
   (*ii*) Injuries inflicted by others or homicidal

(*iii*) Accidental injuries

(*iv*) Defence wounds

(*v*) Fabricated wounds

4. Depending upon time of death:

(*i*) Ante-mortem

(*ii*) Post-mortem

Abrasion, Bruise or Contusion, Laceration, Incised Wound, Punctured Wound, Firearm Wound

An abrasion is a destruction of the skin, which usually involves the superficial layers of the epidermis only. They are caused by a lateral rubbing action by a blow, a fall on a rough surface, by being dragged in a vehicular accident, fingernails, thorns or teeth bite. Some pressure and movement by agent on the surface of the skin is essential. An abrasion is a superficial injury, commonly known as a 'graze' or 'scratch'.

This type of wound damages only the epidermis (uppermost skin layer), and should not therefore bleed. However, abrasions do usually extend into the dermis causing slight bleeding. A fresh abrasion is bright red in colour. It dries and forms a scab in about 12-24 hours. A fresh scab is red in colour but becomes reddish brown in about 2-3 days. The abrasion heals from the periphery by new growth of epithelium in about 4-7 days by which time the scab falls off. Healing is complete by about 10 days depending on the size of the abrasion and the area involved.[3]

Bruises or contusions are injuries which are caused by a blow from a blunt weapon, such as a club (lathi), whip, iron bar, stone, ball, finger, fist, boots etc.[4] It is due to an infiltration or extravasation of blood into the tissues following rapture of small vessels. Contusions may be present not only in skin but also in internal organs, such as the lung, heart, brain and muscles.

3 Dr. Parikh, C.K. (2006). *Parikh's Textbook of Medical Jurisprudences, Forensic Medicine and Toxicology*. 6th Edition, Page 4.3. New Delhi, CBS Publishers & Distributors.

4 Franklin, C.A. (1988). *Modi's Textbook of Medical Jurisprudence and Toxicology*, Twenty-first Edition, p. 250. Bombay: N.M. Tripathi Pvt. Ltd.

When a large blood vessel is injured, a tumour-like mass called haematoma is formed. When fresh, a bruise is reddish in colour, it becomes blue within few hours up to 3 days. Gradually, it changes in colour and subsides by two weeks. The margin of a bruise is diffused and not sharp due to diffusion of the extravasated blood in the surrounding tissue.[5]

A laceration is a wound in which the skin, mucosa or underlying tissues are torn as a result of application of hard blunt and rough weapons and objects.

Incised wounds are cuts or slashes produced by the sharp edge of a weapon like knife, sword, dagger, razor, tangi, katari etc. Length of an incised wound is greater than breadth and depth.[6] Chop wounds are caused by a blow with a moderately sharp splitting edge of a fairly heavy weapon like hatchet, an axe, a sabre or a cleaver, striking at a body part overlying bone.[7]

Stab wound is penetrating injury caused by sharp and/or pointed objects, such as knife, dagger, nail, needle, spear, arrow, screw driver, etc. penetrating the skin and the underlying tissues that is deeper than its length and width on skin. This can occur by driving the object into the body or from the body's pressing or falling against the object.

Firearm wounds are produced by the projectiles discharged from firearms. They produce punctured wounds.

Thermal Injuries

Thermal injuries may be due to exposure to heat or cold which may have generalized effects or localized effects according to the nature of exposure. Frost bite occurs due to exposure to dry cold, as in cases of mountaineers or polar expeditionists. In trench foot or immersion foot or hand, necrosis of the finger, toes or hands and feet may occur at a low temperature, if the limbs are wet due immersion.[8]

5 Nandy, Apurba (1995). *Principles of Forensic Medicine*, 1st Edition, p. 215. Kolkata, New Central Book Agency.

6 *Ibid,* p. 223.

7 Dr. Parikh, C.K. (2006). *Parikh's Textbook of Medical Jurisprudences, Forensic Medicine and Toxicology*. 6th Edition, Page 4.15. New Delhi, CBS Publishers & Distributors.

8 Nandy, Apurba (1995). *Principles of Forensic Medicine*, 1st Edition, p. 268. Kolkata, New Central Book Agency

Self-inflicted or Suicidal, Homicidal, Accidental Injuries, Defence Wounds and Fabricated Wounds

Self inflicted wounds are superficial, multiple, grouped together, parallel to each other, placed over the approachable parts of the body more commonly on the anterior aspects of the forearms, inner aspects of the thigh and front of lower abdomen and anterior and lateral aspects of upper arms. Suicidal wounds are usually placed in front and sides of the neck or sometimes in front of the wrists, to cut the radial artery to bleed to die. Homicidal wounds may be on any part of the body including unapproachable parts. Accidental wounds may be caused when somebody falls upon the sharp edge of a cutting weapon there is no mark of resistance on the body or no sign of struggle at the place.[9] Defence wounds result due to the immediate and instinctive reaction of the victim to save him, either by raising the arm to prevent the attack, or by grasping the weapon. If the weapon is blunt, bruises and abrasions are produced on the extensor or ulnar surfaces of the forearms, wrists, backs of the hands and knuckles. The size and shape of the bruises depends upon the attacking object. Fractures of the carpal bones, metacarpals and digits may occur. Fabricated wounds are those which may be produced by a person on his own body, or by another with his consent. Fabricated wounds are mostly incised wounds, and sometimes contusions, stab wounds and burns. Lacerated wounds are rarely fabricated. Incised wounds are usually superficial, multiple and parallel.

All those injuries or wound if caused before death then these are ante-mortem in nature and if caused after death then they are post-mortem in nature.

RECORDING OF INJURY REPORT – DUTY OF MEDICAL OFFICER

In all Government hospitals a medical officer or a casualty medical officer may be asked to examine an injured person. The details of this examination must be entered in an Accident Register which is a confidential record and if required by a court of law has to be produced in the Court. In this register which is maintained by all government hospitals, irrespective of

9 *Ibid*, pp. 224-225

whether the case is seen as an outpatient case or admitted in the wards a careful entry of the following particulars is made – (1) Serial number (2) Place, date and the time of examination (3) Name, age, sex, occupation and address of the injured person (4) Identification marks (5) Name and address of the accompanying person (6) Name and number of Police Constable (7) A brief summary of how the injury was caused as told by the injured person (8) Detailed description of the injuries (9) Opinion and medical officer's signature.[10]

After that the doctor will examine the injured person as such and prepare a report in this regard, which is called technically "injury report." But before examination of the injured, the doctor should take consent from the injured person. It is better that he should take written consent from the person in presence of witness and this should bear signature or thumb impression of the injured and the witnesses present. If the injured is a female then examination should be undertaken in presence of another female. The consent should be free and voluntary. The consent should be informed consent, i.e. it is to be given knowing that the report may go in his/her favour or against.[11] The injury report should contain the name of hospital and date and hour of examination, the case reference, name and address of the subject examined and may also contain brief history of the case. Minimum two identification marks of the person should be recorded. The height, weight, general built of the person should be noted.[12]

An injury report generally contains the following information with serial numbers – type of injury, size, site or location on the body, weapon used or mode of infliction, whether simple or grievous or dangerous, remarks and inference. At the left hand top corner of the injury report, the medical officer should write the full name of the injured person and the name and number of the police constable accompanying him and also the exact time of the examination, viz., hour, date, month and year. Then he starts the examination of the injured. While describing the injuries he should carefully note their nature and number, the character of their edges, their

10 Franklin, C.A. (1988). *Modi's Textbook of Medical Jurisprudence and Toxicology*, Twenty-first Edition, p. 273. Bombay: N.M. Tripathi Pvt. Ltd.

11 Nandy, Apurba (2001). *Investigation of Human Offences on Human Body*, 1st Edition, p. 79. Kolkata, Academic Publishers.

12 *Ibid*, p. 80.

size as regards length, breadth and depth. Presence of any extraneous material in the wound should be carefully noted and carefully preserved to be handed over to Police later. If necessary, he should use a magnifying lens. The other factors which have a varying effect on the nature of injury are the movement and position of the assailant and the victim and should be carefully studied. All the injuries should be measured and the exact measurements in centimeters must be given; they should never be guessed. In describing these points technical terms should be avoided as far as possible.[13]

APPRECIATION OF MEDICAL EVIDENCE

In every trial for the offence of causing hurt to human body, opinions of medical officers are Invited to ascertain the cause of injuries, whether the injuries are anti-mortem or post-mortem, the probable weapon used, the effect of injuries, medicines etc. The medical opinion has great bearing and is of great assistance in the trial of criminal cases. It greatly helps the prosecution in establishing its case by soliciting corroboration from it by showing that the injuries could have been caused by the alleged weapon of offence by the accused persons in the manner alleged. The accused persons with the assistance of medical evidence try to demolish the prosecution story by showing that the injuries could not have been caused by the alleged weapon of offence in the manner alleged by the prosecution.

Ordinarily, the value of medical evidence is only corroborative. It proves that the injuries could have been caused in the manner alleged and nothing more. The use, which the defence can make of the medical evidence, is to prove that the injuries could not possibly have been caused in the manner alleged and thereby discredit the eyewitnesses. Unless, however, the medical evidence in its turn goes so far that it completely rules out all possibilities whatsoever of injuries taking place in the manner alleged by eye witnesses, the testimony of the eye witnesses cannot be thrown out on the ground of alleged inconsistency between it and the medical evidence.[14]

13 Franklin, C.A. (1988). *Modi's Textbook of Medical Jurisprudence and Toxicology*, Twenty-first Edition, pp. 273-274. Bombay: N.M. Tripathi Pvt. Ltd.

14 *Solanki Chimanbhai Ukabhai v. State of Gujarat*, AIR 1983 SC 484 : 1983 Cri.L.J. 822; see also *Khambam Raja Reddy & another v. Public Prosecutor, High Court, A.P.*, (2006)11 SCC 239, *State of U.P. v. Dinesh*, (2009)11 SCC 566

The term medical evidence has not been defined in the Evidence Act, but the opinion of an expert from the field of science, which covers medicine also, is admissible under Section 45 of the Evidence Act. Interestingly, while Section 45 makes admissible the opinion of an expert, it does not say anything about the weight to be attached or given to the opinion of an expert. In case of medical evidence, it has to be weighed by taking into consideration, its corroboration or conflict with oral evidence as the case may be. In this context the observations of the Supreme Court in *Madan Gopal Kakkad v. Naval Dubey*[15] are relevant wherein it was held that a medical witness called in as an expert to assist the court is not a witness of fact and the evidence given by the medical officer is really of an advisory character given on the basis of the symptoms found on examination. The expert witness is expected to put before the court all materials inclusive of the data which induced him to come to the conclusion and enlighten the court on the technical aspect of the case by explaining the terms of science so that the court although, not an expert may form its own judgment on those materials after giving due regard to the experts opinion because once the expert's opinion is accepted, it is not the opinion of the medical officer but of the court.

In *State of Haryana v. Bhagirath*[16] it was held that the opinion given by a medical witness need not be the last word on the subject. Such an opinion shall be tested by the court. If the opinion is bereft of logic or objectivity, the court is not obliged to go by that opinion. After all opinion is what is formed in the mind of a person regarding a fact situation. If one doctor forms one opinion and another doctor form a different opinion on the same facts it is open to the Judge to adopt the view which is more objective or probable. Similarly if the opinion given by one doctor is not consistent with probability the court has no liability to go by that opinion merely because it is said by the doctor. Of course, due weight must be given to opinions given by persons who are experts in the particular subject.

15 (1992) 3 SCC 204 : 1992 SCC (Cri) 598

16 (1999) 5 SCC 96 : AIR 1999 SC 2005, See also *Abdul Sayeed v. State of M.P.*, (2010) 10 SCC 259, *Rakesh v. State of M.P.*, (2011) 9 SCC 698),

CONCLUSION

Medical documentary evidences like medico-legal reports on injuries or wounds prepared by the medical practitioners are very important for the courts in making their judgments. Medico-legal training and experiences strengthen the abilities of the medical expert witnesses. Medical officers are to be trained for how to write a "certificate" or "report", so that all the supporting facts to conclude the opinion are mentioned properly and with possible scientific deviation and limitation without giving undue weightage to the observes facts.

❑❑❑

4

Insurance and Victim Compensation

Need For Reforms in Health Insurance in India, With Special Reference to Irdai (Health Insurance) Regulations, 2016

Shreya Mishra

Abstract

The health sector in India is in a very bad shape, owing to the differences in the nature of facilities on offer by public hospitals as well as private hospitals. Also, due to the lack of a universal health insurance policy in India, most of the health insurance is in the hands of private companies. Due to lack of basic infrastructure in many districts, people are compelled to undertake long distance journeys to get medical treatment, and consequently, end up paying huge amounts of money as out-of-Pocket expenses. The Chapter takes into account the various factors which make the implementation of reforms in health insurance necessary. Special emphasis has been laid on the IRDAI (Health Insurance) Regulations, 2016. To support the findings, a comparative approach has also been adopted in the Chapter and the health insurance systems of two countries, Sweden and Sri Lanka have been analyzed. The central aim of the Chapter is to suggest long-term solutions for the betterment of the health sector in general, and health insurance schemes in particular.

Keywords: *Health Insurance, Regulations, Comparison, Sweden, Sri Lanka*

INTRODUCTION

It was a proud moment for India when it was announced in 2014 that India had become polio-free, and in 2015 that India had become successful in eliminating maternal and neonatal tetanus. It not only demonstrated India's commitment as a nation to pursue health reforms aggressively as a long-term goal, it demonstrated India's emergence as a country with improved access to better sanitation, immunization and facilities for both children, pregnant mothers and newborn infants, some of the most vulnerable groups. India has taken a momentous step by introducing "Mission Indradhanush", a step towards immunizing all the children under the age of 2 years and pregnant women in India against seven vaccine-preventable diseases by 2020. But the picture is not altogether rosy. According to the Ministry of Statistics and Programme Implementation which was responsible for monitoring the progress on Millennium Development Goals (MDGs) for 2000-2015, India was able to fulfill only four out of eight MDGs.[1] Among the list of Millennium Development Goals (MDGs) for 2000-2015 were two health-related goals: Goal 5 being "Improve Maternal Health", and Goal 6 being "Combat HIV/AIDS, Malaria and TB".[2] Non-fulfillment of these two goals is a serious issue. Although the MDGs have been replaced by Sustainable Development Goals (SDGs), it is pertinent to mention that India lags behind in its efforts to achieve SDGs by 2030. SDG-3 is "Good Health and Well Being". According to the Global Burden of Disease

1 Venkat, V. (2015, September 15). India yet to achieve U.N. Millennium Development Goals. *The Hindu*, Retrieved from http://www.thehindu.com/news/national/india-yet-to-achieve-un-millennium-development-goals/article7654764.ece.

2 (2015). *Millennium Development Goals India Country Report 2015* (pp. 1-245, Rep.). New Delhi: Government of India, Ministry of Statistics and Programme Implementation, Central Statistics Office (Social Statistics Division). Retrieved from http://mospi.nic.in/sites/default/files/publication_reports/mdg_2july15_1.pdf.

(GBD) 2016 Study, India's ranking was at a low 127 among 188 countries in respect of the achievement of the SDGs.[3] Thus, it can be inferred that many obstacles remain in the path of development.

WHY INDIA NEEDS HEALTH INSURANCE FOR ALL?

India represents the second-largest population in the world, and with the rise in population, it is being seen that people in larger numbers are falling ill owing to various causes. Diseases borne through the air, water, or soil contamination have also spread in many areas; but the number of diseases as a result of erratic lifestyles is also a concern that needs to be addressed. Non-communicable diseases (NCDs), such as diabetes, asthma, cancer, cardiovascular diseases etc. account for more than half of all the deaths. In 2011, the figure was 53 percent[4], but as of 2017, this figure has increased to 61 percent of deaths[5]. When it comes to communicable diseases, the scenario is not any better. Being a tropical country, India has to face the menace of growth of mosquito population in many places, and these mosquitoes often carry fatal diseases such as dengue, chikungunya, malaria, etc. Malaria-endemic areas in the country are home to about 95 percent of the population[6], and often the facilities do not cover this huge number of people. As of 2015, India ranked 3rd among 15 countries having the highest incidence of malaria.[7] Dengue has been really fatal for many people. Every year, the number of deaths due to dengue is rising. In 2017,

3 Sharma, N. C. (2017, September 16). 6 million died of non-communicable diseases in India in 2016: study. *Livemint*. Retrieved October 16, 2017, from http://www.livemint.com/Politics/0gsKN2nO4zroKh2QgpkogN/6-million-died-of-noncommunicable-diseases-in-India-in-2016.html.

4 India. (2010). Retrieved from http://www.who.int/nmh/countries/ind_en.pdf?ua=1.

5 Dey, S. (2017, September 20). Non-communicable diseases cause 61% of deaths in India: WHO report. *The Times of India*. Retrieved October 16, 2017, from https://timesofindia.indiatimes.com/life-style/health-fitness/health-news/non-communicable-diseases-cause-61-of-deaths-in-india-who-report/articleshow/60761288.cms.

6 National Vector Borne Disease Control Programme. Retrieved from http://www.nvbdcp.gov.in/malaria3.html.

7 Azad, S. (2015, September 18). India 3rd in no. of malaria deaths: WHO. *The Times of India*. Retrieved October 16, 2017, from https://timesofindia.indiatimes.com/city/dehradun/India-3rd-in-no-of-malaria-deaths-WHO/articleshow/49017287.cms.

the number of dengue cases rose by 11, 832 when compared to 2016.[8] Other diseases such as Swine Flu have also proved fatal. As of 2017, 22, 186 cases of Swine flu have been reported. Since 2009-2010, when Swine flu was first discovered in India, it has claimed almost 1000 lives annually.[9] The existence of both NCDs and communicable diseases can be attributed to different factors. The rise in the number and incidences of NCDs has been attributed to four major factors- tobacco consumption, erratic diets, lack of physical activity and resultant obesity, and overconsumption of alcohol[10]. In other words, the rise in NCDs could mainly be attributed to the kind of choices one makes in his/her daily routine, and these are largely personal choices.

The rise in the number of communicable diseases, on the other hand, could be a mixture of both personal and community choices, the latter bordering on policy shifts. Open Defecation is a major concern in India because it leads to many diseases such as typhoid, cholera, diarrhoea, etc. It was not a concern till the population was less and the earth could absorb the human wastes[11], but over the years, many people have realized the ill-effects of open-defecation. Despite that, it is indeed shocking that over 60 percent of the world's population that defecates in the open lives in India[12]. This has been attributed to both cultural as well as infrastructural issues. Culturally, many people in villages find it "unhygienic" to defecate in the house in a

8 Dengue cases in India up by over 11, 500 from last year, south Indian states worst hit. (2017, August 1). *The News Minute*. Retrieved October 16, 2017, from http://www.thenewsminute.com/article/dengue-cases-india-over-11500-last-year-south-indian-states-worst-hit-66073.

9 Swine flu killed 1,100 so far this year, reveals health ministry data. (2017, September 2). *The Times of India*. Retrieved October 16, 2017, from https://timesofindia.indiatimes.com/india/swine-flu-killed-1100-so-far-this-year-reveals-health-ministry-data/articleshow/60332205.cms.

10 Supra Note 5.

11 Royte, E. (2017, August). Nearly a Billion People Still Defecate Outdoors. Here's Why. *National Geographic*. Retrieved October 16, 2017, from https://www.nationalgeographic.com/magazine/2017/08/toilet-defecate-outdoors-stunting-sanitation/.

12 60% of people defecating in the open in world live in India: WHO report. (2014, August 4). *Hindustan Times*. Retrieved October 16, 2017, from http://www.hindustantimes.com/india/60-of-people-defecating-in-the-open-in-world-live-in-india-who-report/story-gHdORFHYsmJycRQkjyuiJM.html.

bathroom. Some of them who have toilets in their homes do not use them for various reasons, such as lack of water supply[13], or erratic construction. India's public healthcare is largely dependent on a governmental hierarchy, perhaps the most crucial level of which is represented by the Primary Health Centers (PHCs), which cater to three or four villages. This hierarchy has many players: Auxiliary Nurse Midwives (ANMs), Community Health Centers (CHCs), high-end public hospitals etc. According to a World Bank report[14], the PHCs are critically lacking in the infrastructural support and are not fulfilling important functions required of them, such as: health education, welfare services, vaccination, etc.

With so many problems in the background, it has become increasingly difficult for India to improve its health situation. It does not help that the country's public spending on health is just a little over 1 percent of the Gross Domestic Product (GDP), according to the latest Economic Survey.[15] Economic Survey has attributed this to an inherent weakness in the Indian economic model, characterized by lethargic supply of essential public services. This is ironic as India had adopted a 'mixed economy' model. Moreover, the Constitution of India declares India to be a "Socialist" country. Delivery of essential public services is a duty of any Socialistic country, but unfortunately, these services have not reached where they are needed the most. With such a meagre spending by the government on public health, it is no surprise that India does not have a concrete medical insurance policy or scheme which would benefit everyone by reducing to

13 Chauhan, C. (2017, May 14). No water in 60% toilets puts question mark over Modi govt's Swachh Bharat mission. *Hindustan Times*. Retrieved October 16, 2017, from http://www.hindustantimes.com/india-news/no-water-in-60-toilets-built-under-swachh-bharat-mission/story-3rdu1Hv1UZbabYQhb68OTP.html.

14 Radwan, I. (2005). *India- Private Health Services for the Poor* (HNP Discussion Paper, pp. 1-68, Discussion Paper). Washington: The World Bank. doi:http://siteresources.worldbank.org/HEALTHNUTRITIONANDPOPULATION/Resources/281627-1095698140167/RadwanIndiaPrivateHealthFinal.pdf.

15 The global average is close to 6 percent. Economic Survey says India's public spending on health well below global average. (2017, January 31). *The Times of India*. Retrieved October 16, 2017, from https://timesofindia.indiatimes.com/business/economic-survey/economic-survey-says-indias-public-spending-on-health-well-below-global-average/articleshow/56897993.cms.

a great extent their out-of-pocket expenses on availing medical facilities. The National Health Policy 2017 aims at increasing public health spending to 2.5 percent of the GDP, but much remains to be seen in terms of health insurance for all. It is said that health is wealth, but it is increasingly been observed in India that it is wealth which is largely saving lives of people, the most important reason in India being the overall lack of medical insurance. In 1995 in India, 91.4 percent of the total private expenditure on health comprised of out-of-pocket expenditures or out-of-pocket payments (OOPs).[16] As of 2014, this percentage stood at 89.2.[17] According to the World Health Organization (WHO), OOPs are "direct payments made by individuals to health care providers at the time of service use. This excludes any prepayment for health services, for example in the form of taxes or specific insurance premiums or contributions and, where possible, net of any reimbursements to the individual who made the payments."[18] The amount of OOPs serves as an important indicator for determining the state of healthcare in any country as it refers to the 'direct payments' by the individuals or families themselves. In Socialistic economies, the amount of OOPs can indicate the success or failure of adopting a welfare-State approach. For instance, the classic example of a country which adopts this approach is Cuba, where the government finances more than 80 percent of total spending on healthcare (95.5% in Cuba)[19]. It can be easily be inferred that of the different strata in a society, lack of proper health insurance most acutely impacts the lowest strata of the society, comprising people with either no jobs or jobs with meagre wages. They are compelled to

16 Out-of-pocket health expenditure (% of private expenditure on health). The World Bank. Retrieved October 16, 2017, from https://data.worldbank.org/indicator/SH.XPD.OOPC.ZS.

17 *Ibid.*

18 Out-of-pocket payments, user fees and catastrophic expenditure. World Health Organization. Retrieved from http://www.who.int/health_financing/topics/financial-protection/out-of-pocket-payments/en/.

19 Mascarenhas, A. (2017, April 21). Of India's healthcare spend, 2/3 out of patients' pockets: Study. *The Indian Express*. Retrieved October 17, 2017, from http://indianexpress.com/article/india/of-indias-healthcare-spend-23-out-of-patients-pockets-study/.

depend on public healthcare, and many such people have to spend long hours waiting in queues or waiting in dilapidated hospitals and closed PHCs, or they suffer because of shortage in Community Health Centres (CHCs), also known as the "first-level referral hospitals"[20]. Often, patients die because of these long hours of wait, and lack of facilities.[21] Health Insurance in India is generally looked after by companies such as L&T Health Insurance, Cholamandalam MS Health Insurance, Apollo Munich Health Insurance, etc. But it is not equivalent to a government-mandated provision of health insurance for all, as very few people avail these insurance services. In 2016, the Insurance Regulatory and Development Authority of India (Health Insurance) Regulations were enacted, which incorporate important provisions.

THE INSURANCE REGULATORY AND DEVELOPMENT AUTHORITY OF INDIA (HEALTH INSURANCE) REGULATIONS 2016: SALIENT FEATURES

The Insurance Regulatory and Development Authority of India (IRDAI) were established in pursuance of the enactment of the IRDA Act, 1999. The authority is responsible for regulating the insurance industries in India. In 2016, a major step was taken to initiate changes in the regulatory mechanism for insurance in India. Thus, the Insurance Regulatory and Development Authority of India (Health Insurance) Regulations, 2016 [hereinafter as 'Health Insurance Regulations, 2016' or 'Regulations'] were enacted. Some important changes have been introduced through these regulations. As per the regulations, health insurance products cannot be offered without proof of valid registration granted under the IRDA

20 Chatterjee, P. (2015, August 19). Death rate goes up with distance from district hospital. *The Indian Express*. Retrieved October 17, 2017, from http://indianexpress.com/article/india/india-others/death-rate-goes-up-with-distance-from-district-hospital/.

21 Sharma, S. (2016, September 5). Why are the poor deprived of proper healthcare in India. *Hindustan Times*. Retrieved October 16, 2017, from http://www.hindustantimes.com/india-news/why-are-the-poor-deprived-of-proper-healthcare-in-india/story-i8VZjCC6HXgqYuYRMACTHM.html.

(Registration of Indian Insurance Companies) 2000.[22] Furthermore, the marketing and offer of any such product is contingent on its filing with the IRDA in accordance with the Product Filing Guidelines.[23] The element of confidentiality in a proposal form has been introduced[24] to make the insurance products more attractive and to make a person seeking such product feel secure. The Regulations have laid down specific factors which are to be kept in mind for pricing of the health insurance products offered by Life, General and Health Insurers. These principles are supposed to be different for individual and group/family insurance products.[25] In addition, the insurance products could be designed for target groups varying from one insurance product to another. For instance, health insurance products could be age-group-specific, gender-specific, location-specific, and so on.[26] An interesting feature is the designing of 'Pilot products', which has been introduced to support innovative ideas relating to health insurance products; and could be designed with the approval of the authority and offered for a period not exceeding 5 years.[27] The Regulations ensure that care is taken for the patients who undergo AYUSH treatment (i.e. treatment under Ayurveda, Yoga and Naturopathy, Unani, Siddha and Homeopathy) in "government hospital or in any institute recognized by government and/ or accredited by Quality Council of India or National Accreditation Board on Health"[28], although the provision comes with a rider in the form of the word 'may', which attaches a certain amount of discretion to the policies of the insurer. Another interesting feature is that although insurers are

22 S.3 (a), Insurance and Regulatory Development Authority (Health Insurance) Regulations, 2016.

23 S. 4(a), Insurance and Regulatory Development Authority (Health Insurance) Regulations, 2016.

24 S. 9, Insurance and Regulatory Development Authority (Health Insurance) Regulations, 2016.

25 S. 10, Insurance and Regulatory Development Authority (Health Insurance) Regulations, 2016.

26 S.11, Insurance and Regulatory Development Authority (Health Insurance) Regulations, 2016.

27 S. 11(b), Insurance and Regulatory Development Authority (Health Insurance) Regulations, 2016.

28 S. 18, Insurance and Regulatory Development Authority (Health Insurance) Regulations, 2016.

not allowed to offer any discounts to the policyholders, they may offer discounts in certain cases, such as for health check-ups or pharmaceuticals or outpatient treatments.[29] To ensure uniformity, Regulations make mandatory provisions of inclusion of standard definitions (to be issued by the IRDA) for phrases, terms, nomenclature and procedures used across the policies of Life Insurers, General Insurers and Health Insurers, except in case of Personal Accident and Travel policies.[30]

On the administrative level, some innovative features are in the form of mandatory access to cashless facility for treatment by Network Providers, provision of Identification Cards, Smart Cards.[31] To make reimbursement by medical establishments hassle-free, medical establishments could be licensed under a law at any level (local, State or National).[32] The most important provision from a legal point of view is, perhaps, the provision detailing Health Services Agreements.[33] A typical Health Service Agreement could be in the form of a direct or tripartite arrangement amongst health services provider, the Third Party Administrator and the insurer.[34] The Agreements shall mandatorily cover the tariff applicable with respect to various kinds of healthcare services that will be provided by a Network Provider.[35] In addition to this, Agreements empower an insurer to cancel or modify the agreement in case of discovery of fraud, misrepresentation, inadequacy of service or any kind of default on the part of Third Party Administrator.[36] In addition, inclusion of an opt-out clause, a clause for cancellation of a claim, and a clause enabling inspection of the premises of the Network Provider are also mandatory.[37]

29 S. 19, Insurance and Regulatory Development Authority (Health Insurance) Regulations, 2016.

30 S. 20 and 21, Insurance and Regulatory Development Authority (Health Insurance) Regulations, 2016.

31 S. 30, Insurance and Regulatory Development Authority (Health Insurance) Regulations, 2016.

32 *Ibid.*

33 S. 31, Insurance and Regulatory Development Authority (Health Insurance) Regulations, 2016.

34 *Ibid.*

35 *Ibid.*

36 *Ibid.*

37 *Ibid.*

HEALTH INSURANCE IN INDIA: A COMPARISON WITH SWEDEN AND SRI LANKA

Although the Regulations display a comprehensive arena of provisions, the Health Insurance system in India cannot rely solely upon the Regulations. The Regulations are a part of the Health Insurance system in India. In order to improve the situation, it is important to take note of some of the best practices in the world. The author has chosen to compare the health insurance systems of two widely different countries: Sweden and Sri Lanka. Sweden has been chosen because the health insurance system there is among the most famous. Sri Lanka has been chosen because of its similarities with India and its differences in the fact that it has been able to successfully eradicate Malaria.[38]

It is important to compare certain basic features of different health insurance systems. For instance, neither the IRDA Act, 1999 nor the Health Insurance Regulations, 2016 specify whether the health insurance could be availed of by only citizens or they could be availed by citizens as well as foreigners, including refugees and asylum seekers. It is not clear as to what 'All' entails when 'Health Insurance for All' is talked about in the country. This is a drawback, as the non-citizens feel left out, and asylum seekers and refugees are generally already in bad conditions. Some countries do give certain benefits to people who seek asylum and to those who are undocumented. In this regard, health insurance policy of Sweden is notable. Some facilities of health insurance are available to asylum-seeking children as well as asylum-seeking adults.[39] Another problem that has surfaced in India is with respect to the growing attention towards primary and tertiary health care, and a simultaneous lack in attention towards preventive healthcare. In this regard, a common problem today is lack of good oral practices. Growing number of fast food chains and irregular lifestyles have contributed to the growth in bad

38 World Health Organization, Regional Office for South-East Asia. (n.d.). *WHO certifies Sri Lanka malaria-free* [Press release]. Retrieved October 17, 2017, from http://www.searo.who.int/mediacentre/releases/2016/1631/en/.

39 The Swedish Health Care System. International Health Care System Profiles. Retrieved October 17, 2017, from http://international.commonwealthfund.org/countries/sweden/.

oral practices, leading to problems such as cavities, plaque, halitosis, etc. In India, the situation of not only the people, but of medical facilities in dentistry is equally bad. The national density of dentists is extremely low at 2.4 dentists per lakh population.[40] Of the 593 districts in India, 175 districts do not have a properly qualified dentist.[41] Moreover, although the comparative costs of going to a dentist in a government hospital and going to a dentist at a private clinic cannot be denied, it is an unfortunate truth that many government hospitals lack proper infrastructure and many a times lack basic equipment, such as hand piece, forceps, etc.[42] In a good dental clinic, costs are often skyrocketing. But faced with the choice of quality over cost-effectiveness, a patient ultimately opts for the former in order to avoid any risk or complications. Consequently, the choice between public dental care and private dental care is getting diluted, with the latter being more popular with the patients. The case of Sweden in this regard can provide some insights. In Sweden, dental care is subsidized by the government, and the dental care benefits are available to expatriates too, provided they have completed a year's residence in Sweden.[43] Yet another issue revolves around the status of the elderly in India. Although the government has launched schemes such as the Integrated Programme for Older Persons[44] and Rashtriya Vayoshri Yojana[45], these schemes have

40 Bansal, S. (2016, July 18). WHO report sounds alarm on 'doctors' in India. *The Hindu*. Retrieved October 17, 2017, from http://www.thehindu.com/data/WHO-report-sounds-alarm-on-%E2%80%98doctors%E2%80%99-in-India/article14495884.ece.

41 WHO report questions qualification of 'doctors' in India. (2016, July 18). *Hindustan Times*. Retrieved October 17, 2017, from http://www.hindustantimes.com/india-news/alarm-after-who-report-questions-qualification-of-doctors-in-india/story-RPAEhrxCmTU7kE1MnL5VRI.html.

42 Yasmeen, A. (2016, July 22). Deep cavity in govt. dental care. *The Hindu*. Retrieved October 17, 2017, from http://www.thehindu.com/news/cities/bangalore/Deep-cavity-in-govt.-dental-care/article14502233.ece.

43 Swedish healthcare: all you need to know. (2013, March 27). *The Local*. Retrieved October 17, 2017, from https://www.thelocal.se/20130327/46910.

44 Integrated Programme for Older Persons (Revised Scheme effective from 01.04.2015). Retrieved October 17, 2017, from http://socialjustice.nic.in/SchemeList/Send/43?mid=48565.

45 Government of India Ministry of Social Justice & Empowerment, Press India Bureau. (2017, March 23). *'Rashtriya Vayoshri Yojana' to be launched on 1st April,*

certain loopholes. For instance, the target group under Rashtriya Vayoshri Yojana is confined to senior citizens belonging to BPL (Below Poverty Line) category. Furthermore, over a span of 3 years, the scheme intends to benefit 5, 20, 000 senior citizens over a span of 3 years; this number of beneficiaries is significantly lower in comparison to the actual population of senior citizens in the country, which is 10.38 crore as per the Census of 2011.[46] Also, schemes such as the Senior Citizen Health Insurance Scheme (SCHIS) do not cover AYUSH treatment, although the Healthcare Insurance Regulations, 2016 provide for the same.[47] There is a stark contrast in Sweden with respect to the healthcare of senior citizens. In Sweden, the support system for the senior citizens is in an integrated form, with the municipalities responsible for the financing and organization, and the county councils being responsible for routinized health care.[48] In addition, Sweden has implemented a dedicated law called The Social Services Act for safeguarding the rights of the senior citizens.[49] In general, most of the facilities related to health care are provided for under the Swedish legislation. Thus, it can be noted that although India has implemented the IRDA Act, 1999 as well as many Regulations (including the Healthcare Insurance Regulations, 2016), the Indian legislation does not explicitly mention specific facilities for different ailments and/or different target groups.

Although India can definitely attempt at emulating certain practices in Sweden, it is even more important to take into account and learn from the achievements of our neighbours. One such neighbour, the "Tear of India"[50], which has delivered outstandingly is Sri Lanka, which has been successful in eradicating Malaria. This is notwithstanding the fact that

2017 in Nellore, Andhra Pradesh [Press release]. Retrieved October 17, 2017, from http://pib.nic.in/newsite/PrintRelease.aspx?relid=159804.

46 *Ibid.*

47 15 insurers offer products covering AYUSH treatment, but centre's schemes do not . (2017, July 28). *The New Indian Express*. Retrieved October 17, 2017, from http://www.newindianexpress.com/nation/2017/jul/28/15-insurers-offer-products-covering-ayush-treatment-but-centres-schemes-do-not-1634841.html.

48 Supra Note 39.

49 *Ibid.*

50 Sri Lanka Health Insurance. Pacific Prime. Retrieved October 17, 2017 from https://www.pacificprime.com/country/asia/sri-lanka-health-insurance/.

due to Sri Lanka being located in the vicinity of the equator, the county has a highly tropical climate, and both "receptivity and vulnerability to mosquitoes"[51]; it was among the most malaria-affected countries during from 1970s[52]. India, in comparison, is a large country, but most parts of India have a subtropical climate and are thus, prone to outbreaks of mosquito-borne diseases, such as Malaria. Thus, it remains to be analyzed if we can imbibe certain Sri Lankan practices into our own system, so that it would benefit our large population. In order to understand the intricacies of elimination of such a disease, it is important to take into account the healthcare system in Sri Lanka.

Sri Lanka has an insurance legislation similar to India[53], which provides for the establishment of the Insurance Commission of Sri Lanka (similar to the IRDA in India) and many other regulations form part of the legislation. Recently, the Sri Lankan cabinet has approved the change in the name of the regulator from 'Insurance Board of Sri Lanka' to 'Insurance Regulatory Commission of Sri Lanka'.[54] Although health represent just 2% of the GDP of Sri Lanka, it is remarkable that more than 90% of the inpatient services relating to preventive, rehabilitative and curative health services are provided by public sector hospitals.[55] Moreover, unlike the condition in India, where people, especially those living in rural areas have to travel as long distances as 50 km[56], Sri Lankan government has ensured that health care facilities are available within a short distance of 3-5 kilometres,

---

51 *Malaria-Free Sri Lanka* (pp. 1-19, Rep.). (n.d.). New Delhi: World Health Organization Regional Office for South-East Asia. Retrieved October 17, 2017 from http://www.searo.who.int/srilanka/areas/malaria/malaria-free-sri-lanka.pdf?ua=1.

52 Supra Note 38.

53 Regulation of Insurance Industry Act, 2000.

54 John, J. (2017, July 17). Sri Lanka: Cabinet approves renaming of insurance regulator. *Asia Insurance Review*. Retrieved October 17, 2017, from http://www3.asiainsurancereview.com/News/View-NewsLetter-Article?id=39726&Type=eDaily.

55 *National Malaria Plan for Elimination Prevention of Sri Lanka 2014 - 2018* (pp. 1-62, Publication). Ministry of Health Sri Lanka. Retrieved October 16, from http://www.malariacampaign.gov.lk/Downloads/AMC%20NSP.pdf.

56 In a study, it has been found that "89 percent of India's population lived within 50km of a district hospital, while only 57 percent lived within 50km of a "well-resourced" hospital". Supra Note 20.

on an average.[57] The government-controlled insurance initiatives in Sri Lanka in addition to increased amount of surveillance, establishment of mobile malaria clinics, community awareness and education, and a sense of urgency helped Sri Lanka to overcome the menace of Malaria.[58] The crux of the eradication programme lay in the aim of eliminating the parasite instead of the vector mosquito.[59] The difference lies in the amount of political will and the sense of ownership as opposed to a sense of entitlement, at the end of the day.[60]

CONCLUSION AND SUGGESTIONS

It can be inferred from the above discussion that despite the efforts of the government in implementing legislation such as the IRDA Health Insurance Regulations, 2016, the healthcare system and the health insurance system still lag behind, whether in terms of preventive or curative healthcare. It is evident that India needs to invest more on healthcare in terms of portion of GDP including the expenditure on developing basic infrastructure, recruiting more doctors, installing more beds in hospitals etc. India faces certain obstacles in the form of a huge population to take care of, but the government cannot deny its basic duty to provide health insurance. It may be difficult to emulate practices of countries like Sweden, which in addition to being a developed Scandinavian country has much less population as compared to India; but sustained efforts towards promising health insurance can go a long way in safeguarding the future of people in India. India can also learn from its neighbour Sri Lanka, as both countries have similarities in terms of problems created by the climate, administration, etc. The author proposes the following suggestions in the light of the above mentioned discussion:

1. India should invest significantly more than 1% of its GDP on its healthcare system. India can imbibe a combination of practices in other countries in this regard.

57 Supra Note 55, p.5.

58 Senthilingam, M. (2016, September 7). Can Sri Lanka show the world how to end malaria? *CNN*. Retrieved October 17, 2017, from http://edition.cnn.com/2016/09/07/health/sri-lanka-declared-free-of-malaria/index.html.

59 Supra Note 51, p. v (foreword).

60 Supra Note 58.

2. The government should invest in upgrading the CHCs and PHCs, and should provide more facilities such as basic medicines, vaccination and immunization processes, recruitment of more general physicians, etc. The district administration should pave way for establishment of CHCs and PHCs
3. The government should make sure that at least preventive health care is insured. For example, government can bear costs or subsidize the costs of minor accidents, dental treatment, blood tests, etc.
4. In case of diseases which have an epidemic nature (such as Malaria, Chikungunya, Dengue) in particular areas, the government should constantly monitor the diseases through constant surveillance. The government should involve the PHCs and the CHCs in this process as it would be better to utilize an existing setup.
5. The government should make efforts to upgrade and retrofit the existing public hospitals in order to serve a two-fold purpose: firstly, to bridge the gap between the public and the private hospitals; and secondly, to make the public hospitals accessible on subsidized rates for both BPL and APL (Above Poverty Line) category people.
6. The IRDA Act, 1999 should be amended to incorporate a provision detailing the scope and extent of the insurance offered by Life Insurers and/or General Insurers, by elaborating whether 'all' people including asylum seekers, stateless persons and refugees would be considered for the purpose of health insurance.

Victim's Right to Health Under State Victim Compensation Schemes in India

Dr. Sukdeo Ingale

Abstract

This chapter describes the existing position of the victim's right to health at national and local levels by outlining State Victim Compensation Schemes in India. Recently, after 2010 all the States and Union Territories in India have implemented Victim Compensation Schemes to provide monetary help to the victims of few crimes. Some of these schemes do provide compensation for mental agony to women and children as well as hospital expenses. However there is a long way to go ahead in this direction. In this chapter, the development of victim's right to health through State Victim Compensation Schemes in India is reviewed and the analysis of all Compensation Schemes is summarized. Suggestions are also provided for further reforms in such schemes for effective and efficient protection of victims' right to health. This chapter advances an agenda for research and action grounded in the struggle for victim's right to health and rehabilitation.

Keywords: *Right to Health, State Victim Compensation Schemes, Victim's Right to health*

INTRODUCTION

The victim's right to health has to be focused on priority basis as it has the greatest impact on the most disadvantaged section of society. Similarly enjoyment of the human right to health is crucial to the realization of many other fundamental human rights and freedoms recognized in a particular legal system. Hence such an approach in the development of right to health will not only help in emergence of a novel thought of line in newly budding field of victimology but also in the implementation of right to health in true spirit.

The interconnection between health and human rights is receiving increasing attention in contemporary society. Fundamental dimensions of health rights and human rights are integral and important components of the evaluation of the standard of life in a particular society. Hence more protection needs to be given to some protective groups like children, women, prisoners, victims, etc who has to face many impediments in enjoyment of their rights and freedoms. Now the human right to health is recognized by every civilized country in the world. Nevertheless, the resources necessary to achieve respect for these rights are lacking in many countries. Same is true with Indian society. Therefore, the links between victimization and the care for a victim's physical and mental health are still absent in India. We shall do our best in minimizing these constraints and to adopt a human rights approach to the victim's right to health.

Recently, the social, economic, cultural, ethical, and political climate at international level has given rise to an international movement which is re-evaluating the measures for the protection and rehabilitation of victims of crime and abuse of power. As a result, victims' right issues are being actively discussed in both the private and public platforms in all the countries. In India, the field of right to health has grown quickly, but its boundaries have yet to be traced. Even today, after such Compensation Schemes, India fails to protect victim's right to access health care and protect them against threat to their mental and physical health after victimization. Against this backdrop, present chapter describes current status of affairs about recognition of victim's right to health in the light of State Victim Compensation Schemes in India.

WHAT INCLUDES IN RIGHT TO HEALTH?

Everyone has the right to a standard of living adequate for the health and well-being of himself and of his family, including … medical care and necessary social services.[1] As the WHO constitution recognizes, the enjoyment of the highest attainable standard of health is one of the fundamental rights of every human being without the distinction of race, religion, political belief, economic or social condition. In the human rights

1 Article 25 (1) Universal Declaration of Human Rights.

discourse and practice the right to health has been and continues to be a contentious arena. However, we shall note that when we talk about the right to health we are not just talking about the physical or mental well-being of a person. The right to health encompasses not just the absence of disease or infirmity but "complete physical, mental and social well being".[2]

As regards to the responsibility of government, there are some basic requirements, which the government must provide as minimum requirements, for protection of right to health. It includes availability of and informed accessibility to economically affordable, quality medical treatment with respect and courtesy to all without any discrimination. In this regard the right to health imposes three types of obligations on the State,[3] it includes-

1. **To respect the right:** It requires States to refrain from interfering with it directly or indirectly – for example, denying access to healthcare services or discriminating in providing healthcare services,
2. **To protect the right:** It requires States to prevent third parties from interfering with the right to health, which may require states to enact legislation to ensure that individuals comply with the appropriate standards or prohibit doing acts harmful to the health of others,
3. **To fulfill the right:** It requires states to adopt progressive legislative, administrative, budgetary and other measures to fully realize the right to health by adopting national policies and schemes.

In short the protection of the right to health requires that governments must generate conditions in which everyone can be as healthy as possible. It is equally, rather more, applicable in the case of the victims of crime.

2 Preamble to the Constitution of the World Health Organization. Accessible online at http://www.who.int/ about/definition/en/print.html.

3 United Nations Committee on Economic Social and Cultural Rights, General Comment No.14: The right to the highest attainable standard of health (Article 12) (2000) E/C.12/2000/4, p 27.

ORIGIN OF THE STATE VICTIM COMPENSATION SCHEMES

The principle of compensating victims of crime has for long been recognized by the Indian Legal System though it was recognized more as a token relief rather than as a part of the punishment or substantial remedy. After constant judicial activism in this regard, recently all States and Union Territories have notified and implemented Victim Compensation Schemes in India. The first state implementing such scheme was Sikkim (June, 2011) shortly followed by Bihar (July, 2011) and Chhattisgarh (August 2011). Recently Madhya Pradesh (March, 2015) and Telangana (March, 2015) has notified scheme as the last states in the queue. All Union Territories also have Victim Compensation Schemes notified on different dates during 2012 - 2013.

The compensation given under these State Victim Compensation Schemes is given for different purposes like loss of life, permanent disability, rehabilitation, rape, funeral expenses, medical expenses, mental agony, etc. We will limit ourselves to the compensation for mental agony and medical expenses. In this regard it has to be noted that only few States have made provision for both, mental agony and medical expenses. The right to compensation for mental agony is limited to the women and children victims only. The amount of compensation for these purposes does differ considerably from one scheme to another.

AMOUNT OF COMPENSATION FOR MENTAL AGONY AND MEDICAL EXPENSES

It is surprising to note that only seven States [Haryana (expenses at actual to the maximum extent of ₹ 15,000) Karnataka (Maximum ₹ 25,000), Maharashtra (expenses at actual to the maximum extent of ₹ 15,000), Meghalaya (expenses at actual to the maximum extent of ₹ 15,000), Mizoram (Maximum ₹ 5,000 to 25,000; only on Hospitalization), Punjab (100% medical expenses for acid attack victims) and Tamil Nadu (at actual to the maximum extent of ₹ 1,50,000)] have made provisions for separate amount of compensation for medical expenses. Only one State (Madhya Pradesh) has made provision of free medical treatment in government hospital for all victims of crimes. Maximum States (20 in number including Assam, Bihar, Chhattisgarh, Gujarat, Himachal Pradesh, Jammu and Kashmir, Jharkhand, Karnataka, Kerala, Maharashtra, Manipur, Mizoram, Nagaland, Odisha, Sikkim, Tripura, Uttar Pradesh, Uttarakhand, Kolkata and Delhi) and all Union Territories have a provision which requires the District Legal Service Authority to consider 'loss caused to the victim, medical expenses to be incurred on treatment, minimum sustenance amount required for rehabilitation including such incidental charges as funeral expenses' while deciding overall amount of compensation.

All the States and Union Territories have provision for compensation for severe mental agony to the victims of crime. However, this compensation is limited to women and or children only and it is payable only if they are victimized due to few types of offences. Only one state (Uttar Pradesh) has made provision of this compensation for all types of crimes. The State of Jammu and Kashmir, West Bengal, Jharkhand, Manipur and Odisha (₹ 10,000 by each State), Chhattisgarh (₹ 20,000), Himachal Pradesh (₹ 24,000), Gujarat, Rajasthan and Sikkim (₹ 25,000) Nagaland and Uttarakhand (₹ 1,00,000) have limited this compensation for 'human trafficking' only. The scheme of Arunachal Pradesh (₹ 10,000) has made provision for 'human trafficking, etc.' The State of Assam (₹ 15,000) has limited this compensation to the cases of human trafficking, kidnapping, cruelty U/S 498(A) IPC, etc. The State of Mizoram (₹ 20,000) and Bihar (₹ 25,000) has made such provision for human trafficking, kidnapping etc. The State of Tripura (₹ 20,000) has made provision of such compensation for Child abuse/Human Trafficking. The State of Goa (Upto ₹ 1,00,000) has limited this compensation to human trafficking and rape cases, Acid cases. The State of Haryana, Telangana, Meghalaya (₹ 50,000) and Tamil Nadu (₹ 1,00,000) has made such provision for Human Trafficking, Kidnapping and Molestation etc. The State of Karnataka (₹ 1,00,000) has limited this compensation to the cases of human trafficking and made payable to the victims who themselves or their parents have suffered separation / dislocation and disturbance. The state of Punjab, Delhi and all Union Territories (₹ 50,000) has limited this compensation to the cases of human trafficking, child abuse and kidnapping.

In *Laxmi v. Union of India and others*[4] the Hon'ble Apex Court has dealt with the issue of amount of compensation to the victims of acid attack. After detailed discussion, the Court came to conclusion that the amount of compensation in all the State Victim Compensation Schemes is inadequate and hence directed all the State Governments to provide ₹ 3 lakh as a minimum amount to the acid attack victims.

In *Parivartan Kendra v. Union of India and Ors.*[5] the Hon'ble Apex Court has considered the question of granting compensation to the victim for medical care for rehabilitation of victims of acid attack. In this case the Hon'ble Court found that, "… Even in those States where the Scheme has been implemented a meagre compensation ranging between ₹ 25,000 to ₹ 2 lakhs is provided for medical care. And many States have not provided any compensation for rehabilitation at all." Recently on 7 December, 2015 in *Parivartan Kendra & Anr v. U.O.I & Ors*[6] the Hon'ble Supreme Court has reiterated above opinion and further observed that, "Keeping in view the impact of acid attack on the victim on his social, economical and personal life, we need to enhance the amount of compensation. We cannot be oblivious of the fact that the victim of acid attack requires permanent treatment for the damaged skin."

WHO CAN CLAIM COMPENSATION UNDER THE SCHEMES

It is interesting to study who can be the 'applicant' for the victim compensation Schemes in India. The term 'applicant' is defined only in the schemes provided by the State of Kerala, Telangana and Himachal Pradesh. The meaning of 'applicant' as provided by the State of Kerala and Telangana is same which run as "applicant means a victim or the dependent of a victim who applies for compensation." The State of Himachal Pradesh defined 'Applicant' as "the victim or the person making an application on behalf of the victim where he or she, due to physical or mental incapacity, is unable to submit the same or where the victim has died, includes his legal heirs."

4 (2014) 4 SCC 427.

5 (2016) 3 SCC 571.

6 2016(1) R.C.R. (Criminal) 336.

If read with definitions of the term 'victim', 'dependent' or 'applicant' as provided by all other states and Union Territories, it is very surprising that the state of Himachal Pradesh is the only state which allows 'a person' "to make an application on behalf of the victim where he/she, due to physical or mental incapacity is unable to submit the same." It can be interpreted in a broader perspective as giving *locus standi* to some public spirited individuals, institutions and NGOs to act on behalf of the victim. On other hand, the State of Kerala is the only state which expressly prohibits any other person / institution to apply for compensation on behalf of the victim.[7] The fate of victims in other States will depend on the approach of the Hon'ble Courts while interpreting these schemes as there is no explicitly enabling or prohibiting provision in this regards in the schemes provided by other states. All other states defined either the term 'victim' or 'dependent' to indicate who can claim compensation under the scheme.

Definition of Victim:

The State of Haryana, Punjab and Tamil Nadu have not provided any definition for the term 'victim' in their schemes. After careful scrutiny of all the compensation schemes, one can come across with total nine different definitions of the term 'victim'. The definitions provided by other states are as follows:

Firstly, the state of Assam, Delhi, Himachal Pradesh, Maharashtra, Meghalaya, Rajasthan, Tripura and all Union Territories have adopted definition of the term 'victim' as provided under section 2 (wa) of the Code of Criminal Procedure.[8] Before going further it is to be noted that the

7 Clause 7 (9) of the victim compensation scheme provided by the state of Kerala runs as "The District Legal Service Authority shall not allow any participation or representation by a legal practitioner or any other person or institution or Non-Governmental Organization on behalf of the victim/claimant."

8 Section 2 (wa) runs as "Victim means a person who has suffered any loss or injury caused by reason of the act or omission for which the accused person has been charged and the expression victim includes his or her guardian or legal heir."

state of Haryana, Punjab and Tamil Nadu has notified victim compensation schemes without providing any definition for the term 'victim' (though the state of Haryana and Tamil Nadu provides definition of dependent). In the absence of definition under the notification of Victim Compensation Scheme it is expected that the Hon'ble Courts will read definition of 'victim' under section 2 (wa) of CrPC.

Secondly, the state of Andhra Pradesh and Goa defined the term victim as "Victim means any person who himself or herself has suffered loss or injury as a result of crime and requires rehabilitation." There is willful exclusion of the words "the expression victim includes his/her guardian or legal heir" which is provided under section 2 (wa) of CrPC. After considering definition of 'dependent' as given in Andhra Pradesh Victim Compensation Scheme, it results in exclusion of legal heir other than 'the spouse or a natural parent or a child of the deceased'. This definition of victim will make situation more difficult in Goa as there is no definition of 'dependent'. The definition in Telangana is similar except suffix added as 'includes guardian or legal heir of such person' which make it similar to definition under section 2 (wa) CrPC. One more difference in the first and second definition of victim is that the second definition includes 'and requires rehabilitation'. The result is that the person becomes victim under definition of Andhra Pradesh, Goa and Telangana only if the person is injured or suffered loss to the extent that he/she requires rehabilitation. But the term rehabilitation is not defined and hence the conditions/ qualifications to become victim are not clear.

Thirdly, the State of Gujarat, Odisha and West Bengal defined victim as "Victim means a person who himself has suffered loss or injury as a result of crime and requires rehabilitation and the expression victim also includes his/her dependants." Apparently the definition seems to be very clear. It has intrinsic infirmity as the term 'dependent' is not defined by the State of Gujarat and Odisha. The term 'dependent' is defined by the State of West Bengal as a person who fully depends on the earnings of the victim. The scope of definition of victim is very wide as there is no limitation as to relation or family membership. It may also include father in law and mother in law depending on the earning of daughter in law. This issue could be more understood while elaborating the term 'dependent'.

Fourthly the state of Chhattisgarh, Jammu and Kashmir, Jharkhand, Manipur, Nagaland, Sikkim and Uttar Pradesh defined the term victim as "Victim means a person who himself has suffered loss or injury as a result of crime and requires rehabilitation and this includes dependant family members also." But none of the State bothered to define the term 'dependent' as the term is limited by the expression of 'family members'. Here the issue can be about a person who is family member but has no blood relationship.

Fifthly the State of Kerala and Madhya Pradesh defined victim as "victim means a person who has suffered any loss or injury caused by reason of the act or omission on the part of the accused and who requires rehabilitation under this scheme and includes the guardian or legal heir of such person, but does not include a person who is responsible for injury to such person." This definition differs from all other definitions because of a suffix 'but does not include a person who is responsible for injury to such person'. This definition can be appreciated as it excludes husband (and his relatives) in the cases of dowry death and related offences. But it can be criticized as it is not clear whether a person will lose his/her right under these schemes if the offence is committed due to contributory negligence on the part of such person. S*ixthly,* the State of Karnataka defined the term victim as "Victim means a person who himself has suffered loss or injury as a result of crime and, require rehabilitation and includes his dependents who had suffered loss or injury as a result of the crime and who require rehabilitation". This definition includes a clause providing that the term victim "... includes his dependents who had suffered loss or injury as a result of the crime and who require rehabilitation." This means that the loss or injury to victim will not *ipso facto* designate his dependents as 'victim' unless the dependents will cause loss or injury independent and other than the loss or injury to the victim.

Seventhly, the state of Bihar has defined the term victim as "Victim means a person who himself has suffered loss or injury as a result of crime causing substantial loss to the income of the family making it difficult to meet their both ends without the financial aid or has to spend beyond his means on medical treatment of Mental/Physical injury and require rehabilitation." This definition requires fulfilling two essential conditions. *Firstly*, that the crime shall 'cause substantial loss to the income of family' or the term 'substantial' is further qualified by 'making it difficult to meet their both ends without the financial aid'. *Secondly* that he 'has spent beyond his means on medical treatment …'. It means that the victim is not entitle for compensation under this scheme if crime will not result in causing 'substantial loss' to a family which was, before such crime, able to meet their both ends and the crime 'make it difficult to meet their both ends' or if victim has spent 'within' his means. It is totally external element to the Criminal Law (Amendment) Act, 2008 and section 357 A of CrPC. There was no such legislative intent while formulating policy of Criminal Law (Amendment) Act, 2008 or the Scheme for Relief and Rehabilitation of Victims of Rape, 2005 (revised in 2010) as recommended by National Commission for Women. Similarly it has to be noted that 'spend beyond his means' is also not easy to ascertain and establish.

Eighthly, the state of Uttarakhand defined victim as "victim means a person, who himself has suffered loss or injury as a result of crime, Acid attack, Human trafficking, Serious accident etc and require rehabilitation and includes dependent family members." This is the narrowest definition among all eight definitions of victim provided under different victim compensation schemes in India. The clause 'suffered loss or injury as a result of crime' is followed by 'acid attack, human trafficking, serious accident etc'. It will defeat legislative intent, which can be ascertained from Schedule 1 of the scheme, if we will limit this scheme to such a category of offences only. Though definition of victim has specific mention of the term 'serious accidents', the clause 5 (6) of the same scheme provides that "the cases covered under Motor Vehicle Act, 1988 (Act No. 59 of 1988) wherein assistance is to be awarded by the Motor Accident Claims Tribunal, shall not be covered under the Scheme."

Ninthly, the state of Mizoram defined victim as "Victim means a person who himself has suffered any loss or injury caused by reason of the act or omission for which the accused person has been charged; and causing burns or maiming or disfiguring or disabling or causing grievous hurt as a result of acid attacks and require rehabilitation and the expression 'victim' includes dependent family members". In this definition the special mention of 'and causing burns or maiming or disfiguring or disabling or causing grievous hurt as a result of acid attacks' shows legislative intent to focus on the menace of acid attack. But the scope of definition is limited when read with the definition of 'dependent' as provided under the scheme of victim compensation. The term 'Victim' is discussed by the Hon'ble Allahabad High Court in *Manoj Kumar Singh v. State of U.P. & Others*[9] on 11 November, 2016. In this case the Hon'ble Court have reviewed decisions of many other High Courts and the Court opined that

"It may be seen that all the judgments which we have noticed discuss the definition of 'victim' as 'Means X and includes Y' and while interpreting the phrase 'Means X', the term 'any loss or injury' has been discussed elaborately and for this purpose, the provisions of section 2 (y) of the Code along with sections 23 (wrongful loss) and 44 (injury) of the Indian Penal Code have been taken into consideration. Like-wise for the phrase 'Includes Y', the meaning of term 'legal heir' has been analyzed taking aid of the law dealing with principles of inheritance and succession which are used to determine civil rights."

The same formula was also discussed and applied with caution by the Hon'ble Delhi High Court in *Ram Phal v. State and Ors.*[10] on 28 May, 2015 and the court held as follows-

"(ii) The 'means X and includes Y' clause in Section 2 (wa) cannot be interpreted so as to result in the included meaning Y excluding the actual meaning X of the term being defined; thus 'legal heirs' who are included within the definition of the term 'victim' cannot exclude those who actually fall within the definition of 'victim' by virtue of emotional harm suffered, such as the father or siblings of a deceased victim or other categories of persons (based on proximity) noted previously."

After close perusal of all above judgments of various High Courts, it is noticeable that all the judgments deal with definition of 'victim' in respect of an offence committed by offender without considering the impact of the nature of an offence of which one is a victim. There are various forms of offences as provided under Indian Penal Code as well as other Special Laws. An offence may be against body, mind, property, etc. In that context injury caused by the offence would vary. Further, there may be crime

9 CRL. Misc. App. No. 67 of 2013. [Non-reportable].
10 221 (2015) DLT 1

against society, which can be termed as a victim less crime because there is no victim in particular. None of these judgments consider the above aspect.

Recently, while deciding issue of right to appeal as a victim, the Hon'ble Allahabad High Court has used definition of victim provided under section 2 (wa) of CrPC. According to Hon'ble Allahabad High Court[11] the first part of the definition of 'victim' as given under Section 2 (wa) is required to be construed in its literal sense and no liberal interpretation is required, Accordingly, only such person would be treated as "victim', who is the subject-matter of trial being direct sufferer of crime in terms of loss or injury caused to his own body, mind, reputation and property and such loss or injury is one of the ingredient of the offence for which the accused person has been charged and, therefore, any other person cannot be accepted as victim within the first part of Section 2 (wa) for the purposes of maintaining appeal. The second part that is "includes his or her guardian and Legal Heir" would come into play when the actual sufferer is absent or suffers disability.

This is obvious as the issue is not about right to compensation which is regulated as per different State Victim Compensation Schemes. It is not that easy for Hon'ble Apex Court to arrive at such a conclusion with respect to meaning of the term 'victim' in case of deciding the claims of compensation as the definitions provided under different State Victim Compensation Schemes are diverse and sometime contradicting to each other.

Definition of Dependant

Now let us discuss the definition of the term 'dependent'. The victim compensation schemes provided by the state of Punjab, Uttarakhand, Karnataka, Chhattisgarh, Jammu and Kashmir; Jharkhand; Manipur; Nagaland; Sikkim; Gujarat; Goa, Himachal Pradesh, Rajasthan and Assam has no definition of the term 'dependent' even though the term is used frequently under the schemes provided by all these states. The term 'dependent' has nine definitions provided by other states under different schemes in India. It can be explained in short as follows-

11 *Manoj Kumar Singh v. State of UP* CRL. Misc. App. No. 67 of 2013. [Non-reportable].

Firstly, the definition provided by the State of West Bengal is denoting the most 'literal' meaning of the term. It runs as "Dependents mean a person who fully depends on the earnings of the victim." But the term is not qualified by any word which denotes near blood relation, marital relation, family relation, etc and hence the definition becomes more vague and any remote relative or illegitimate child or 'second' spouse can be included in this definition. *Secondly*, the most simplest definition is given by Madhya Pradesh, Kerala, Delhi and All union Territories which run as "Dependent includes wife, husband, father, mother, unmarried daughter and minor children of victim as determined by the authority empowered to issue dependency certificate or any other authority authorized by Government in this regard." Here it is not clear whether the term 'father' and 'mother' includes 'father-in-Law' and 'mother-in-law' respectively; specially when daughter-in-law is the only earning person after death of their son.

Thirdly, the state of Maharashtra, Tamil Nadu and Haryana defined the term 'dependent' as "wife, Husband, father, mother, unmarried daughter, minor children and includes other legal heirs who, are found fully dependent on the victim." Here it is not clear whether the phrase "who are found fully dependent on the victim" is limited to 'other legal heirs' or it is equally applicable to 'wife, Husband, father, mother, unmarried daughter, minor children' also. *Fourthly* the definition provided by the State of Telangana is similar to above second definition which run as "Dependent includes wife, husband, father, mother, unmarried daughter and minor children of victim as determined by the authority empowered to issue dependency certificate or any other authority authorized by the Government in this regard and found fully dependent on the victim by the District Legal Services Authority" the difference here is that 'other legal heirs' are not included in this definition.

Fifthly, while talking about the term dependent; the scheme provided by the State of Odisha runs as "Provided where the victim is a minor, his/her parents would be dependants in case they are found to have been affected by the crime or in case the perpetration of crime has left a scar on their dependant family members". The minor and parents needs to prove that they have been affected by the crime or in case the perpetration of crime has left a scar on their body. The definition also includes a phrase 'dependant family members'. Hence the definition can be interpreted as – "a minor and parents would be dependents in case they are found to have been affected by crime" and include "other family member on whose body the perpetration of crime has left a scar." In short this definition is also difficult to interpret and will unnecessarily curtail number of really dependent members of family. *Sixthly*, the definition provided by Andhra Pradesh runs as "Dependent means and includes those who at the time of the deceased's death was either the spouse or a natural parent or a child of the deceased." It is not clear whether this definition intend to exclude adoptive and surrogate parents. Here it is not necessary to show that the spouse or a natural parents or a child was depending on the deceased victim.

Seventhly, the State of Tripura defines the term 'dependent' as "Dependent means any of spouse, dependent children up to age of 21 years (including legally adopted children) and dependent parents." Here the children are entitled for compensation only up to the age of 21 years which is discriminating and against the spirit of compensation laws. *Eighthly*, The State of Mizoram defines dependent as "dependants would mean husband/wife, dependent children up to the age of 21 years (including legally adopted children) dependent parents, dependent daughter of any age and physically or mentally challenged children of any age." This definition is similar to the above definition provided by the State of Tripura. The only difference is this definition includes 'dependent daughter of any age and physically or mentally challenged children of any age.' This special mention of 'physically or mentally challenged children of any age' is unique provision of this definition as it is not included in the compensation scheme provided by any other state. But use of the term 'children of any age' attached to the 'physically or mentally challenged' restricts utility of this provision. It is suggested that the term 'children of any age' should be substituted for 'person of any age.' *Ninthly*, now the widest definition is given by the state of Bihar which runs as "Dependent means member of family of the victim, namely Husband/Wife; Mother/Father, Brother/Sister, Son/Daughter, Grand Mother/Grand Father, Father-in-Law/Mother-in-Law and it includes any other person who is leading life on the income of the victim." There is no any other scheme providing such definition of dependent which includes Brother/Sister, Grand Mother/Grand Father,

Father-in-Law/Mother-in-Law and 'any other person who is leading life on the income of the victim.'

CONDITION PRECEDENTS OF ELIGIBILITY FOR COMPENSATION

There are six major conditions used in different victim compensation schemes which limit scope; and hence utility, of the scheme. Following are such conditions which needs to be reconsidered to make the schemes more efficient and meaningful-

Firstly, all victim compensation schemes has a condition that –"the victim or claimant must co-operate with the police and prosecution." But the term 'non-co-operation with police and prosecution' is not easy to be defined. There can never be uniform understanding of this term. But the author has not come across with any case where application for compensation is denied on the ground that the victim or claimant is not co-operating with the police or prosecution.

Secondly, the victim compensation schemes of Delhi, Maharashtra, AP, Odisha, Punjab, Rajasthan, Goa, J and K, W.B., Sikkim and all Union Territories provides that "He / She should not have been compensated for the loss or injury under any other scheme of the Central/State Government, Insurance Company or any other Institution." There is a similar condition excluding cases covered under the Motor Vehicles Act, 1988 in the victim compensation schemes of Maharashtra, Bihar, Chhattisgarh, Gujarat, Haryana, Jammu and Kashmir, Kerala, Odisha and Tripura. In the state of Odisha the cases covered under Schedule Caste and Schedule Tribe (Prevention of Atrocities) Act, 1989 and Protection of Civil Rights Act, 1955 are not allowed to be considered for compensation under Victim Compensation Scheme.

The Hon'ble Supreme Court has dealt with such conditions and diluted it by constructive interpretation. For example *Mohini* v. *The State (Govt. of NCT of Delhi)*.[12] In this case the Delhi State Legal Services Authority declined to award any compensation under the Scheme in view of clause 4 of the Delhi Victim Compensation Scheme. Clause 4 of the scheme reads as follows:

12 W.P. (C) 3754/2015 decided on 14.09.2015 [Non-reportable].

"4. Eligibility for compensation- The victim or his dependent(s) shall be eligible for the grant of compensation after satisfying the criteria that he/she should not have been compensated for the loss or injury under any other scheme of the Central Government or the Government of National Capital Territory of Delhi."

When it was challenged the Hon'ble Delhi High Court held that-

"Section 357A (5) CrPC provides that the District Legal Services Authority after due enquiry will award 'adequate compensation'. The stress is on 'adequate compensation'. To knock out an applicant under the Scheme merely because some meagre or token compensation was received by the applicant under some other statutory provisions would be unfair and contrary to the very object of the Scheme."

Hence the Hon'ble Delhi High Court concluded that – "the victim can be said to 'have been compensated for the loss and injury' from some other scheme when he has received compensation equivalent to or more than what is the minimum stipulated in the Schedule to the Scheme. Such an applicant would not be entitled to receive any compensation under the present Scheme. However, where the amount received is less than the minimum stipulated under the Schedule, it cannot be said that he has been compensated for the loss and injury and the concerned authority shall grant appropriate compensation under the Scheme but taking into account the amount of compensation already received by the victim/dependent."

Thirdly, the compensation schemes of AP, Assam, Bihar, Maharashtra, Chhattisgarh, Goa, Punjab and Sikkim, have very strange condition that "the loss or injury sustained by the victim or his dependents should have caused substantial loss to the income of the family making it difficult to meet their both ends without the financial aid or has to spend beyond his means on medical treatment of mental or physical injury". There is similar condition in Tripura which runs as "The victim suffers substantial loss of income as a result of the crime or is unable to take care of expenses of medical treatment for injury caused on account of crime." Slightly different but similar condition is required to be fulfilled in Odisha, Rajasthan, and Sikkim which requires that, "Loss or injury sustained by the victim have caused substantial loss to the income of the family making it difficult to live as before without the financial aid or has affected his/her dignity or personality or the medical treatment of mental/physical injury should have caused financial stress for the family."

Fourthly, the victim compensation schemes of Maharashtra and Telangana has a very objectionable condition that "the employees of the Central or State Government, Boards, Corporations and Public Undertakings and income tax payees shall not be eligible for compensation under this Scheme". The State of Kerala has similar condition which runs as "employees of Central or State Governments, Boards, Corporation Public Sector Undertakings and- those whose family income exceeds the creamy layer limit fixed by the respective Governments from time to time are not be eligible".

Fifthly, some schemes used 'income' as a limit for applicability of the Scheme. The victim compensation schemes of Haryana and Telangana have limited scope of the schemes to a person from a family having income not exceeding Rs. 4.5 Lac per annum (37, 500 per month). On similar line the scheme of the state of Madhya Pradesh says, "If annual income of victim is more than 5 Lacs- only 50% of amounts in scheme should be payable". On other hand the precondition in the state of Mizoram is, "Only BPL family would be considered for eligibility under the Scheme." *Sixthly*, the victim compensation scheme of only one State (i.e. Karnataka) expressly prohibits participation or representation by any person on behalf of victim. The provision runs as- "The District Legal Service Authority shall not allow any participation or representation by a legal practitioner or any other person or institution or Non-Governmental Organization on behalf of the victim/claimant."

It has to be noted that except first condition as mentioned above was recommended by the Scheme for Relief and Rehabilitation of Victims of Rape, 2005 (revised in 2010) as recommended by National Commission for Women. A careful reading of all above conditions shows that most of the condition precedents have no nexus with the aims and objectives of the scheme. Some of the conditions are direct threat to the idea of restitution and compensation. On the basis of above discussion it can be safely concluded that Victim Compensation Schemes in India are intrinsically different from each other and renders the majority of victims of crime ineligible for the compensation under schemes.

CONCLUSION

The most popular tool evolved for protection and rehabilitation of victims of crime in India is monetary help by way of compensation. The States in India have tried to protect victim's right to health through different compensation schemes. A careful reading of all these schemes shows that most of the condition precedents in these schemes have no nexus with their aims and objectives. Some of the conditions are direct threat to the idea of restitution and compensation. The schemes are limited to very marginal number of victims by way of very stringent definitions of the term 'victim', 'dependent' and 'applicant'. On the basis of above discussion it can be safely concluded that Victim Compensation Schemes in India renders the majority of victims of crime ineligible for the compensation under schemes and thereby fails to protect right to health. Hence the present author is of a opinion that the definition of the words like 'victim', 'dependant', and 'legal heir' are required to be construed in a manner that it sub-serve the purpose of the main enactment and, in any case, does not defeat the same.

We have a long way to go ahead in this direction. To start we can increase ambit of the Compensation Schemes by providing free medical help and treatment to the victims of crime. In most of the cases of offences against women and children, the Hon'ble Supreme Court has directed for medical care of victim at the expenses of Government.[13] It is suggested that all victim compensation schemes shall have a provision of free medical care of the victims by all Government as well as Private Hospitals and Health Care Centres. Presently similar provision is made for victims of acid attack for first aid or medical treatment under section 357 C of Cr.P.C which is inserted by way of the Criminal Law (Amendment) Act 2013. It is further suggested by the present author that the Private Hospitals or Health Care Centres may recover the amount through Victim Compensation Schemes.

One more suggestion for further reform in this regard is about National level uniform law for compensation to victims of crime. A comprehensive

13 *Indu Devi v. The State of Bihar and Ors.* Civil Writ Jurisdiction Case No.5286 of 2017.

enacted law for victim compensation applicable to whole India is a dire necessity. A National level comprehensive law should be enacted providing for fair treatment, medical and psychological assistance and adequate compensation to all victims of crime throughout India irrespective of residence of a person in particular State. Or the better way can be central government enacting law as well as prescribing minimum limit of compensation amount for each category of crimes and empowering states to decide amount of compensation, more than such minimum limit, on the basis of funds available to the states.

❑❑❑

5

Health Legislative Perspective

Surrogacy and its Regulation: An Overview of Legislative and Judicial Responses in India

Dr. Aneesh V. Pillai

Abstract

In the past two decades, there has been a stunning change in the field of surrogacy practices in India. As a result India has emerged as a world capital for surrogacy practice and is become a favourite destination for foreigners for ART services particularly for surrogacy practices. Hence, the surrogacy practice is developed as a well established business in India, with an estimated annual turnover of more than billion dollars. Despite this growing prominence of the Indian surrogacy industry in recent years, it is strange but true that the surrogacy practices in India remain largely unregulated1. This paper seeks to examine the various legislative attempts in India to deal with the subject of surrogacy and also it examines the judicial approach towards the issues related to surrogacy practices.

Keywords: *Surrogacy; ART; Laws; Judicial view.*

1 KLJ.

INTRODUCTION

Raising a family is the most important aspect of life for almost all individuals. However, due to the increasing rate of rate of infertility, many couples face a challenge in reproducing their own genetic offspring. With the advancement of science and technology, various methods and techniques have emerged to help such couples to enable them to have a genetic offspring. Such methods and techniques are collectively termed as Assisted Human Reproductive Technologies (ART) and it includes mainly Artificial Insemination, In Vitro Fertilization and Surrogacy. Among these methods 'surrogacy' is most widely used and being preferred by couples and individuals who cannot have a child otherwise as a last resort. 'Surrogacy' is an "arrangement in which a woman agrees to a pregnancy, achieved through assisted reproductive technology, in which neither of the gametes belong to her or her husband, with the intention of carrying it to term and handing over the child to the person or persons for whom she is acting as surrogate (Draft ART Regulation Bill, 2014).

Due to the varying approach towards ART and its strict regulations in certain countries, the couples or individuals who wish to beget a child through ART especially with the help of surrogacy prefer to travel across countries and avail such services from a country which either does not have a legal prohibition or has the minimum restriction for ART. In the past two decades, there has been a stunning change in the field of surrogacy practices in India. As a result India has emerged as a world capital for surrogacy practice and is become a favourite destination for foreigners for ART services particularly for surrogacy practices. Hence, the surrogacy practice is developed as a well established business in India, with an estimated annual turnover of more than billion dollars. Despite this growing prominence of the Indian surrogacy industry in recent years, it is strange but true that the surrogacy practices in India remain largely unregulated (Pillai, 2017). This paper seeks to examine the various legislative attempts in India to deal with the subject of surrogacy and also it examines the judicial approach towards the issues related to surrogacy practices.

SURROGACY

Surrogacy is a practice in which a woman agrees to become pregnant through artificial methods and to bear the child for another person or persons to whom she will transfer custody at or shortly after birth. The woman who agrees to bear the child is known as Surrogate mother and to whom he transfer the custody of the child after its birth are termed as Intended couple/Commissioning parents. Surrogacy practices can be classified as altruistic or commercial surrogacy. An altruistic surrogacy is one in which the birth mother does not receive any financial or material gain from the arrangement. In contrast, commercial surrogacy is where the birth mother receives a fee or some other monetary gain in return for acting as the surrogate (Brown, 2008).

During the past twenty years, the practice of surrogacy has gained respect as an attractive reproductive alternative for infertile couples who wish to conceive a child biologically related to at least one of them (Ragone, 1994, p.13). Due to its various advantages when compared to adoption as well as other reproductive technologies, the concept of surrogacy has gained wide recognition all over the world particularly in India. Developments in the procedures such as artificial insemination and invitro fertilization, have made surrogacy a viable alternative means of reproduction in infertile couples (Behm, 1999). Though surrogacy is widely accepted as a method for begetting a child, it has also been criticized on account of various grounds such as, it violates the human rights and dignity of surrogate women and it would lead to commodification of women, exploitation, prostitution36 and slavery. Further, it is said that surrogacy would have an adverse impact on the rights of the child and lead to baby selling, sex selection and creation of designer babies. These concerns in surrogacy can be resolved only through an adequate legislative framework.

REGULATION OF SURROGACY IN INDIA: LEGISLATIVE RESPONSE

The popularity of surrogacy as a means for begetting a genetically related child has increased tremendously all over the world. Though surrogacy is gained popularity and is rapidly developed as an industry in India, the

Government has been very slow in responding to the changing situations. In the absence of a legislative action, the Indian Council for Medical Research has come up with certain ethical guidelines for regulating assisted human reproductive technologies in general and it also includes guidelines for surrogacy practices.

In 2000, the ICMR adopted, "Ethical Guidelines for Biomedical Research on Human Participants", in which they prescribed certain guidelines to deal with ART in general. So also in the same year, "Statement of Specific Principles for Assisted Reproductive Technologies, 2000" was released by ICMR. Further in 2002, the ICMR submitted a Draft National Guidelines for Accreditation, Supervision & Regulation of ART Clinics, 2002 to the Ministry of Health and Family Welfare. This draft was later modified and adopted by the ICMR officially in 2005 after consultation with the National Academy of Medical Sciences, practitioners of ART, and the Ministry of Health and Family Welfare (Smerdon, 2008-09).

The Government of India, realising the increasing need to regulate ART practices and surrogacy in the country took steps for adopting a binding legal framework. As a result, the Assisted Reproductive Technology (Regulation) Bill and Rules, 2008 were drafted (Pillai, 2015). The Law Commission of India submitted its Report No. 228 in August 2009, entitled 'Need for Legislation to Regulate Assisted Reproductive Technology Clinics as well as Rights and Obligations of Parties to a Surrogacy'. The Report noted that, 'Surrogacy involves conflict of various interests and has inscrutable impact on the primary unit of society viz. family. Non-intervention of law in this knotty issue will not be proper at a time when law is to act as ardent defender of human liberty and an instrument of distribution of positive entitlements. At the same time, prohibition on vague moral grounds without a proper assessment of social ends and purposes which surrogacy can serve would be irrational. Active legislative intervention is required to facilitate correct uses of the new technology i.e. ART and relinquish the cocooned approach to legalization of surrogacy adopted hitherto. The need of the hour is to adopt a pragmatic approach by legalizing altruistic surrogacy arrangements and prohibit commercial ones' (228th ILC Report, 2009).

Further an updated Bill was introduced in 2010 and 2013. However, these Bills also failed to become an Act (Jargilo, 2015-16). In 2014, Dr. Kirit Premjibhai Solanki, a Member of Parliament from Gujarat, has taken an initiative to introduce a Bill for regulating surrogacy in the Lok Sabha. This Bill was named as The Surrogacy (Regulation) Bill, 2014 and it was introduced in the Lok Sabha on 08. 08. 2014 (Surrogacy Programs, 2016). However it was also a futile attempt.

On 27th October, 2015 the Department of Health Research of the Indian Ministry of Health and Family Welfare, Government of India, filed an affidavit in the case of Jan Balaz before the Supreme Court. The Central Government stated in the affidavit that, India does not support commercial surrogacy and the scope of surrogacy will be limited to Indian married infertile couples only, and not to foreigners (Jargilo, 2015-16). On the basis of this Central Government has adopted the Surrogacy (Regulation) Bill, 2016 thereby imposed a ban on commercial surrogacy and limited surrogacy only for Indian hetero sexual married couples.

THE SURROGACY (REGULATION) BILL, 2016: FEATURES

The object of this Bill is to regulate surrogacy services in the country, to prohibit the potential exploitation of surrogate mothers and to protect the rights of children born through surrogacy. This is because, due to lack of legislation to regulate surrogacy, the practice of surrogacy has been misused by the surrogacy clinics, which leads to rampant of commercial surrogacy and unethical practices in the said area of surrogacy. The Bill contains 51 Sections and is divided into 8 Chapters. This Bill contains provisions in relation to intended couples, surrogate mother, regulation of surrogacy clinics, protection of the welfare of the child, penalties for prohibitions, and constitution of Central and State Surrogacy Boards.

INTENDED COUPLES

According to the Bill, the intended couples must be married hetero sexual couple between the ages of 23 to 50 years in case of female and between 26 to 55 years in case of male. They must be Indian citizens and must have completed 5 years of their marital relationship. The intended couples must obtain a certificate of proven infertility in favour of either or both members of the intending couple from a District Medical Board. They should not have any surviving child biologically or through adoption or through surrogacy earlier. However, in cases where the intending couple have a child and who is mentally or physically challenged or suffers from life threatening disorder or fatal illness with no permanent cure and approved by the appropriate authority with due medical certificate from a District Medical Board, are eligible for accessing surrogacy services.

SURROGATE MOTHER

According to the Bill the prospective surrogate woman must be a close relative of the intending couple and an ever married woman having a child of her own and between the ages of 25 to 35 years on the day of implantation. Such woman can provide gametes or carry the surrogate pregnancy only once in her life time. She should produce a certificate of medical and psychological fitness for surrogacy and surrogacy procedures from a registered medical practitioner. The surrogate mother should give a written informed consent for participating in the surrogacy procedures. The Bill also states that prior to the beginning of surrogacy procedures the intended couple shall make an insurance coverage of such amount as may be prescribed in favour of the surrogate mother.

SURROGATE CHILD

In order to protect the welfare of the child, the Bill states that before the commencement of surrogacy procedures the intended parents has to obtain an order concerning the parentage and custody of the child to be born through surrogacy from a court of the Magistrate of the first class or above, on an application made by the intending couple and surrogate mother. The Bill states that any child born out of surrogacy procedure shall be deemed to be a biological child of the intending couple and the said child shall be entitled to all the rights and privileges available to a natural child under any law for the time being in force. Further the Bill mandates that, the intending couple shall not abandon the child, born out of a surrogacy procedure, whether within India or outside, for any reason whatsoever, including but not restricted to, any genetic defect, birth defect, any other medical condition, the defects developing subsequently, sex of the child or conception of more than one baby and the like.

REGULATION OF CLINICS

The Bill states that only a registered surrogacy clinic should conduct or associate with, or help in any manner, in conducting activities relating to surrogacy and surrogacy procedures. Such clinics shall not conduct, offer, undertake, promote or associate with or avail of commercial surrogacy in any form. While offering surrogacy services the clinics shall employ only those who possess the prescribed qualifications. Further the Bill states that, the clinics should refrain from activities which are aimed to induce or likely to induce a woman to act as a surrogate mother and promoting commercial surrogacy in general. The Bill also states that the clinics should conduct or cause abortion during the period of surrogacy without the written consent of the surrogate mother and on authorization of the same by the appropriate authority concerned. Lastly, the Bill prohibits the surrogacy clinics from storage of any human embryo or gamete for the purpose of surrogacy.

PROHIBITIONS

The Bill expressly prohibits the practice of commercial surrogacy and its related component procedures or services in any form or run a racket or an organized group to empanel or select surrogate mothers or use individual brokers or intermediaries to arrange for surrogate mothers and for surrogacy procedures, at such clinics, laboratories or at any other place. The Bill also prohibits abandoning or disowning or exploitation of child or children born through surrogacy; and sale and import of human embryo for the purpose of surrogacy. The punishments for indulging in such practices are imprisonment for a term which shall not be less than ten years and with fine which may extend to ten lakh rupees.

The punishment for any registered medical practitioner, gynaecologists, paediatrician, human embryologists or any person who owns a surrogacy clinic or employed with such a clinic or centre or laboratory and renders his professional or technical services to or at such clinic or centre or laboratory, are imprisonment for a term which shall not be less than five years and with fine which may extend to ten lakh rupees. Any intending couple or any person who seeks the aid for commercial surrogacy or for conducting surrogacy procedures for commercial purposes shall be punishable with imprisonment for a term which shall not be less than five years and with fine which may extend to five lakh rupees for the first offence and for any subsequent offence with imprisonment which may extend to ten years and with fine which may extend to ten lakh rupees. All the offences prescribed under this Bill are cognizable, non-bailable and non-compoundable.

SURROGACY BOARDS

The Bill mandates that the Central and the State governments shall establish a National Surrogacy Board and the State Surrogacy Boards respectively. Functions of the Surrogacy Board includes (*a*) to advise the Central Government on policy matters relating to surrogacy; (*b*) to review and monitor the implementation of the Act, rules and regulations; (*c*) to lay down code of conduct to be observed by persons working at surrogacy clinics; to set the minimum standards of physical infrastructure, laboratory and diagnostic equipment and expert manpower to be employed by the surrogacy clinics; etc.

The Surrogacy (Regulation) Bill, 2016 is considered as an important step towards the regulation of surrogacy practices in India. The Bill focuses on preventing commercial surrogacy, exploitation of surrogate mothers and child born through surrogacy. It also provides a detailed regulatory framework for Surrogacy Clinics. However this Bill raises several questions and concerns related to the issues such as Ban on Commercial Surrogacy; Restriction for International Surrogacy; Who can act as a surrogate mother; Waiting period for using surrogacy; Maternity relief for both intended mother and surrogate mother; Designer baby; Need for Certificate of eligibility; Rights of intended couples; and about surrogacy contracts

(Pillai, 2017). Most of these concerns have been discussed in detail and has made several recommendations for modifications by Department-Related Parliamentary Standing Committee on Health and Family Welfare, Rajya Sabha in its 102nd Report on the Surrogacy (Regulation) Bill, 2016 (102nd Report, 2017). Thus it can be seen that the Bill cannot become a law in its original position and it will undergo several changes including legalization of commercial surrogacy before enacting it as legislation.

SURROGACY: JUDICIAL ATTITUDE

The subject of surrogacy has been discussed by Indian judiciary in several cases. However there was no single case which directly discussed the issue of legality of surrogacy either altruistic or commercial and about the legality of surrogacy contracts. Some of the important cases in which different issues connected with surrogacy were discussed as follows:

1. ***Nirmala Case*:** The case of Nirmala was the first case in India which discussed an important issue connected with surrogacy. In fact this case fuelled the debate on the practice of surrogacy in India. In this case, Nirmala, a poor Indian woman has brought the question whether agreeing to act as surrogate would amount to an act prohibited by Immoral Traffic (Prevention) Act, 1986, to limelight in the country. Nirmala was a poor woman of Chandigarh and was ready to be a surrogate mother for 50,000 rupees to save her paralyzed husband. Later she found out that her act would amount to adultery and she would be detained under Immoral Traffic (Prevention) Act, 1986. Hence with the help of a lawyer she filed a petition in the District and Sessions Court praying that to declare, since the child born to her by the unidentified partner was without sexual intercourse and through surrogacy and was with her husband's consent there was no violation of Immoral Traffic Laws (Pillai, 2015). The Court while accepting her prayer stated that, surrogacy cannot be considered as adultery and it does not violate any provision of the Immoral Traffic (Prevention) Act, 1986.
2. ***Baby Manji Yamada v. Union of India and Another*:** This case has brought into limelight one of the risks involved in surrogacy practice and the need for an appropriate legal frame work to cover

those risks. In this case, a Japanese couple Ikufumi and Yuki Yamada entered into a surrogacy contract with a married Indian woman. An embryo created from Ikufumi Yamada's sperm and an egg harvested from an anonymous Indian woman and then implanted the embryo into surrogate's womb. Meanwhile in June 2008, the Yamadas divorced. A month later, on July 25, 2008, Baby Manji was born to the surrogate mother. Though Ikufumi Yamada wanted to raise the child, his ex-wife, Yuki, did not want the child as she was unrelated to the baby biologically, genetically and legally. The surrogacy contract did not cover such a situation of refusal by one of the intended parents. There was no law existing in India to clarify and solve this matter. The grandmother of the baby Manji, Ms Emiko Yamada came from Japan to take care of the child and filed a petition in the Supreme Court of India under Article 32 of the Constitution. The Court relegated her to the National Commission for Protection of Child Rights constituted under the Commissions for Protection of Child Rights Act, 2005 (Baby Manji, 2008). Finally, baby Manji left for Japan in the care of her genetic father and grandmother (Pillai, 2015). It is to be noted here that, in this case the Supreme Court has not addressed the issue of legality of surrogacy practices, however proceeded with the presumption that it is legal.

3. ***Jan Balaz v. Anand Municipality and Others*:** This case has highlighted the issue of citizenship and nationality of a baby born in India through surrogacy. In this case, the petitioner, a German national was the biological father of two babies born through surrogacy to a surrogate woman named Marthaben Immanuel Khristi, a citizen of India. The petitioner applied to the Indian Passport authorities for obtaining a passport for the babies. The passport authorities initially issued two passports in the name of both the babies. However, later the Government of India, Ministry of External Affairs, through Regional Passport Office issued a letter directing the petitioner to surrender both the passports to the office. The petitioner surrendered the passports accordingly. Thereafter a petition was filed by the petitioner before the Gujarat High Court seeking a direction from the Court to the Regional

Passport Officer to return those Passports so that he could take the babies to Germany for acquiring German Citizenship.

The petitioner submitted that though he and his wife were German citizens, the children were not born in Germany, and so they would not get German citizenship, especially when German law does not recognize surrogacy (Pillai, 2015). The Gujarat High Court held that, 'the only conclusion that is possible is that a gestational mother who has blood relations with the child is more deserving to be called as the natural mother because she has carried the embryo for full term in her womb and nurtured the babies through the umbilical cord. Both the egg donor and the gestational surrogate are Indian nationals, and hence the babies are born to an Indian national'. The Court also added that, 'in the present legal framework, have no other go but to hold that the babies born in India to the gestational surrogate are citizens of this country and therefore, entitled to get the Passports' (Jan Balaz, 2010)

The need for a legislation to deal with the subject of surrogacy was emphasized by the Court in the following words, 'A comprehensive legislation dealing with all these issues is very imminent to meet the present situation created by the reproductive science and technology which have no clear answers in the existing legal system in this country. Legislature has to address lot of issues like rights of the children born out of the surrogate mother, legal, moral, ethical; Rights, duties and obligations of the donor, gestational surrogate and host of other issues'(Jan Balaz, 2010).

4. ***Kalaiselvi v. Chennai Port Trust*:** The Madras High Court addressed the question whether a woman employee working in the Chennai Port Trust is entitled to avail maternity leave even in case where she gets the child through arrangement by Surrogate parents? The petitioner has claimed maternity leave under Rule 3-A of the Madras Port Trust (Leave) Regulations, 1987, which provides leave to a female employee on her adoption of a child. By extending the protection of this rule to the case of surrogacy the Court observed that, "When once it is admitted that the minor child is the daughter of the petitioner and at the time of the application, she

was only one day old, she is entitled for leave akin to persons who are granted leave in terms of Rule 3-A of the Leave Regulations. The purpose of the said rule is for proper bonding between the child and parents. Even in the case of adoption, the adoptive mother does not give birth to the child, but yet the necessity of bonding of the mother with the adoptive child has been recognized by the Central Government. Therefore, the petitioner is entitled for leave in terms of Rule 3-A" (Kalaselvi, 2013)

Regarding the application of Maternity Benefit Act, 1961 to cases of surrogacy, Justice K Chandru observed that, "it is unnecessary to rely upon the provisions of the Maternity Benefit Act for the purpose of grant of maternity leave, since that act deals with actual child birth and it is mother centric. The Act does not deal with leave for taking care of the child beyond 6 weeks, i.e., the post natal period. The right for child care leave has to be found elsewhere" (Kalaselvi, 2013).

In the case of ***P. Geetha v. The Kerala Livestock Development Board Ltd. & Others***, the Kerala High Court stated that, "there ought not to be any discrimination of a woman as far as the maternity benefits are concerned only on the ground that she has obtained the baby through surrogacy. It is further made clear that, keeping in view the dichotomy of maternity or motherhood, the intended mother is entitled to all the benefits an employee could have on post-delivery, *sans* the leave involving the health of the mother after the delivery. In other words, the child specific statutory benefits, if any, can, and ought to, be extended to the intended mother" (Geetha, 2015). It is to be noted that under the Maternity Benefit Act, 1961 there is only one provision which can be considered as child specific benefit, i.e. the provision for nursing breaks. An analysis of both these cases thus shows that the application of Maternity Benefit Act, 1961 to surrogacy is completely ruled out by Indian Courts (Pillai, 2015a)

However in the case of ***Dr. Mrs. Hema Vijay Menon v. State of Maharashtra***, the Court while granting maternity leave observed that, 'In our view, the case of the mother who begets a child through surrogacy procedure, by implanting an embryo created by using either the eggs or sperm of the intended parents in the womb of the surrogate mother, would stand on a better footing than the case of an adoptive mother. At least, there cannot be any distinction between the two. Right to life under Article 21 of the Constitution of India includes the right to motherhood and also the right of every child to full development. If the government can provide maternity leave to an adoptive mother, it is difficult to digest the refusal on the part of the Government to provide maternity leave to a mother who begets a child through the surrogacy procedure (Hema, 2015).

In the case of ***Rama Pandey v. Union of India & Ors***, Delhi High Court also observed that, 'to curtail the commissioning mother's entitlement to leave, on the ground that she has not conceived the child, would work, both to her detriment, as well as, that of the child. Non-provision of leave to a commissioning mother, who is an employee, would, be in derogation of the stated Directive Principles of State Policy as contained in the Constitution' (Rama, 2015)

5. ***Amy Antoinette Mc Gregor & Anr v. Directorate of Family Welfare*:** This case dealt with issue of sex selection in surrogacy practices. The petitioner approached Delhi High Court with a prayer to select the sex of their child during the surrogacy procedure in order to balance their family comprising a male and a female child. Also the petitioners challenged the constitutionality of the Pre- Conception and Pre-Natal Diagnostic Techniques (Prohibition of Sex Selection) Act, 1994. The Court rejected both the prayers of the petitioner (Amy, 2016). It is to be noted here that in all these cases Indian judiciary recognized the legality of surrogacy practice and surrogacy contracts, though not explicitly stated.
6. ***Union of India and Ors. v. Jan Balaz and Ors.*:** This is an ongoing case before the Hon'ble Supreme Court of India. The Union of India preferred an appeal against the judgement of Gujarat High Court in Jan Balaz v. Anand Municipality and Others. The Hon'ble Apex Court took serious note on the various issues and concerns raised by surrogacy practices in India. Some of the questions for which the Court looking an answer are: a) Whether in commercial

surrogacy the surrogate mother is the only mother of surrogate child? b) Whether a lady who donates her egg in connection with a commercial surrogacy mother can be said to be mother? c) Whether both "surrogate mother" and "genetic mother" (who has donated the egg) can both be said to be mother of the surrogate child. d) Whether commercial surrogacy involved sale of a child in view of the fact that surrogate mother relinquishes her parental rights for money? e) Whether commercial surrogacy amounts to renting of a womb? f) Whether commercial surrogacy is immoral and is opposed to public policy and therefore void Under Section 23 of the Contract Act. g) Whether commercial surrogacy as practiced in India amounts to economic and psychological exploitation of surrogate mother? h) Whether commercial surrogacy is inconsistent with the dignity of Indian womanhood and therefore violative of Article 21 of Constitution? i) Whether commercial surrogacy involves trafficking in human beings as it involves sale of a surrogate child, relinquishment of the surrogate's parental rights for money and involves rent of womb thus violating Article 23 of the Constitution. j) Whether commercial surrogacy should be prohibited?, etc. It is to be noted that the answer for these questions can e provided by a legislative action, the whole issues and concerns about the surrogacy will be solved.

CONCLUSION

The development of surrogacy as a success full method for begetting a child has proven beneficial for many childless couples and individuals. Considering the importance of surrogacy practice and its development as a million dollar business in India, it is necessary to enact a comprehensive favourable legislation for surrogacy practice with a prime focus to prevent exploitation of surrogate women and protection of rights and interests of surrogate child as well as intended parents. Such a law should address the following issues:

1. Who can access the surrogacy practice for begetting a child? Whether for hetro-sexual married couple, same sex couple, singles, aged, disabled etc. should be clearly defined.

2. What should be the qualification of women to act as a surrogate for another? Whether a single women or married women, disabled, prisoner, aged, etc can act as a surrogate should be identified.
3. The format and method of entering into surrogacy contract and a process to review the terms and conditions of the contract to prevent exploitation of surrogate mother.
4. The rights and duties of surrogate mother as well as intended parents need to be mentioned.
5. The right to compensation for the surrogate mother and its payment should be legalized and regulated to ensure the exploitation.
6. The rights and interests of surrogate child should also be described.
7. There should be provisions to deal with the issue of breach of contract by either surrogate mother or intended parents both during the surrogacy pregnancy and after the delivery.
8. The various acts such as refusal to accept the child and abandonment of the child; sex determination; sex selection; designing of babies should be declared as an offence.
9. There should be provision to deal with the situation of abandonment of surrogate child by the intended parent for ensuring the welfare of such child.
10. There should be adequate provisions to deal with surrogacy involving foreign couples and to avoid the possible dangers of such use.

REFERENCES

1. 102nd Report on the Surrogacy (Regulation) Bill, 2016 (2017), Retrieved from www.prsindia.org/ uploads/.../Surrogacy/SCR-%20 Surrogacy%20Bill,%202016.pdf.
2. *Baby Manji Yamada* v. *Union of India and Another*, (2008) 13 S.C.C. 518.
3. Behm, Lisa L. (1999). Legal, Moral & International Perspectives on Surrogate Motherhood: The Call for a Uniform Regulatory Scheme in the United States. 2 *DePaul J. of Health Care L.* 557.

4. Brown, Catherine (2008). The Queensland Investigation into the Decriminalization of Altruistic Surrogacy. 29 (2) *Queensland Lawyer*, 78-83.
5. *Dr. Mrs. Hema Vijay Menon v. State of Maharashtra*, 2015 SCC OnLine Bom 6127.
6. Draft The Assisted Reproductive Technology (Regulation) Bill, 2014, (2017) Retrieved from http://www.prsindia.org/uploads/media/draft/Draft%20Assisted%20Reproductive%20Technology%20(Regulation)%20Bill,%202014.pdf.
7. *Gregor & Anr v. Directorate of Family Welfare*, 2016 SCC OnLine Bom 8812.
8. *Jan Balaz v. Anand Municipality and Others* , A.I.R. 2010 Guj. 21
9. Jargilo, Izabela (2015-16). Regulating the Trade of Commercial Surrogacy in India. 15 *J. Int'l Bus. & L.* 337.
10. *Kalaiselvi v. Chennai Port Trust*, 2013 SCC OnLine Mad 811
11. *P. Geetha v. The Kerala Livestock Development Board Ltd. & Others*, 2015 SCC OnLine Ker 71
12. Pillai, Dr. Aneesh V. (2015). *Surrogate Motherhood and the Law*. New Delhi: Regal Publications.
13. Pillai, Dr. Aneesh V. (2015a). Right to Maternity Protection of Surrogate Mother and Intended Parents in Surrogacy: An Emerging Paradigm. Paper presented at the International Seminar on Human Rights: National and International Perspectives, National University of Advanced Legal Studies, Kerala.
14. Pillai, Dr. Aneesh V. (2017). The Surrogacy (Regulation) Bill, 2016: A Critical Appraisal. *Kerala Law Journal*, (1) 13.
15. Ragone, Helena (1994). *Surrogate Motherhood: Conception in the Heart*. USA: Westview Press.
16. *Rama Pandey v. Union of India & Ors*, https://indiankanoon.org/doc/125365715/
17. Smerdon, Usha Rengachary. (2008-09). Crossing Bodies, Crossing Borders: International Surrogacy between the United States and India. *Cumberland Law Review* 39(1) 15.

18. Surrogacy Programs (2016), Retrieved from http://www.wecaresurrogacy.ca/surrogacy-law-india/.
19. *Union of India (UOI) and Ors. v. Jan Balaz and Ors.*, MANU/SC/1362/2015

Abortion in India: Issues & Concerns

Mrs. Soumya James

Abstract

The term abortion is defined as an untimely delivery voluntarily procured with an intention to destroy the foetus. It may be procured at any time before the natural birth of the child. In India our substantive criminal law and the special laws relating to abortions made it as an offence invoking criminal liability subject to the exceptions expressly provided in such laws. The special laws relating to the abortion issues are MTP Act, POCSO Act, PCPNDT Act etc. The purpose of my research in this area is to conduct a study about the existing laws and ambiguities and practical implications if any, with reference to the various judicial decisions in this regard. The major issues in which my focus is being made under this chapter are the issue of consent given by the women undergoing abortions especially in the cases of minors and women suffering from mental illness, criminal liability of medical practitioners and quacks in performing an illegal abortions and the liability of women undergoing such abortions under the existing laws, how far such penal laws adversely affect an ethical and qualified medical practitioners in rendering their services in a lawful termination of pregnancy on account of their fear of prosecution, privacy issues in case of rape victims specially in case of minor rape victims due to the existence of conflicting provisions of POCSO Act and MTP Act. Another burning issue which my research focused and requires a massive attention of authorities in the area of termination of pregnancy is sex selective abortion. Though there are laws in our country to prevent such gender violence which is happening within the mother's womb, it is now a commonly accepted practice of family planning in our society. Therefore my attempt is also extended to identify the lacunas and practical implications in the existing laws with the help of various judicial decisions and reports.

INTRODUCTION

Abortion occurs when the life of foetus or embryo is destroyed in the women's womb or the pregnant uterus empties prematurely. There are different types of abortions such as natural, accidental, spontaneous and artificial or induced abortions. Natural abortion means abortion due to bad health, defect in generative organs of the mother, shocks fear, joy etc.; accidental abortion means those abortions happens due to pathological reasons where pregnancy cannot be completed and the uterus empties before the maturity of foetus; spontaneous abortion means natural death of an embryo or a foetus before the foetus is sufficiently developed to survive. Chromosomal abnormalities cause at least half of the spontaneous abortions; the last and the final one which I mentioned above is an artificial or induced abortion which is an untimely delivery voluntarily procured with an intention to destroy the foetus. It may be procured at any time before the natural birth of the child. This type of abortion is a crime unless and until it is covered under the exceptions provided by law. Therefore we can say that the first three types of abortions are not punishable whereas the last one is a criminal offence punishable by law i.e. artificial or induced abortion.

In *queen Empress v. Ademma*, [(1886) ILR 9 Mad 369] defined the term induced abortion [by quoting the words of Glanville Williams in his book, the Law of Abortion: Current Law Problems Vol.5pp.128, 138(1952)] as "an untimely delivery voluntarily procured with intent to destroy the foetus. It may be procured at any time before the natural birth of the child."

In India the laws regulating the termination of pregnancy can be broadly classified into two:

- **General laws:**
    1. **Constitutional law:** Right to life and Personal liberty under Article 21 of the Constitution
    2. **Laws under IPC:** Law relating to Miscarriage under S.312 to s. 316 of IPC ; Criminal law Amendment Act 2013 with regard to 375 & 376 IPC

- **Special statutes:**
  1. Medical Termination of Pregnancy Act 1971 (MTP)
  2. Protection of Children from Sexual Offence Act 2012 (POCSO)
  3. Pre – Conception and Prenatal Diagnostics Techniques Act 1994(PCPNDT)

MAJOR ISSUES & CONCERNS

1. **Issue of consent in abortion cases:** Requirement of spousal consent in the termination of pregnancy: In India the courts are already made it clear that abortionist i.e. the medical professionals practicing in this area requires the consent of the concerned adult woman for termination of pregnancy and not others. Her close relatives whether it is her husband, boyfriend, parents and in-laws have no right to consent to termination or to refuse to consent to an abortion. But in 2011 the Supreme Court in *Samar Ghosh v. Jaya Ghosh* [26 March 2011(Appeal (C) 151/2004)] gave a decision which creates a lot of confusion regarding the spousal consent requirements. The facts here is that, the parties are husband and wife. They were in an unsatisfied and unhappy strained marital relationship. Husband argued that he couldn't adjust with his wife as she unilaterally decided not to have a child which caused a lot of pain and mental agony to him. Therefore he pleads divorce on grounds of cruelty.

   Here the court admitted the arguments of husband after a detailed study of English law from 1950's to support its findings that withholding sex, unilateral decision to terminate a pregnancy could amount to mental cruelty and held that where a wife terminates a pregnancy without her husband's knowledge or consent, the abortion might constitute cruelty grounds for a divorce. In the words of SC: "If the wife undergoes vasectomy or abortion without medical reason or without the consent or knowledge of her husband, such an act may lead to mental cruelty". It is really a shocking observation from the part of the honourable court because the court in this case believed that a woman can undergo vasectomy. That observation of the honourable court itself illustrates the Judges limited understanding of reproductive health issues.

It is important to note that though the above said ruling of the SC does not change the requirements provided in s.3 of the MTP Act, it would adversely affect a woman's autonomy by upholding spousal interest in a woman's decision regarding her body. Therefore it led to a lot of confusions. The main difficulty that may arise here is that the men may use this ruling as a weapon to accuse women of terminating nonexistent pregnancies to substantiate fake cruelty charges in divorce matters. Ultimately, the spousal consent requirements reflect patriarchal norms that rob women of bodily autonomy and equality. Therefore it can be assumed as a spousal "stake" in a women's reproductive health. Not only that this decision could deter those women who may be in an abusive relationships from seeking abortion services. Moreover, the most important thing we have to consider is that the medical professionals may also have a legitimate fear of legal repercussions if they support a termination that amounts to cruelty.

Though the above decision of the SC created a lot of confusions and practical difficulties, there is a decision of the HC of Punjab and Haryana in *Dr.Mangla Dogra &others v. Anil Kumar Malhotra & others* (CR No.6337/20) which relieves the existing confusions in this regard to a certain extent. In this case the wife decided to terminate her pregnancy but the husband refused to sign the consent form given by the hospital authorities. Later he filed a suit for the purpose of prohibiting her legally from terminating the pregnancy without his consent. However she terminated the foetus at 6 weeks and 4 days. Subsequently the husband filed a suit against his wife, her parents, her brother and the doctors who conducted her termination and demanded 30 lakhs as compensation for mental pain and agony caused to him. He argued that a woman cannot obtain a termination unless the pregnancy endangers the women's health. The doctors argued that they abided by the MTP Act and conducted the surgery in a registered facility.

Here the HC use several sections of MTP to reach the conclusion that for the termination of pregnancy, the consent required must be given by that woman who undergoes termination and none other except in cases of minors and unsound persons. Firstly, S. 3(4) (b) clearly states that the pregnant woman has the sole right to consent to an abortion. Further, the judgment cites Explanation II of S.3 (2) of MTP Act which states that a married woman can obtain a termination in case of contraceptive failure because of the "grave injury to the mental health of pregnant women". Finally the court examines sections of the Act pertaining to MTP clinics and found that the doctors conducted the procedure in a safe and legal setting.

The court also examines the consent form and states that the Act "nowhere provides for the express or implied consent of the husband. The wife is the best judge…" Ultimately the court concludes that the husband cannot compel her to conceive and give birth to his child.

In examining whether the husband has any recourse against the doctors who performed termination, the court looks to S.8 of the MTP Act, which provides explicit protections to medical practitioners who provide services in "good faith" under the Act. In this case the court stands strongly in favour of women's right to bodily integrity. The court states, "It is the right of a woman to give birth to a child, but it is not the right of a husband to compel his wife to give birth to a child for the husband." The court also pointed out that "a woman is not a machine in which raw material is put and finished products comes out". She should be mentally prepared to conceive, continue the same and give birth to a child. The unwanted pregnancy would naturally affect the mental health of pregnant women.

Moreover, the court also clarifies the criminal liability of medical profession in abortion cases i.e. the medical professionals had committed no crime in failing to obtain the spousal consent. Though it provides a relief to doctors, the court pointed out that the doctors had to defend themselves in the court if any such case was registered and added them as a respondent party. This may lead the medical professionals to think to avoid such types of headaches by refusing to provide their service in conducting abortion or contraceptive measures.

When we analyze the above mentioned cases, we can clearly understand that the outlook of the SC in Samantha's case though created some issues and implications, the rulings of the Punjab Haryana court in *Dr.Mangla Dogra &others v. Anil Kumar Malhotra & others* succeeded to a certain extend in removing the confusions regarding the spousal consent requirements in abortion and thereby reaffirmed the women's exclusive right in reproduction and health.

One more case I would like to refer in this regard is the decision of the Haryana and Punjab High Court in *Ashok Kumar v. Anupama Sharma* on 21st January 2015.[1] In this case, the husband accused wife of terminating the pregnancy without husband's knowledge and consent for the purpose of establishing cruelty in a divorce proceedings. However he had no proof of abortions. Fortunately, in this case the court found that the husband was at fault in the dissolution of marriage. Here these types of cases show that the husbands may mould such types of fake allegations against their wife to absolve themselves of from their responsibility in divorce proceedings. Moreover they can allege unilateral termination against their wife because of the reason that proving spousal consent may be impossible.

(*a*) **Consent of minor:** As per s.3 (4) (a) of MTP Act provides that the consent of the guardians are required to terminate the pregnancy of minor. Therefore in case of a minor rape survivor, normally her parents are entitled to give consent to terminate the pregnancy of their daughter for and on behalf of her. But what will happen if the minor is not consented to terminate her pregnancy. In such case the issue we have to sort out is whose interest will prevail i.e. whether the interest of the minor or their parents? The MTP Act does not specify about whose interest be given priority in such situations. However in 1993, the Madras HC in *Krishnan v.*

1 FAO-M No.29/2018.

Rajan Alias Madipu Rajan & another had dealt this issue. In this case, a 15 year old girl's father contented that the continuation of the pregnancy of her minor daughter would cause to her many complications physically, psychologically and socially. Therefore he prayed for termination of her pregnancy. But the minor was not consented to terminate the foetus. The question for the consideration of the court in this case is that whether a minor rape survivor posses a right to continue her pregnancy against the interest of her parents? Here the Madras HC held that a minor rape survivor can decide whether to continue her pregnancy or not even against the wishes of her parents in this regard because in the opinion of court this case represents an exception to the presumption of mental anguish caused by pregnancy in Explanation. I to s.3 of MTP Act. By this decision the court gave much importance to the rights of adolescent's autonomy and bodily integrity and observed that recently, the teenage mothers have no more risks during pregnancy and labor and their babies would be safe and comfortable like their more mature sisters babies if they have had given good parental care. The court also mentioned about Smt. Kasturba Gandhi that she was married at the age of 13 and had her first baby at the age of 15 and second baby at the age of 17. By this example the court tried to legitimize the anti abortion arguments and discredit the accepted medical facts. This decision faced a lot of criticism which is said to be a disastrous one as it ignores widely accepted medical research, jurisprudence from around the world. This highlights the need for improved judicial training and general activism.

(*b*) Induced or fraudulent consent: In India we can see a lot of instances where the women were forced or coerced by their husbands and relatives to terminate pregnancies. As per the provisions of MTP Act, it is essential to ensure the consent of the women for termination of her pregnancy. Here the most important thing what the hospital authorities have to ensure is whether the consent given by the concerned woman is freely and without any inducement or coercion. If it is proved that the consent given by the women is out of coercion or undue influence of any person, then that person can be prosecuted under section 313 of IPC. In *Mohit Gupta &other v. State of NCT of Delhi & another* [135(2006) DLT 390], a woman who underwent termination of pregnancy at 19th week wanted to charge her partner under S.313 IPC. She argued that she was not consented to termination and whatever happened was without her consent and knowledge. She stated that she was unconscious at that point of time and never saw the consent form. On the other hand the husband stated that she was terminated the pregnancy with her own knowledge and consent. After making a deep study on the facts and contentions of both sides, the court came to the conclusion that the consent form might be signed by some other person and not the concerned woman. To arrive at this conclusion the court considers several factors. Firstly at the 19th week the termination can be complicated so there arose a question that why she waited till the 19th week if she is a willing participant. Secondly, the court found a "million reasons" which makes the husband to push his wife for an abortion. The court held that there is sufficient material on records to give rise to a gross suspicion with regard to the commission of such an offence.

(*c*) Consent in termination of pregnancy of a mentally retarded person: The consent of women is an essential element for termination of her pregnancy. As per the provisions of MTP Act, likewise in the case of minor here also the guardians are entitled to give consent for and on behalf of the mentally retarded person. In *Suchita Srivastava & another v. Chandigarh administration* [(2009) SLP(C) 5845/2009] the SC observed that while deciding an issue of consent for the medical termination of a mentally retarded woman, the court must examine the facts of each case and held that where a woman is not a minor but had a "mild" mental illness, the court has to ensure her reproductive rights including her right whether to continue the pregnancy or not. However in *Anand Manharlal Brahmbhatt v.State of Gujarat* [Special Cr.Appeal No.4204/2015], the HC held that where a women who in the opinion of medical experts was not able to make decisions for herself or if she is not in a position to understand the fact that she is pregnant, the state is entitled to provide consent for termination. In this case, the police picked up a wandering "mentally ill woman" and took her to the hospital for a checkup. The test revealed that she became pregnant for 14 weeks. In the opinion of medical experts she was suffering from severe Schizophrenia and therefore not able to take care for herself. The medical team recommended the termination of pregnancy. Therefore the hospital authorities tried to intimate her relatives but couldn't locate them. Under these circumstances the magistrate directed a government hospital to terminate the pregnancy and it was done. But the decision of the magistrate in deciding the termination was challenged in the HC for not consulting with additional expenses and to determine whether the pregnancy entitled from rape. Here the HC relied on the decision of the SC in Suchita Srivastava and observed that the aim of the MTP Act is to focus mainly on the women's health and here in this case the mental health of the woman does not make it safe for her to continue the pregnancy. The doctors have the opinion that the medicine the woman is supposed to take would harm the fetus and thereby it complicates the delivery and woman's health. Therefore the HC upheld the decision of the magistrate in this regard and in the words of HC "a woman with mild mental illness is better equipped to make decision than woman with severe Schizophrenia". In this case the court made a clear distinction of the consent giving capacity of a women suffering from mild mental illness from a woman suffering from severe Schizophrenia. By this decision the court made a good effort in protecting the women's health both physical and mental and thereby upholds the intention of MTP Act and Fundamental rights obligation.

2. **Issue of emergency contraception:** Anti abortion groups argued that the use of emergency contraception is also a form of termination of pregnancy. The Kerala HC provides an adequate observation in this regard in the case *Krupa prolifers v. State of Kerala*. [2009 WP (C) 37462/2008] Here in this case the petitioner claimed from the court to issue three orders. Firstly, an order to ban all the advertisements for the i - pill brand of emergency contraception. Secondly in their point of view, emergency contraceptive pill results in the termination of pregnancy. Therefore it should not be made without prescription; thirdly, they urged the court to ban the sale and distribution of i-pill brand of emergency contraception.

   In the words of court, it is "not required to go into the morality aspect, but only to consider the medical consequences of the i-pill drug.... Whether it is a contraceptive tablet or it is a medicine for causing abortion. The court found that the MTP has not given a precise definition for the term 'pregnancy'. Therefore the court relied upon 'the undisputed medical science' in deciding whether an emergency contraception result in the termination of pregnancy or not. According to medical science, the process of implantation takes place between 5 to 7 days after fertilization. Hence in the first 72 hours when the emergency contraceptive is to be taken, the fertilized egg has not yet been implanted. At this state the emergency contraceptives merely prevents the implantation from taking place and thereby prevent pregnancy. The court also relies upon the report of the consortium on national emergency contraception which found in that most women in India had little knowledge of emergency contraceptive pills. While delivering the judgment the court pointed out that many women resort to "quacks or old women" for abortions at great risk to their health and lives.

   In the above case, the court provides an adequate meaning to the term 'pregnancy' under MTP Act. According to the view of SC the pregnancy is a stage at which the fertilized the fertilized eggs are implanted into the lining of uterus five to seven days after fertilization (i.e. in the pre embryonic stage). The court in this case relied on the medical science and avoids the moral arguments of certain groups from their religious point of view while deciding the legality of conception and abortion. Finally this judgment acknowledges the link between access to emergency contraception and preventing unsafe abortions.

3. **Issue of criminal liability in abortion cases:** The Indian penal code 1860 is the basic criminal law of our country that has made the induced abortion as a punishable offence under sections 312 to 316 of the code.

   - Section 312 : Causing miscarriage
   - Section 313 : Causing miscarriage without women's consent
   - Section 314 : Death caused by an act done with an intent to cause miscarriage
   - Section 315 : Act done with intend to prevent child being born alive or to cause it to die after birth
   - Section 316 : Causing death of quick unborn child by act amounting to culpable homicide

   Sec. 312 of the IPC deal with an unlawful termination of pregnancy. Under this section, a voluntarily causing miscarriage is a punishable offence. It permits termination of pregnancy only to protect the life of mother. Instead of using the term abortion the offence under IPC is mentioned as miscarriage. The act has not given any definition to the term miscarriage and unborn child. MTP Act 1971 however liberalize the laws relating to abortions which provides certain exceptions to the provisions of IPC.As per the Act, all abortions and miscarriages are criminal unless they are undertaken to save the life of a pregnant women. Not only that the act provides a time limit in conducting the termination of pregnancy. A medical practitioner is allowed to conduct the termination only up to the 12 weeks of pregnancy and it requires the opinion of more than two medical practitioners for the termination of a foetus having the growth between 12 to 20 weeks and it can be done only on the following reasonable grounds:

- A risk to the life of a pregnant women
- A risk of grave injury to her physical and mental health
- If the pregnancy is caused by rape
- The existence of a substantial risk that if the child is born, it would suffer from physical or mental abnormalities so as to be seriously handicapped.

Another important factor in the area of law relating to abortion is that only a registered medical practitioner has the right to terminate the pregnancy and in that case he will be exempted from liability only if he has done the act in good faith for the benefit of the woman in order to save her from causing grave injury to her body and mental health which is stated under *S.3(1)of MTP Act, "Notwithstanding anything contained in the Indian Penal Code (45 of 1860), a registered medical practitioner shall not be guilty of any offence under that Code or under any other law for the time being in force, if any pregnancy is terminated by him in accordance with the provisions of this Act."*

In *Murari Mohan Koley v. State of West Bengal* [(2004) 3 CALLT 609 HC], the court considered the question whether a registered Medical professional protected under s.3 (1) of the MTP Act from the criminal liability charged against them under s.313 & 314 of the IPC. In this case, a well reputed doctor conducted a termination of pregnancy. Unfortunately the surgery resulted in the death of woman. The doctor claimed protection under s.3 (1) of the MTP Act on ground that he was a trained service provider and working at a registered facility. The court held that, to get the protection under s.3 (1) of the MTP Act on ground that he was a trained service provider and working at a registered facility. The court held that to get the protection under s.3(1), the doctor has to prove that he has done the termination in good faith and the trial Judge will determine whether the accused person acted in good faith or not.

Dr. Usha Sharma v. State [17th Nov 2006 Delhi HC] was a clear case of negligence leveled against a registered MTP Centre. In this case the A.Sikri J. held that s.3 (1) automatically shields the provider from criminal charges under s.313 &314. However they are still answerable for medical negligence charges and could face other criminal charges under IPC. In the words of HC, in order to claim the protection under s.3 (1) of the MTP against a criminal charge leveled against a doctor under s.313 & s.314 of IPC, he has to establish or prove the following requirements:

- The facility providing termination services must be a registered one under the MTP Act.
- The accused doctor must be a qualified medical practitioner in this regard;
- He must perform the termination in good faith;

The criminal liability of a doctor in conducting abortions can be exempted by invoking **Section.8** of MTP Act 1971 if he proved that he has acted in good faith with an intention to protect the woman from grave injury to her body and mental health. Here what amount to good faith from the part of a doctor is not mentioned or defined under the act. However from **S.3 (2)** and **S.5** of the MTP Act, we can clearly assume that the doctors are required to have at least any of the following good faith opinion for termination of pregnancy:

- The pregnancy would harm the mental or physical health of woman; or
- The fetus would have serious anomalies; or
- The termination will immediately save a women's life if the pregnancy is more than 20 weeks

Therefore, we can say the burden of proof is on the doctor/ service provider to prove that he has conducted the termination of pregnancy in good faith and for that he has to record in writing the reason for termination.

***Criminal liability of quacks*:** The protection of s.3 (1) provided for the medical practitioners under the MTP Act against the charges under s.313 & s.314 of the IPC will only be extended to a registered medical practitioner. The court imposes severe punishments to those who are not a qualified and registered practitioner and who performs termination in an unregistered facilities.

In *State v. Riyazuddin & others* [Dec 3rd (2014) HC Cr.Appeal. No.577/2013], the accused was working at a health clinic as a compounder. He performed an unsafe surgery to terminate the pregnancy which resulted in the deadly perforations in survivor's uterus. He contended that he did not act as a doctor and had no intention to cause harm to the patient. But here the state submitted before the court the medical records, the stocks regulations and other documents which show that the clinic compounder acted as doctor and performed surgeries. The court held that though he had no intention to cause harm to the patient, being an unqualified provider, he had the knowledge that an unskilled surgery can result in serious injury and death. Therefore he was held to be guilty of offence punishable under s.314 of the IPC and sentenced him to 5 years imprisonment and a fine of Rs.1 lakhs for violation of IPC S.314 and to an additional 3 years imprisonment for violation of MTP Act. By this decision we can clearly understand that an unqualified providers practicing in an unregistered facilities are not entitled to have protection of s.3 (1) of the MTP Act/of general negligence claims. They are entitled to receive severe punishment.

Another major issue in this regard is that the criminal liability of a doctor in conducting abortions can be exempted by invoking section.8 of MTP Act 1971 if he proved that he has acted in good faith with an intention to protect the woman from grave injury to her body and mental health. But the women who undergone an abortion contrary to the provisions of existing laws cannot avoid her criminal liability. Therefore, if an abortion on demand is not allowed or restricted, then the women will go for an unsafe abortion which leads to mortality and the death of women and thereby it infringes their right to health and right to live with human dignity.

4. **Issue of abortion in rape cases:** Another blasting issue we can't ignore is the abortion in rape cases. whether the termination of pregnancy is permissible only in those cases of rape that are reported to the police or whether it is allowed in all cases irrespective of the fact that it is an already reported case or not. In India 99% of the cases are remained unreported due to the fear of social stigma.

As per Explanation 1 to Sec.3 of IPC, an Abortion is possible only in case of rape. To conduct an abortion in rape cases, it must be proved that the carriage and pregnancy was a result of rape committed by man. But according to the canons of Criminal Jurisprudence, a man is presumed to be innocent unless his guilt is established in a court of law beyond reasonable doubt. Here the question arises is that how can a women be proved that his pregnancy is due to the result of an offence committed by a man punishable under section.365 unless and until his guilt is proved and established in a court of law beyond reasonable doubt. In such case she has to wait till the guilt of the accused is established by the court of law. Otherwise, if in such case the man charged of rape is acquitted from that offence, the women will be liable under section 312 of the code for causing illegal abortion. If she waits for the verdict of the court in proving the guilt of the accused for the offence of the rape, then also she has to face some practical implications which make the abortion impossible. The long process of investigation procedure and the prosecution of the accused and the verdict of the court on the basis of the evidence would take a minimum of 3 to 4 years of time for its disposal by the court of law.

The offences under sec.312 to 316 are non cognizable and bailable. Sec.155 of CrPC deals with the provision relating to the investigation of Non Cognizable offence. According to the Law, a Police Officer cannot arrest an accused without a warrant and cannot investigate the alleged offence of miscarriage without the order of the magistrate. Unfortunately it a very long formal and complex procedure in which the enforcement authorities need to do a lot of exercise. [K.D.Gaur (1991)] Not only that the woman who demands abortions are generally pregnant unmarried girls or widows caught in a difficult situations. The long formal complexity of procedure and ambiguity in the law only provides the victim harassment, agony, torture rather than a remedy to her problem.

Therefore the courts in India consistently ensured that rape survivors especially minor rape survivors shall have unfettered access to abortion services. Most recently the SC in Chandrakanth's case has allowed for an exception to 20 week abortion limit in S.3 (2) (b) of MTP Act for a minor rape survivor by applying the "victim best interest test" after evaluating the medical opinion and societal status. It is a fact that the MTP Act does not require the rape survivors to obtain judicial approval for termination. However the hospitals, police and magistrates routinely block rape survivor's access to abortion. As a result the HC across India consistently hear these cases delaying access to abortion services.

The SC in Chandrakanth's and Srivastava's case states that the rape survivors should have an immediate access to services under s.3 of the Act while using the best interest test'. In *K.M. Mahima v. State of others*[2], the court affirms the rape survivor's right to access abortion services without judicial approval. The court gave more priority to women's health and underscores the importance of urgency in abortion matters. In this case, the HC held that an adult rape survivor filled a petition before the magistrate for permission to terminate her pregnancy and for an order compelling the hospital to preserve the products of the conception for the criminal investigation. The magistrate dismissed the petition stating that the MTP arms the woman with the power to determine whether she wants to continue her pregnancy.

On appeal the HC agreed the magistrate's decision regarding permission for an abortion. However the HC found fault with the magistrate's refusal to have the woman's arguments regarding preservation of evidence. The court stated that "merely by saying that the petitioner has an independent right of getting her pregnancy terminated was not sufficient as her main object was not only to get her pregnancy terminated but also preserve the foetus for conducting DNA test. The time wasted in not giving such directions by the court below may cause a situation revealing in injury to the mental health of the complainant as the termination of the pregnancy regarding 20 weeks may prove dangerous to her life as a consequence of which she would suffer the mental agony and torture of giving birth to a child of rape."

2 FAO-M No.29/2018.

Even in the case of a rape victim the time limit for conducting an abortion is only up to 20 weeks. Here the problem is that these sort of restrictions and the prohibition of committing abortion on demand of the victim on ground of time bar may force the victims either to commit suicide or to approach unskilled medical practitioners such as quacks which may adversely affect her health and therefore a gross violation of the right to access to health care in right time.

In *Jamana Suthar v. State of Rajastan & others*,[3] the HC denied abortion to a minor rape survivor who was 25 weeks pregnant. A doctor reported that the pregnancy did not pose a threat to her health and that the foetus could be viable at 25 weeks. Additionally the court questioned the minor's rape allegations. Finally the court specifically stated that the mental and physical health protections in s.3 of the MTP Act cannot be used to justify a S.5 abortion. These type observations of the court would cause a lot of hardship to the victims.

Fortunately the above mentioned types of decisions are now impossible due to the landmark decision given by the Honourable SC in *Chandrakanth Jayanthilal Suthar &another v. State of Gujarat*.[4] Further the MTP Act only says a woman has to allege to justify a termination under s.3 and woman need not prove that she has been raped to justify termination.

In an another case, *Kavitha v. State of Haryana & others*,[5] a 12 year old rape survivor and her family wanted to terminate her 34 year pregnancy. The court constituted 2 panels of doctors to examine whether a termination at 34 years constituted an emergency life saving measure under s.5 of MTP Act. The medical team reported that the pregnancy did not pose an imminent danger to the girl's life and that at 34 weeks the abortion would be riskier than delivery. The court also says that the termination at this stage would likely result in a live baby and held that the termination is illegal under

3 103 (2003) DLT 143.

4 (WP(c) 6683/2009), 6th Aug 2009.

5 (2015)8SCC 721.

the MTP Act where the abortion would pose health risks to the minor. Therefore the court did not allow for the abortion, but it expresses its great sympathy for the rape survivor. In the light of forced pregnancy, the court ordered the hospital to provide a private room, free health care, mental health care services and Rs.2 lakhs to support her child. This decision may have been difficult after the SC's holding in *Chandrakanth's* case.[6]

Just a few days before the SC's order in *Chandrakanth's* case, the HC of Punjab and Haryana similarly refused a 14 year old girl's application for termination at 25 weeks in *Sweetha v.State of Haryana & others*.[7]

Finally on September 2015 the landmark judgment of SC pronounced in *Chandrakanth's* case which represented a major progress on the abortion rights in India. In this case a minor was raped by her doctor and she became pregnant. The petitioners argued that the opinion given by the medical experts shown that the victim was "psychologically devastated" and physically too weak to deliver a child and the medical opinion concluded that the pregnancy posed a serious threat to her life. They also pointed out that the termination of pregnancy at 24 weeks is still safe and that the procedure would not harm the girl's health. Unfortunately the HC rejected her family's application for termination. On appeal to the SC, it reviewed the medical opinion and allowed for termination if the girl consented.

In the words of SC, "looking at the peculiar facts of the case, we direct that Ms. Maitri Chandrakant Suthar be examined by three senior most available Gynecologists of the Civil Hospital..." and other doctors "shall decide whether there is a serious threat to her life if the child is not aborted. If the team of the afore-stated doctors is of the view that termination of the pregnancy is immediately necessary to save life of Ms. Maitri, the concerned doctor of the Civil Hospital shall perform necessary surgery, without taking any permission from this Court, if the petitioner and Ms. Maitri desire to go through to such abortion."

6 Letters Patent Appeal No.538/2008, 8th April.

7 (2015) 8 SCC 721.

At the same time, the court also showed sympathy to the unborn child in this case. The court observed that it was really a difficult decision because "Whatever be the circumstances in which the child was conceived, whatever the trauma of the young mother, the fact remains that the child is also not to blame for being conceived."

It is very important to note that the SC in the above said case relied on the opinion of medical science and avoid religious and moral grounds to determine that the minor rape survivor can access to abortion.

MTP Act 1971 provides a privilege of confidentiality in abortion cases which enables many unethical unscrupulous and profit mongering medical professionals to conduct most of the illegal abortions in a very secrecy and they exploits helpless victims of pregnancy by extorting huge amount of money for procuring abortions. Therefore it is clear that illegal abortions, suicides of pregnant women are the results of rigidity ambiguity and conflicts in and among the legal provisions.

Dr.V.S.Chandra Shekhar an independant consultant on women's health had the following view;

"attention need to be drawn to the poor access to safe abortions and its consequence on the women's health and rights, particularly on unmarried adolescents and women, in general face in accessing safe services. If confusing laws deny access to safe abortions, adolescents will go for unsafe procedures which are harmful for women health."

The existing ambiguities in the legal provisions especially in the criminal law makes the doctors in a dilemma that they may refuse to carry out the termination of pregnancy for fear of persecution under penal provisions. Therefore the Paramjeet Singh Dhaliwal J. While dealing with the rape case of a minor, observed that, "to remove this fear of prosecution in the mind of doctors, the authorities concerned should issue procedural guidelines so they may act without fear in the interest of the patient."[8]

8 (2015) CWP 19343/2015, 16 Sept

Issue of Conflicting Provisions in the MTP Act & POCSO Act

The protection of children from sexual offenders Act and Criminal Law Amendment Act 2013 made it mandatory for the hospitals, local bodies or individuals to report any kind of offence or even a suspicion of offence in the case of minor. Therefore it is the duty of the doctors and hospital authorities to intimate the police officials in the cases of rape, physical injury and abuses committed to a minor by anyone if it comes to the knowledge of them.

In *M. Kala v. The Inspector of Police*[9] a 14 year old girl approached a government hospital for an abortion. The doctors refused to perform the surgery. Her parents challenge the hospital's refusal in the HC. The court held that under POCSO, the doctors have an immediate obligation to inform the police when a pregnant minor request a medical termination of pregnancy. The court also ordered the government hospital to perform the termination of the minor's pregnancy because the minor and her parents already consented to terminate the pregnancy and above all it was clearly a case of rape.

The POCSO Act demanded the doctors to report the pregnancy of minors to the police. However the POCSO violates a girl's privacy and it deter young women in consensual relationship from seeking safe abortion services. MTP rules ensure strict privacy to those women and girls undergoing abortions. But the POCSO demanded the doctors to violate patient's confidentiality and to risk their patient's trust. Until the government has corrected these contradictions, it is important to immediately report any POCSO case to the police to avoid criminal liability under POCSO.

In the words of Nozer Sheriar, Secretary General of the federation of obstetrics and Gynaecological societies of India told 'The Hindu':

"There need to be more clarity on the issue. We had some cases recently where abortion conducted on girls below the age of 18 years became an issue and the doctors were harassed by police for not reporting as these amounted to rape. In India 22% of India's population comprise young adolescents. Therefore adolescent's right to access to health facilities would become a major issue due to the ambiguity and conflict in the existing statutes."

---

9 *R & Anr. v. State of Haryana & Ors,* 30th May CWP-6733/2016

5. Issues under PCPNDT Act

The main objective of PCPNDT Act 1994 is to prevent the medical termination of female foetuses due to a disastrous decline in the ratio of girls in India. By this act the disclosing or revealing the sex of the foetus with the help of latest technologies such as ultra sonography or through any other fertility treatments is now a penal offence punishable under law. S. 27 of the PCPNDT Act provides, "Every offence under this act shall be cognizable, non bailable and non compoundable." By virtue of S. 28, a court can take cognizance of a PCPNDT offence where the appropriate authority has made a complaint or when an individual has lodged a complaint with the appropriate authority and 15 days have passed In *Dr. Saraswati v. State of Maharashtra*, 2013,[10] the question before the Bombay HC for consideration is whether a doctor is entitled to apply for bail application when a criminal charge is framed against him under IPC, PCPNDT & MTP Act? Generally the offence under IPC constitutes non-bailable offences and here in this case, a doctor conducted a sex selective abortion on a woman even after the cancellation of her registration under the MTP Act 1994. The woman died as a result of complications related to the surgery. The court in this case noticed that the accused doctor's sonography machine has already been seized by the appropriate authority under PCPNDT Act and also cancelled the registration of her clinic under the MTP Act for previous misconduct. Therefore the court denied bail to her.

On the basis of the existing laws in India we can undoubtedly say that the performance of a sex selective abortion attracts criminal liability to the defaulters. But the point we have to analyze here is that whether a mere agreement to perform a sex selective abortion attracts any criminal liability. This issue was considered by the Delhi High court in *Abhilasha Garg & Another v. The Appropriate Authority*[11] and held that a mere agreement to do an act which may constitute a violation of S.3 (2) by itself is not punishable under the

10 WP-8750/2015, 24th March.

11 CRL APP No.3350/2013.

MTP Act. There has been an actual act of terminating the pregnancy and not an agreement to terminate such pregnancy". In this case the court's perspective is that the MTP Act only criminalizes illegal abortion and not a promise to abort.

However in *Dr. Varsha Gautham w/o Dr.Rajesh v. State of UP* (26th may 2006), the Allahabad HC had made a contrary view. In this case the appropriate authority has not filed a complaint against a doctor who has agreed to perform a sex selective abortion to a TV Journalist while conducting a sting operation. Not only that his clinic has not been registered under the MTP Act or PCPNDT Act. The Government filed an FIR against the doctor. The doctor contented that S.28 of the PCPNDT Act allows for judicial intervention only when an appropriate authority has filed a complaint. The doctor also argued that a mere agreement to perform abortion is not same as actually performing it. The court examined S.6(c) of PCPNDT Act and held that " all aspects of sex selection, starting from the initial activity of determination of sex by prenatal diagnostics procedures and thereafter all the steps taken by any person or a specialist for facilitating selection before or after conception would be brought under the ambit of this amendment." The court in this case convicted the accused doctor to one and a half years of imprisonment for attempted sex selective abortions in consideration of 'grave social consequences' of sex selection. Because the court noticed that the sex selective abortions are very much rampant in the village areas and in the words of court "there are no eligible females for marriages". While giving severe punishment to the accused on ground of 'attempted sex selective abortion', the HC has mentioned the SC's order in *CEHAT v.UOI*[12] for justifying its sentence in this case.

So from these provisions we can clearly understand that the police officials are vested with the wide powers to circumvent the PCPNDT Act. They can conduct a raid without the knowledge of the appropriate authority. In *Dr. Aravind Pal Singh v. State of Punjab & Anothers*[13] the court held that the police have a right to

12 WP(C) 182/2010.

13 [(WP(C) No.344/2002; (2003) 8 SCC 412.

investigate offences alleged under the PCPNDT Act. The PCPNDT Act 1994 requires the ultra sonography centres to be registered under it. The act has also empowered the government authorities to conduct inspections in these clinics.

In *Center for Enquiry into Health and Allied Themes v. UOI*[14] the SC issued an order which confers an obligation on the states to improve the implementation of PCPNDT Act 1994 immediately and without delay. In addition to that, the Code of Ethics regulation issued by the Medical Council of India on 2002 specifically states that, sex determination and termination of pregnancy of a normal foetus merely on the ground that the foetus is a female one amounts to female feticide and shall be treated as professional misconduct from the part of medical professionals. So as far as medical professionals concern a termination of pregnancy on the basis of sex determination is not merely a professional misconduct but impose upon them a criminal liability in case of violation. As a result of imposition of criminal liability we cannot deny the fact that it might create even an unnecessary fear of prosecution in the minds of medical professionals and due to that they may express reluctance in conducting abortion services. Many feminist have the opinion that this act failed to remove the Indian custom of treating women as a secondary citizen and practically in their view it restricts the women's access to safe abortion services.

In *Voluntary Health Association of India v. UOI*[15] the Supreme Court pointed out the importance of eliminating the termination of pregnancy on the basis of sex determination. In the words of court, "all involved in the female feticide deliberately forget to realize that when the foetus of a girl child is destroyed, a woman of future is crucified. To put it differently, the present generation invites the suffering on its own and sows the seeds of suffering for the future generation as in the ultimate eventuate the sex ratio gets affected and leads to manifold social problems." It also stated that the termination of a female foetus impliedly resulted in the killing of a woman. In India the law prohibits it, scriptures forbid

14 Crm.No.335959-M/2008.

15 AIR 2003 SC 3309.

it, philosophy condemns it, ethics deprecate it, morality decries it, and social science adhores it and still it is very much rampant in our society. Therefore, the SC in this case, issued an order directing the states to establish supervisory committees, conduct clinical raids and expedite litigations under the Act.

Through various cases, our judiciary considered the blasting contemporary issue of falling sex ratio in the Indian society seriously. But even then also it failed to focus on the unfair discrimination faced by the already born female children because in many of the judgments, the judiciary use the word 'unborn girls'. Not only that, even though India is developing and gaining achievements in various fields, we cannot close our eyes against the fact that thousands of women are dying here as a result of unsafe abortion.

6. Overlapping human rights of mother & unborn child

Under Constitutional law the issue is with regard to the overlapping of Fundamental rights of mother and the right of an unborn child. The right of a carrying woman involves and includes following rights:-

- Right to dignity of a women
- Right to health
- Right to access to healthcare facilities in the right and deserved time
- Right to abortion/reproductive choice
- Right to privacy

All the above said rights are the rights of women emanated from the right to life and personal liberty provided under Article. 21 of the Constitution. If so the major issue arises here is about the issue of the right of an unborn child i.e. whether an unborn child acquires any legal status in India? Or whether an unborn child can be treated as a human being? If law treats it as a human then we cannot deny its right to live. Therefore the termination of a foetus or an unborn child from the mother's womb amounts to murder or nearly a wrong as Murder punishable under IPC.

At the same time our existing laws in India does not permit the termination of pregnancy after twenty weeks. In Nikita's case, the first abortion debate in India regarding the time limit of 20 weeks has been started and argued to raise the time limit for termination from 20 to 24 weeks. Because in medical science the stage of viability arises after 7 months that is about 28 weeks. Here the viability means the ability of the foetus to survive outside the mother's womb. Secondly, it does not give any autonomous right to the women to conduct abortion. Because the decision to conduct an abortion is solely and primarily depends upon the willingness and approval of medical practitioner and on the proof of risk of women's life or proof of child being born with abnormalities. Therefore abortion laws relating to IPC and MTP Act 1971 infringes the women's right to make reproductive choice, right to privacy, right to health, right to dignity of a women.

Thus the overlapping of the rights of mother and the unborn child is a matter we have to think seriously while deciding an abortion case. The question when a life starts is even now a controversial issue. Neither any statutes nor any laws mentioned about the starting point of life of a foetus or at which stage a foetus can be treated as a human being. Considering the various statutes in India, we can clearly understand that an unborn child has been recognized as a legal person by fiction but such unborn child acquires right only after being born alive. Therefore an unborn child's interest is merely a contingent interest. E.g.: S.13 of the TP Act 1882. Therefore in my opinion, state is required to interfere in the abortion matters only after the stage of viability.

In *Suchita Srivastava & another v. Chandigarh Administration,*[16] the SC held that the state has an obligation to ensure a women's reproductive rights a component of her article 21 right to personal liberty, dignity and privacy.

In *Lakshmi mandal v. Deen Dayal Harinagar Hospital* [(WP(C) 8853/2008], the Delhi HC ruled that preventable maternal death represents a violation of Article 21 of the constitution. The HC

16 WP(C) 349/2006

required the NCT of Delhi to implement the service guarantees in the National Rural Health Mission including safe abortion services to prevent maternal deaths. This is a land mark judgment which created a state obligation to take steps to end preventable maternal death including death caused as a result of inadequate access to safe abortions.

CONCLUSION

A case study conducted among a group of 67 women in a village of Maharashtra (a case study on 'Abortion needs of women in India' (Manish Gupte, Sunitha Bandewar & Hemalatha in Reproductive Health Matters May 1997 5(9) pp.77-86) clearly shows that 64% of the women had the opinion that abortion is not legal; 18% of the women knew that abortion was legal in India and only one woman knew that an abortion was allowed in India but not on ground of fatal sex determination. On the basis of the study it was well settled that most of the women were not aware about the eligibility and time limits for abortion. 9% of the women incorrectly believed that the law required the service provider to obtain the consent of the husband for abortion. From this case we can assume that there is a wide gap between formal rights of the women regarding abortion and social realities. Even now also it's a controversial issue that how far these rights can be achieved in its fullest and fruitful sense in their implementation through law.

For every 1000 boys born in India, there are only 914 girls (Source: Indian Census 2011). In India the birth of a girl is always seen as a burden for the family because most families are expected to pay a dowry when a daughter gets married. If the parents are not financially sound, then having a second daughter would be considered by them as a calamity. This is due to the attitude that the girl is not going to earn money in future and parents have to pay a lump some amount as bride price for her marriage. The statistics shows that despite strict abortion laws, the number of girls is still declining. It is a shocking fact that our country is having the highest number of maternal deaths in the world i.e. in 2010, 56000 women and girls were died in India due to maternal causes.(Source: TREND IN

MATERNAL MORTALITY 2012) In rural areas, most of the parents are not interested to send the girls to school and providing higher education. Instead of that they prefer boys to have education.

In order to tackle the issue, the Government has to take necessary measures from the social perspective. For e.g.: in Germany, while dealing with the issue of abortion, they are mainly focusing on counseling, employment security, social welfare and financial support to persuade pregnant women to give birth to their children. By this way they achieves some degree of protection for the unborn child (J. Kannan, source Hindu) therefore social actions must be taken which enable each member of the society to learn how to respect women and recognizing their rights to health and self determination.

- Awareness programmes must be conducted among women specially in the rural areas which enable them to realize their right to health.
- Measures must be taken from the part of authorities to provide safe abortion facilities in the rural areas.
- Safe abortion must not be unnecessarily restricted.
- It is necessary to provide counseling to the pregnant women before moving to an abortion especially in case of rape victims. At that time they have to inform about the sources of support for married and unmarried mothers, about help on social and psychological problems resulting from pregnancy or other issues
- An effort from the part of judiciary and legislature is necessary to provide clarifications and suitable amendments to already existing ambiguities in the law relating to abortion.
- Considering the various statutes in India, we can clearly understand that an unborn child has been recognized as a legal person by fiction. However such an unborn child acquires right only after being born alive. Therefore an unborn child's interest is merely a contingent interest. E.g.:-S.13 of the TP Act 1882. Therefore in my opinion, state is required to interfere in the abortion matters only after the stage of viability.

In India the time period for termination is limited to 20 weeks that may be raised to 24 weeks(source: amendment bill 2014 by Health & family Welfare ministry)

I am concluding my paper by saying the fact that a mere liberalization of abortion laws in our country will not be an end or a solution to the problems of contemporary society. For that some social measures must be taken by creating awareness to the local about the existing laws, relevance of having a female children, personal responsibility of each person in changing one's own inner attitude towards the rape victims and towards the child borne not out of a illegal or illicit relationship.

REFERENCES

1. Jerome E.Bates. M.S., Edward. S Zadwadki, Criminal Abortion: A study in Medical Sociology published by Charles. C. Thomas, Spring field, Illinois, USA.
2. Summer (1982), Concept of abortion and their relevance to the abortion debate , the Southern journal of Philosophy,Vol. 20, Issue 2, pp.195-207
3. K.D. Gaur, (1995)Abortion & the law in countries of Indian Sub Continent, Asean Region,United Kingdom, Ireland and USA; Journal of Indian Law Institute Vol.37, www.ili.ac.in
4. Jindal Global Law School with support of IPAS Devp. Foundations (2016) Abortion Laws in India: A review of Court cases published by Centre for Health Law, Ethics &Technology.
5. Leela Visaria,Vimala Ramachandra, Bela Ganatra,Shweta Kalyanwala; (2004) Abortion in India: Emerging Issues from Qualitative Studies; Economic & Political weekly Vol.39.Nov pp.5044-5052, http://www.jstor.org/stable/4415809
6. Manisha Gupte, Sunitha Bandewar, Hemalata Pisal (1997) Abortion needs of women in India: A case study of Rural Maharashtra; Reproductive Health matters, May 5(9) pp.77-86
7. Hanah Tanake (2011) Abortion politics in India & the US: Women's Movements & State; An essay submitted to Wesleyan University in partial fulfillment of the requirements for the Degree of Bachelor of Arts with departmental honors in Sociology.

8. International Conference on Population & Development
9. Para 7.2 & 7.3; reproductiverightsreproductivehealth www.un.org/popin/icpd/conference/offeng/poa.html
10. Marcel Vakemans, Upeka Desilva, Manuelle Hurwitz; Access to safe abortion: A tool for assessing legal & other obstacles by International Planned Parenthood Ferderation from choice a world of possibilities.
11. Abortion laws; Haward University http://cyber.law.havard.edu/population/abortion/abortion laws.htm
12. WHO; www.who.int/reproductive-health/publications/safe-abortions
13. Karakkal .M ;(1991) Abortion Law & the abortion situation in India; Issues in Reproductive & Genetic Engineering, 4(3) :pp 223-230.
14. CEDAW Committee, Concluding observations,India, Para-4, UN Doc. CEDAW/C/IND/CO/3(2007).
15. Sushmi Dey; "proposed law set to allow abortion up to 24 weeks, http://economictimes.indiatimes.com.
16. Report of the Committee on Amendment to Criminal Law, Jan 23,2013.
17. Sunanda Bharti; Legal personality of unborn: A jurisprudential analysis under University of Delhi, Delhi-110077.
18. Saumya Rai & Sajid Sheikh (2017) Indian Abortion Laws Need to Change & in the prochoice direction; THE WIRE.
19. Sonali Kokra (Life style editor); why is India's abortion law falling its women on so many fronts. IN-news.
20. The ALAN GUTT MACHER INSTITUTE (A nonprofit corporation for reproductive health research, policy analysis & public education) (1999) 'SHARING RESPONSIBILITY: WOMEN, SOCIETY & ABORTION WORLDWIDE www.agi-usa.org
21. K. Kannan(a former judge of Punjab Haryana HC) (Aug 3rd2016) Atricky debate on Abortion; The Hindu.
22. ABBY. F. JAWNOF(2004) Child & fetal Rights under the CRC;Boston University International Journal Vol. 22 pp. 163.

STATUTES REFERRED

1. Constitutional law.
2. Indian Penal Code 1860.
    - Law relating to Miscarriage.
    - Criminal law Amendment Act 2013 with regard to 375 & 376 IPC.
3. Medical Termination of Pregnancy Act 1971.
4. Protection of Children from Sexual Offence Act 2012.
5. Pre-conception and pre natal Diagnostics Techniques Act 1994.

Arguing for Legalization of Euthanasia: Emerging Issues and Challenges

Dr. Aparna Singh

Abstract

Euthanasia-or simply call it mercy killing is gaining day to day concern of the world and is a highly debatable topic. People are raising voices for legalizing it so that easy death may be procured. But is it still easy to do so? Modern technology has advanced medical science to such extent that now scientists and doctors can better understand the development and complexities of human body. Scientific advancement has led to the prolongation of life-saving treatment for patients but this advancement is still limited to only those who can afford these services. Also, a country like India is still struggling to improve its basic medical facilities. Many countries still treat physician assisting suicide as a crime with stringent provisions to punish such offences. Due regards for this can be given to philosophical thinkers who regarded life as sacred and so physician assisted suicide being against nature.

Still no parameters in the international context are set up to demonstrate whether to legalize it or not. The present Chapter addresses the issues surrounding euthanasia and tries to understand whether it constitutes death with dignity or not. The author also tries to evaluate the current national and international laws on euthanasia in the recent years in specific countries and their outcomes. The main focus is India, being a developing nation, to know the role and obligation of the government related with the current euthanasia practice and its impact on the society.

INTRODUCTION

Human dignity is an expression that is a moral and a legal term. The term is very complex and ambiguous and lacks an adequate definition.

Etymologically, it has Latin roots: humus meaning what is earthly or an earthling and Dignitas is worthiness, worth, beauty. Generally, *humus* means what is proper to the kind that we are or to the species of rational animals, referring in particular to their kindness (humanity) and their fallibility (all too human). **Dignitas** is derived from a Latin root *dignus* meaning worth, fitting[1]. Generally, dignity means the standing of one entitled to respect, i.e. his or her status, and it refers to that which in a being induces or ought to induce such respect: its excellence or incomparability of value[2].

Euthanasia is the termination of a very sick person's life in order to relieve them of their suffering. A person who undergoes euthanasia usually has an incurable condition. In other words, it refers to the practice of ending a life in a painless manner - "a deliberate intervention undertaken with the express intention of ending a life, to relieve intractable suffering".

World Health Organization defines it as "*Palliative care is an approach that improves the quality of patients and their families facing the problem associated with life threatening illness, through the prevention and relief of suffering by means of early identification and impeccable assessment and treatment of pain and other problem physical, psychological or spiritual.*"

It is also important to distinguish between **assisted suicide/dying, euthanasia.** Assisted death is a model that includes both i.e., physician assisted suicide and voluntary active euthanasia. Physician assisted suicide entails making lethal drugs available to the patient to end his own life. The role of the physician is passive in nature; there is no direct participation in the act of ending the life. But in voluntary active euthanasia, the physician takes an active role in carrying out the patient's request. Euthanasia is the act of deliberately ending the person's life to relieve the person from unbearable pain or intolerable suffering. *Mercy killing* happens when someone causes the death of another individual based on the belief that death would be good for the victim.

Euthanasia is becoming a very sensitive & polarizing issue across the world, based on the philosophy of humanism and compassion. Euthanasia

1 http://www.etymonline.com accessed on 31/01/2015.

2 http://eprints.nuim.ie/archive/00000392/01/ human dignity.

includes various forms: Active, Passive euthanasia, Voluntary, Involuntary Non-voluntary euthanasia. There are no international instruments which deal directly with euthanasia. What they deal with majorly is the right to dignity of death. There are also different national legislations dealing with euthanasia.

In the recent years, medico-legal issues of moral character have arisen for consideration by law reform agencies. One such issue arises because medical advancement has considerably reduced the rate of premature morality, but has substantially raised the number of individuals who may survive but lead an unsatisfactory quality of life. There is an inherent tension between the public interest in improving community health services and preservation of life on one hand and the individual's right to personal autonomy on the other. There are various ethical, moral and legal issues involved while practicing euthanasia.

ETHICAL: First and foremost duty of any nation is to preserve and protect the right to life of its people. If euthanasia is legalized, it would undermine this right.

The "*principle of double effect*" which was developed by Roman Catholic moral theologians in 16th–17th century is also questionable as it justifies pain relieving treatment to be given to patients with the intention of providing relief and excuses any unavoidable, unwanted effect, i.e., even the death of the person is tolerable. Euthanasia opponents also raise the issue that due to the large financial cost involved in keeping sick people alive, many patients who are medically unfit would not be properly taken care of. The critics of euthanasia also believe that due to the confusion in the concepts like vegetative state or brain death of the terminally ill person, there may be risk of harvesting organ donation of patients who may not be willing to donate their body parts. Legalizing euthanasia would also invoke the debate to give euthanasia to those who are suffering from psychological disorders or diabetes or other chronic illnesses that are not life threatening.

It is also against the principle of utilitarianism, i.e. maximum happiness to the maximum number of people. The patient who would die a few days later would have to forcefully opt for euthanasia to avoid any sort of burden on his representatives or the hospital because of the large costs involved.

MORAL: Human life occupies an inherent dignity which should be respected. Humans have distinctive capacities for intelligent existence which should be protected at any cost. Other issue relating to morality comprise of self-determination, personhood and autonomy. Those who favour euthanasia say that patient has the right to refuse life-saving treatment but those against it state that even though the patient refuses treatment, it is the physician's duty to provide such treatment. The opponents of euthanasia argue that it is a wrong practice as, since ages societies have denounced the practice of terminating one's life deliberately.

LEGAL: It is still illegal in some countries, ex., in United Kingdom, due to the Suicide Act 1961; the issues are sometimes muddled by the apparent inconsistency in the laws. The opponents of euthanasia present the slippery slope argument that legalizing euthanasia would inevitably lead to legalisation of other forms of euthanasia in guise of voluntary legalized euthanasia. The vagueness in the language of the law and the ambiguity in the language used can lead to confusion and the doctors can make their own interpretation to escape criminal liability. The powers of Attorney could be abused by the guardians of patients. The opponents of euthanasia believe that the countries instead of legalizing euthanasia should increase palliative facilities.

EUTHANASIA: A DEBATE ON DEATH WITH DIGNITY

Advances in medical sciences now allow living and dying to be prolonged. Dworkin's sentiments also reflect a commonly held belief that modern medicine can compel the people to endure life beyond what they perceived to be dignified bounds. As a result, there are repeated calls for bringing legal reforms which should permit euthanasia and assisted suicide.

The ability to preserve life despite trauma and terminal illness has resulted in people raising the demand of right to die with dignity rather than endure a perceived indignity of a dependent existence. The phrase "dying with dignity" forms the basis of euthanasia debate. Human dignity however, is a nebulous concept. One may define it as a calm death without pain and suffering while others define it as an existential maturity, where dying is done in a harmonious and calm way, i.e., with respect for individual autonomy. The argument that human lives possess inviolable & inherent dignity is the traditionalists' attempt to present the sanctity of life as a self-evident moral concept.

Hobbes and Mill have utilized the "natural theory" and propagated the theory that *all men are equal by nature*. Hobbes in reference to equality illustrates "it is obvious that there are many signs of natural inequalities in the society but man should guide himself in the wise way to provide "equal treatment for equals and unequal treatment for unequal[3]." It received its most influential expression in the writings of John Locke. According to him, "good's natural law provided that no one ought to harm another in his life, health liberty or possessions. That law could therefore, be said to give each a natural right to his life, liberty and properties of others"[4]. Kant believed it is the respect of autonomy of rational beings which demonstrates the intrinsic values of all individuals and the esteem and inherent dignity of which each is worthy.

Thus, human dignity is universal and in frangible by state parties or third parties. Human dignity is bound with forms of governance and this is the central feature in modern constitutional states. Therefore, there is certain fundamental value in the notion of human dignity, which some would consider a "pivotal right" deeply rooted in notions of justice & fairness. The protection of human dignity of all individuals was elevated above all considerations as a focal point remedying the colossal failures of all the previous structures, which were derelict in protecting these basic human characteristics during World War- II.

There are two negative rights which are particularly relevant to voluntary euthanasia: right not to be killed, corresponding to the duty not to kill and right to liberty, corresponding to the duty to respect others' rights. The first kind of right rules out euthanasia of any kind. But when such rights are renounced, the duty corresponding to it also diminishes. So, if someone is asking for voluntary euthanasia, he is not only renouncing his negative right not to get killed but asserting his positive right to be killed. Next, the negative right to liberty entails that no one can prevent the person from committing suicide if it causes no harm in the society.

3 http://eprints.nuim.ie/archive/00000392/01/ human dignity.

4 Hugo A. Bedau" *Justice and Equality*", Prentice Hall, U.S.A, 1971, pg. 5,6.

INTERNATIONAL PERSPECTIVE

None of the international human rights instruments define euthanasia directly. This however, does not mean that international human rights laws are inconsistent with euthanasia.

The Preamble of **United Declaration on Human Rights** states that *"recognition of the inherent dignity and of the equal and inalienable rights of all the member of the human family is the foundation of freedom, justice and peace in the world.*[5]*"* Article 3 states that *"everyone has the right to life, liberty and security of persons."* But this idea has proved to be fatal. Indeed, the member nations of U.N. do not have the same views of the very meaning of the term[6] as some members states are on the verge to legalise euthanasia, which is in direct violation of right to life in UDHR. Yet, there is no word from the UN on this matter.

The ICCPR prohibits discrimination under Article 2(1), 3 and 26. Article 26 provides explicitly for equality before law and equal protection of law without any discrimination for all people. So, the *"status"* of an incompetent or disabled person who is not given legal access to accelerated termination of life (once legalised) for sentient, adults and intelligent persons, amounts to "*discrimination*" under *Article 26,* a "*distinction*" under Article 2 and a denial of "*equal rights*" under Article 3. If the right to equality and non-discrimination is violated, Article 2(1) requires all state parties to guarantee an adequate remedy and non-discrimination and equality, the notions that are well entrenched in international law as well as municipal law and the popular consciousness[7].

In article 8 of ECHR, everyone has the right to respect for his private and family life, his home and his correspondence which can be interfered with only under certain circumstances. Under Article 17"Nothing in this Convention may be interpreted as implying for any State, group or person any right to engage in any activity or perform any act aimed at the

---

5 David Miller, "*Blackwell Encyclopedia of Political thought",(*Blackwell, UK, USA.1991), p.3

6 Available at : United Nation ,Universal Declaration on Human Rights (1948) on www.un.org/overview/rights.html as on 10/02/2015.

7 Martin Hailer and Dietrich Ritschl "*The general notion of Human Dignity and the Specific Arguments in Medical Ethics.* " in Kurt Bayertz (ed.) , "*Sanctity of life and Human Dignity*", 1996.

destruction of any of the rights and freedoms set forth herein or at their limitation to a greater extent than is provided for in the Convention."

Contrary to other rights to freedom, Article 2(1) of the ECHR does not include negative right of not to live. The concept of self-determination itself falls into the scope of protection of Article 8(1). The state can restrict euthanasia, however, in accordance with Article 8(2) to protect the life of the other person[8]. In case of *R v. U.K*[9] the European Commission held that the acts of aiding and abetting suicide are excluded from the domain of Article 8 and therefore don't fall under the scope of right to privacy.

In 1983, the former commission held inadmissible the application of the person condemned for lending assistance in the commission of the suicide. It then ruled as follows:

"The commission does not consider the activity for which the applicant was convicted, namely aiding and abetting suicide can be described as falling into the sphere of his private life. While it might be thought to touch directly on the private lives of those who sought to commit suicide, it does not follow the applicant's right to privacy are involved. On the contrary the commission is of the opinion that the acts aiding, abetting, counselling or procuring suicide is excluded from the concept of privacy by virtue of their trespass on the public interest of protecting life as reflected in the criminal provisions of the 1961 Act[10]*."*

The second milestone in recognition of right to assisted suicide was introduced in the case of *Haas v. Switzerland*[11] where the court went from assisted suicide as a quality of personal freedom to that of conventional right to live. This judgment is recognized as proclaiming *"a real conventional right to suicide"*, establishing *"indeed a right to decide one's own death."*

The Court did confirm its jurisprudence in *Pretty v. U.K.* that the choice to avoid an undignified and painful end to life falls within the scope of Article 8. The Court recognized that the right of an individual to decide the manner and moment at which his life should end is one of the aspects

8 Lord Lester and Sarah Joseph, 582.

9 ECHR Pretty (2002), 35 EHRR I.

10 1983 33DR 270.

11 *R. v. United Kingdom*, 1983.

of the right to respect for private life, provided that the person in question is capable of forming his or her own free will in this regard.

Article 4(1) of **American Convention on Human Rights** provides rights for every person to have their lives respected, which shall be protected by law from the date of its conception and no one shall be subjected to arbitrary deprivation of such right.

Australia

The *Right to Terminally Ill Act 1995* legalized medically assisted euthanasia in the northern territory. The validity of the Act was held by the Supreme Court of Australia in the case of *Wake v. Northern Territory*[12]but a legislation to challenge this Act was subsequently passed, known as Euthanasia Laws Act, 1997, repealing the former Act.

Later on, this Act was repealed by "*The Rights of Terminally Ill (Euthanasia Laws Repeal) Bill 2008*". This Bill restores the legitimacy of the Northern Territory Legislation, which established the right of terminally ill persons to request assistance from the medically qualified persons to voluntarily terminate his/her life in a humane manner and to allow for such assistance to be given in certain circumstances without legal impediment to the person rendering such assistance, to provide the possibility of abuse against the misuse of such Act and rights recognised under it.

Netherlands

Netherlands became the first country to legalise physician assisted euthanasia in 2000.

But under the Dutch Penal Code, Article 293-94 makes both euthanasia and assisted suicide illegal if certain guidelines are not followed. Despite these legal provisions, the courts have held that Article 40 of the Criminal Code (i.e. any person who is compelled by *force majeure* to commit a criminal act shall not be criminally liable) provides defence to the doctors charged against Article 293-94. However, this defence is not in favour of the accused if the accused could have avoided the commission of the offence. Hence, euthanasia and assisted suicide are legal only if the criteria

12 Judgement of 20th January, 2011.

laid down in the Dutch *Termination of Life on Request and Assisted Suicide (Review Procedures) Act 2002* are fully observed. The cases would be administered and reviewed by the "*Regional Review Committee for Termination of Life and Request and Assisted suicide*" after the death of the patient.

Belgium

The *Belgian Act on Euthanasia* was passed on May 2002 and became effective from September 23, 2002. It was limited to euthanasia for competent adults and emancipated minors who were in constant and unbearable mental or physical suffering which cannot be alleviated. Another bill was proposed to extend euthanasia to children and individuals suffering from dementia which did not pass. However, on February 13, 2014 Belgium legalized euthanasia by lethal injection for the children. Young children would be allowed to end their life with the help of doctors in the world's most radical euthanasia extensive law.

Thus, Belgium devolved its own model of assessment. The names of the physicians providing euthanasia are kept anonymous. The physician who rejects to perform euthanasia may at the patient's request or at the request of his representative, can transfer the patient's medical record to the physician designated by the physician or his representative.

Switzerland

In 1918, the comment by the Swiss Federal Government on the first federal penal code stated: "In modern penal law, suicide is not a crime. Aiding and abetting suicide can themselves be inspired by altruistic motive." Switzerland and Germany are the two such countries whose Penal Code considers *motive* as an important element in determining the culpability. These countries consider motive of the actor in both the grading of the offence and the sentencing of the crime. Motive means "a desire coupled with the intention to bring about the certain consequences as an end, by means of other consequences which are also desired and intended but only as a means.[13]"

13 (1996), 109 NTR 1.

Switzerland has legislatively permitted assisted suicide since 1937. Switzerland is the only country which provides assisted suicide not only to its citizens but also to the people of other countries within its jurisdiction. For this reason, this country came to be known for *"suicide tourism."*

The legality of assisted suicide is a result of *Article 115* of the Swiss Criminal Code which provides for inciting and assisting someone to commit suicide under the observation that a person who, for selfish reasons, incites someone to commit suicide or who assists that person in doing so will, if the suicide was carried out or attempted, be sentenced to a term of imprisonment of up to 5 years. Consequently, assisting suicide is crime only if the motive is selfish. Ethical guidelines are provided to the physician to follow.

The Swiss Penal Code expressly affixes an obligation upon the judges to mitigate punishment where 'honourable motives' induce the 'homicidal act[14].'The Swiss Penal Code treats homicide upon the "request" as a special classification of homicide. The request must be earnest and urgent. Life imprisonment is permissible punishment upon the finding that the actor possesses the particular reprehensible attitude or he is dangerous[15].

United States of America

Active euthanasia is illegal in U.S.A. Physicians who cause the death of the patients or provide assistance in the suicide may be prosecuted under the homicidal statues which exist in each state. In 1996, in the case of *Washington v. Glucksberg*[16], the court overturned a Washington State law that made assisted suicide a felony based on the equal protection clause of the 14th Amendment. The court's decision depended upon the analysis of Due Process Clause, nation's relevant history and traditions and concluding on the point that there is a commitment to the preservation and protection of all human lives[17]. In his majority opinion, Judge Stephen Reinhardt wrote: "If broad general state policies can be used to deprive a terminally ill individual of the right to make that choice, it is hard to envision where

14 Cook "*Act, Intention and Motive in the Criminal Law*," 26 Yale L.J.660-61.

15 Swiss Penal Code: Article 63.

16 Swiss Penal Code : Article 64.

17 521 U.S.702,117 S.Ct. 2258 (1997).

the exercise of arbitrary and intrusive power by the state can be halted." Reinhardt's analysis relied heavily on language drawn from U.S. Supreme Court abortion case, *Roe v. Wade*[18], because the issues have "compelling similarities". Currently, physician assisted suicide is legal only in one state – Oregon.

In 1973, Dr. Vincent Montemarano was indicted for murder after giving a 57 year old victim a fatal injection of potassium chloride. The jury did not hold him liable. In 1976, California became the first state to legalize the patient's right to refuse prolong treatment. In 1976, the parents of ***Karen Ann Quinlan*** won the right to remove her from a ventilator because she was in a persistent vegetative state. The justices unanimously ruled that this act was necessary to respect Quinlan's right to privacy[19]. In 1990, the Supreme Court in *Cruzan v. Missouri*[20] recognized the principle that a person has a constitutionally protected right to refuse unwanted medical treatment. The Cruzan decision sparked a fresh interest in living wills and in 1990 Congress passed the Patient Self-Determination Act.

INDIA STAND ONEUTHANASIA

A notable feature of the present debate on euthanasia is that it has been conducted entirely within the virtual framework of western philosophies and their ideologies, social patterns, religious and cultural traditions.

Right to health has been incorporated in national as well as international instruments. It is recognised by the Supreme Court under Article 21 of the Indian constitution. Ancillary to it are the provisions enshrined under Part IV of the Constitution and in Articles 39, 47 and 48 where the right to health of workers, women and children employed in the establishments or factories are recognised. In the case of *Parmanand Katara v. Union of India*[21], the Supreme Court held that Article 21 imposes an obligation

18 The Declaration of Independence (U.S. 1776), "We hold these truth to be self-evident, that all men are created equal, that they are endowed by their creator with certain inalienable right, that amongst these are life, liberty and the pursuit of happiness."

19 410 U.S. 113, 93 S.Ct. 705, (1973).

20 1976, 70 N.J. 355A. 2d. 647 Supreme Court of New Jersey.

21 497, US 261 (1990).

upon the states to preserve the life of every individual. Every doctor has the obligation to extend his services in the protection of life. All the government hospitals/institutes have the duty to provide immediate medical care.

EXPANSION OF ARTICLE 21 UNDER "LIFE" VIS-A-VIS "ATTEMPT TO SUICIDE"

Right to life and personal liberty as enshrined under Article 21, enforceable against the state, is very fundamental and pivotal right of the human being around which the other rights of the individual revolve and therefore carries significant importance. The horizons of right to life were expanded by the Supreme Court in the case of *"Maneka Gandhi v. Union of India.*[22]"

The complexity arises as to whether right to life includes right to die or not. There is also the confusion of distinguishing between euthanasia and suicide. In the case of *Naresh Marotrao Sakhare v. Union of India*[23], Justice Lodha made the difference between the two – "...suicide by its very nature is the act of self-killing, an act of self-destruction. It is an act of terminating one's own act without the aid or assistance of any other human agency. Euthanasia or mercy killing implies the termination of life by the intervention of the third person. Mercy killing is not an attempt to suicide and hence not covered under Section 309 of I.P.C. Both these concepts are factually and legally different. Euthanasia or suicide is nothing but homicide. Suicide is nowhere defined. Hence, attempt to commit suicide and abetment of such attempt is bound to pose problems of definition in practice..."

The Supreme Court in *Kharak Singh v. State of Uttar Pradesh*[24] held that right to life includes more than an animal existence. It includes within itself the finest graces of human civilization which makes life worth living and the tradition, culture and heritage of the person concerned.

In the case of *R.C. Cooper v. Union of India*[25], it was held that fundamental rights have both positive as well as negative aspects. For example, freedom

22 1989 AIR 2039, SCR(3) 997.

23 1978, AIR 597, 1978 SCR (2) 621.

24 1996 (1) Bom. C.R. 92, 1995Cri.LJ 96 (1994) (2) Mh. LJ 1850.

25 1963, AIR 129,1964 SCR (1) 332.

of expression includes freedom not to speak. Therefore, stretching this argument, right to life includes right not to live. However, the penal laws in India make the commission of suicide an offence and hence punishable. Stringent provisions are there to punish the person who commits an offence or helps in its abetment. Therefore, the doctor who assists in the termination of life could be punished.

In the case of *State v. Sanjay Kumar*[26], the Delhi High Court held that "… it is still an irony that Section 309 of I.P.C. still continues to exist. Strange paradox is that in the age of votaries of euthanasia, suicide is criminally punishable. The continuance of Section 309 I.P.C. is an anachronism unworthy of a humane society like ours. The very idea is revolting. The need is for humane and socially oriented and conscious penology."

The Bombay High Court in the case of *Maruti Sharipati v. State of Maharashtra*[27] held that Section 309 of I.P.C. is violative of Articles 14 and 21 and therefore struck it down as *ultra vires.* However, this was reversed by *C. Jagadeeshwar v. State of Andhra Pradesh.*[28] In the case of *P. Rathinam v. Union of India,*[29] the Supreme Court held that Section 309 should be removed from the I.P.C. to humanise the penal laws. It is cruel and irrational that the person suffers twice i.e., the agony of an attempt made to commit suicide and thereafter be subject to the penal provisions. Subsequently, Supreme Court in the case of *Gian Kaur v. State of Punjab*[30] held that Section 306 and 309 of I.P.C. are valid on the ground that sanctity of life cannot be over looked. Article 21 guarantees right to life and personal liberty and by no means can be stretched to extinction of life. Withdrawal/withholding treatment was held to be part of life with dignity and permissible when the natural termination of life is certain and the process of natural death has commenced.

The concern to legalise euthanasia is arising from all over the world. In India, the "society to die with dignity" (S.R.D.D.) is making efforts to legalise euthanasia. The judiciary also believes that it is the function of the legislature and it should make law on it.

---

26 1970, AIR 564,1970 SCR (3)530.

27 1986, (10) DRJ 31.

28 1987 (1) Bom. CR 499(1986) 88BOMLR 589.

29 16th April, 1987.

30 1994 AIR 1844 SCC (3) 394.

In March 2011, in the case of *Aruna Ramchandra Shanbaug v. Union of India*,[31] the Supreme Court allowed passive euthanasia but under certain circumstances. It pointed out that "the general legal position all over the world seems to that active euthanasia is illegal unless there is legislation permitting it; passive euthanasia is permitted even without legislations if certain conditions and safeguards are maintained."

"*The Euthanasia (Permission and Regulation) Bill, 2007*"[32]was introduced in the Lok Sabha whereby the statement of objects and reasons states that in case of persons with no hope of recovery, active euthanasia gives a way out and that it is a better alternative "*than committing suicide, which is an offence under the present penal provisions.*" Also, "*before making euthanasia legal, sufficient checks and balances at the institutional level are necessary to ensure that the system is not misused by unscrupulous elements.*" It has to be ensured that the "*life of the patient is taken only after due process has been adhered to and in a humane and compassionate manner in the presence of family members and elected representatives.*" However, the bill lapsed.

The 196th Report of Law Commission on Medical Treatment to Terminally Ill Patients (Protections of Patients and Medical Practitioners), 2006 is one of the most important subjects taken up by the Law Commission for a comprehensive study. It opined that euthanasia and assisted suicide should continue to remain illegal. However, it supported the use of passive euthanasia if sufficient safeguards provided under it are adhered to. This report maintains the established disdain for *active* euthanasia, which is "*comparatively quick and a less painful method of relieving a terminally ill patient from his on-going pain.*"[33]

---

31 (2011) 4 SCC 454.

32 The Euthanasia (Permission and Regulation) Bill, 2007, No. 55. If passed, the bill would provide for a compassionate, humane and painless termination of the life of an individual who are permanently invalid or bedridden because of an incurable disease. Chandrappan (who moved the bill in the house) says, "If there is no hope of recovery for a patient, it is only humane to allow him to put an end to his pain and agony in a dignified manner."

33 Law Commission of India, 196th Report on Medical Treatment of Terminally Ill patients (Protection of Patients and Medical Practitioners), 2006 pg. 15.

If proper safeguards are laid down and the physicians are made to comply with them strictly, then there is nothing wrong in legalising euthanasia. It is a wrong presumption that once euthanasia is legalised, it would lead to the destruction of lives because it would not only be the law which would govern euthanasia but the intention of the parties too. Criticizing something which we are not well aware of is problematic.

SUGGESTIONS

The international standard for grant of euthanasia must be laid down and each signatory member of such international convention or treaty must abide by the same. Under domestic laws, a panel of experts from medicine must be there to diagnose & decide upon the request and consent of the patient to assist in the termination of his life. Countries like India, which are rich in traditional medicinal plants to cure diseases should be motivated to come up with new/hybrid varieties which are more powerful. Medicine prices and treatment costs should be curtailed so that it would be easily accessible for the poor. People who find themselves in distress and depression and decide to end their lives should be motivated to visit psychologists. Categories of patients should be made so that the authority to administer drugs for assisting suicide by physicians should not be abused. Patients with serious irreversible conditions should be kept separately. In case of any abuse, the recommendations from the independent panel of medical experts should be taken into account. A separate fund should be kept by the government for those persons who are unable to afford treatment. Funds can be collected through individual and governmental aiding, both nationally and internationally. Standards must be laid down for providing better conditions of dying. Physician must do only what they are authorised to do by law. Proper opinion polls must be drawn up with the help of NGOs, experts and the people before enacting any legislation for legalising euthanasia. Government should do a peer review on the reported cases of euthanasia and should publish them for public debate according to which laws could be moulded from time to time.

CONCLUSION

With the transformation of the society, the paradigms of right to life were expanded by the legislatures and judiciary. The doctors are charged with the duty to protect the lives of people. The possibility of discovering the miraculous cures for the diseases and symptoms, which were earlier unpredictable, have raised much opposition against euthanasia. Proponents of euthanasia believed that even though there is "sanctity of life", it is not absolute. The government must not only focus on the protection of this right but also, on the right to die with dignity when the circumstances demand so because man is the master of his own destiny. This is the matter of choice and consent. Sometimes, it also becomes the matter of self-respect. When the person suffers from unbearable pain, or is terminally ill, there can be no hope that the alleviation by drugs could help end their pain.

There have been constitutional and procedural challenges regarding the legality of assisted suicide by physicians. Many people reflect the state of ambivalence against the safeguards which are prescribed to be observed under euthanasia. Society feels uncomfortable with the situation where too much power is granted in the hands of physicians to terminate lives. Another argument is that if euthanasia is legalised, then human life would be placed in the hands of a few persons, who on account of their whims would be in the position to terminate lives, being humanitarian, ethically, morally and legally wrong.

But the real world is far different from mythologies and religious theories. Euthanasia in early ages meant "good death." This implied death on emotional and compassionate grounds. Also, patients who are in persistent vegetative state for years with no signs of interaction, it is very miserable for their family members to see them in that stage, because it is their death day-by-day seeing them in such condition.

When an act is performed within the legal framework, it would not amount to an offence. For passing any legislation, the issue is properly analysed, its pros and cons are seen and its probable effects are taken into prior consideration. Legalising euthanasia within the legal framework would not be detrimental to the society till it is well-regulated. Stagnation - whether in society or in life is a problem because it severely hampers the development of the individual & the society. Moreover, suicide, euthanasia and assisted killing are different things because intention of the party matters while doing any act. For suicide and assisted killing or murder, penal laws can be strictly imposed so that they cause no loss to the society, but for euthanasia or mercy killing, stringent provisions should be laid down and if the parties fully comply, there is nothing morally, socially and ethically wrong in assisting a person to end his life. Forms may be different; it may be voluntary active euthanasia or passive euthanasia depending upon the desirability of the legislation of a particular country. Since the society is dynamic, law should continuously be adapted and readapted to serve the needs of the individual and society. The functional aspect of law should be to reconcile & balance the competing interests in the society.

Mental Health Care Act, 2017 – Decriminalizes Suicide and Protecting the Inalienable Rights of Mentally Ill Persons

Diksha Dubey

Abstract

Mentally ill people are painted as stigma in Indian society and thus are deprived of their inalienable rights, which as a human being they are entitled to. This research paper will try to analyze the Mental Health Care Act 2017 which is an offshoot of the international convention signed by India i.e. Convention on Rights of Person With Disabilities, thus by enacting this Act India is fulfilling its international obligations and also addressing the issues which were not addressed by Mental Health Care Act 1987. This article discusses the rights provided in the Act in detail and also compares both the Mental Health Care Act, further analyzing the conditions of mentally ill patients in India. Challenges to the new Act are being discussed in brief. The most important changes brought by this Act is decriminalization of suicide and banning of ECT for minors, so paper deals with a detailed look at both of these aspects. Thus the paper is concluded with a few suggestions to be accommodated in the Act while critically evaluating the Act.

Keywords: *Convention on persons with disabilities, ECT, inalienable rights, Mental Health Care Act.*

Whether an illness effects your heart, your leg or your brain it is still an illness and there should be no distinction

Michelle Obama

Mental Health Care Act 2017 is an offshoot of the Convention on Rights of Persons with Disabilities and its Optional Protocol being adopted by India. The Act imbibes the various rights of mentally ill person and duties concerned with the persons and officials looking after them. Mental illness is treated as stigma in Indian society and thus mentally ill people thereby are deprived of their inalienable and basic rights i.e. their Human rights. Human rights are those rights which each individual is entitled to from the split second he or she is born.[1] The concept of Human rights is deeply rooted in the theory of natural law and further the revival of natural law in 19th century raised its stature. Some of the essential rights are now enshrined in our Constitution in the form of fundamental rights.

The rights of mentally ill person as specified in the Mental health care Act, 2017 are in correlation with fundamental rights and human rights.[2] The rights that mentally ill person are allowed to enjoy are as follows –

1. *He or she has right to access mental health care*[3] but of those organizations that are run by government, though this right is under the ambit of fundamental right of equality that is the mentally ill persons are to be provided with easy access to health care in government run hospitals without any discrimination on the basis of caste creed, colour or sex. Further the services provided must be feasible and appropriate. There are many points that the legislature has taken into consideration like treatment should be in such a manner which supports the community and family of the person, treatment must be readily available according to patients geographical location, persons below poverty line but not in possession of BPL card then too services must be rendered to them[4] and according to the government the specified essential drug list, from that the same list of medicines must be provided to the mentally ill persons.
2. *Right to home,* each individual suffering from mental illness has the right to live freely and not to be shunned or segregated from society and further if he has been abandoned by his family then government will provide the legal aid and facilitate him in exercising to his right to home[5]

---

1 Mangari Rajender, The protection of Human Rights Act and relating Laws (1st ed., Law book agency 2000) 1.

2 Lakshmidhar Mishra, 'Human Rights in Mental Health Care- an Introduction' in D Nagraja and Pratima Murthy (eds.), Mental Health Care and Human Rights (NHRC New Delhi 2008)

3 Mental health Act 2017, S.18 (1).

4 *Ibid.*

5 Mental Health Care Act 2017, S.18.

3. *Right to life with dignity*[6], he or she has all the rights to life and sustain his or her life like a normal human being and also it covers all the rights under Article 21 of Indian Constitution, wherein it is enshrined that no person shall be deprived of his life or personal liberty, life which is certainly more than survival or animal existence.[7] Thus they are entitled to various inalienable rights like right to live in safe and hygienic environment, pollution free air and water[8], has right to proper clothing reasonable facilities for recreation, right to privacy to not be forced for tonsuring and allowed to wear their own clothes if wished for.[9].
4. *Right to equality and non discrimination* – mentally ill persons shall be treated equal to persons with physical illness[10] and the child not to be separated from the mother if he is under three years of age but if the conditions of the mother are such that which will prove harmful for the child then the child can be separated from his mother.
5. *Right to information and confidentiality*[11]though exceptions are provided in case of the medical experts and psychiatrists who are concerned with the treatment or examination of the patient.
6. *Right to refuse and receive calls and to access his or her medical reports*[12]
7. *Right to complaint regarding deficiency in services*[13]
8. *Right to legal aid*[14]

These rights as enshrined in the Act are adhering to the preamble of the Convention on person with disability. This Act unlike Mental Health care Act 1987 covers almost every right, as discussed above. Apart from India's mandate to frame an Act according to the convention, there did already exist a dire need for reforms in earlier Act and to establish new law

6 Mental Health Care Act 2017, S.19.
7 *Upendra Baxi v. State of Uttar Pradesh* [1983] 2 SCC 308.
8 *State of Maharashtra v. Chandrabhan* AIR [1983] SC 549.
9 MP Jain, *Indian Constitutional law* (7th ed., Lexis Nexis, 2014) 1173.
10 Mental Health Care Act, 2017 S.20.
11 Mental Health Care Act, 2017 S. 21.
12 Mental Health Care Act 2017, S. 22, S. 23.
13 Mental Health Care Act 2017 S.25, S, 26.
14 Mental Health Care Act 2017 S.28

protecting the rights of mentally ill persons. With the hype of cases like *Death of 25 chained inmates in Asylum fire in Tamil Nadu in re v. Union of India*[15] and *Veena Sethi v. Union of India*[16], which shocked the conscious of whole nation, and therefore at such a point there were not cries for Judicial Activism but for a proper law which could guard the inalienable rights of individuals.

In death of 25 chained inmates Asylum fire in Tamil Nadu, the patients were burned alive and they also could not escape from the fire as they were tied to their beds, in this case Supreme Court took the suo motu action but still the harsh reality that mentally ill person are paint as stigma in our Indian society could not be removed. In Veena Sethi case, some of the prisoners had to be detained in jail because of lack of institutions and also a few who gained sanity but still remained in jail. Even when mental health Act, 1987 provides that if the person who subsequently found on inquisition to be of sound mind is to be discharged[17] now what appears to be painfully obvious is that these violations continue to occur in India in spite of legal provisions.[18]

There are many instances that had happened in our country before the enactment of Mental Health Care Act 2017 and also during the existence of Mental Health Care Act 1987, which had risked or put the life of mentally ill persons in threat, for a long time. The two cases discussed above are just a few examples, as there are many examples adding to atrocities committed on them, for instance many a times despite the provision of voluntary intake of patients in the hospitals cases are reported of involuntary admission of the patients especially women and girls.

Further they face unhygienic or unsanitary conditions, sexual violence and electric shock treatment.[19] They are treated worse than animals[20] it is

15 Mental Health Act 2017 2017, S.27.

16 2002 3 SCC 31.

17 AIR 1983 SC 339.

18 Mental Health Act 1987, s. 44.

19 Anvar Sadath, Vranda Mysore Narasimha, Mukund Rao and Vijay Kumar, Muralidhar D, *Human Rights Violation. in Mental Health: A Case Report from India* (2014) Journal of Psychiatry < https://www.omicsonline.org/open-access/human-rights-violation-in-mental-health-a-case-report-from india.php?aid=27210> accessed 18th October 2017.

20 Himanshi Dhawani, 'Indian women in mental hospitals 'treated worse than animals'' *Times of India* (India 4th December2014)<.https://timesofindia.indiatimes.com/india/Indian-women-in-mental-hospitals-treated-worse-than animals/articleshow/45368067.cms>accessed 17th October 2017.

seldom highlighted –

"Women and girls with disabilities are dumped in institutions by their family members or police in part because the government is failing to provide appropriate support and services"[21]

Examples of the torture faced by women was studied in India by human rights watch and in their report and a lot of cases were reported like – even after the discharge of women from psychiatric hospital her husband used to take her to private clinic for shock treatment, an old women was admitted to the hospital just because of domestic feud in spite her reports being totally normal and in no way pointed towards bipolar disorder, many a times they are deprived of proper hygiene like a women reported that she did not get soap neither towel and further during laundry of their clothes they had to stay naked for that time.[22]

Though women and girls are explicitly victims of the atrocities but men also are not free from the clutches of tortuous behavior. Cases are reported that the patients are harassed by wards, as their position is not altered unlike doctors and attendant and also they are not trained, like ward man ask the patients for money and make them do manual labor –

"Yahan ka jhaadu maar, warna khana nahin dege (Sweep otherwise, we won't give you food)" — is the threat several patients receive. "The ward boys sometimes ask us to take money from our family and give it to them"[23]

These instances happened in the prevalence of the Mental Health Care Act, 1987 though the Act is not a complete failure but it suffers from some glitches which are covered up by the Mental Health Care Act 2017. The new Act-

---

21 India: Women With Disabilities Locked Away and Abused, https://www.hrw.org/news/2014/12/03/india-women-disabilities-locked-away-and-abused accessed 11th October 2017.

22 *Ibid.*

23 Treated worse than animals, < https://www.hrw.org/report/2014/12/03/treated-worse-animals/abuses-against-women-and-girls-psychosocial-or-intellectual> accessed 11th October 2017.

- Defines informed consent [24]
- Introduces the concept of advance directive which was not present in earlier Act, here the patient can give the directive to the hospital explaining the manner in which he wants to be treated and cared for and this directive may be made by person irrespective of his previous or past mental illness.
- Provisions for outpatient are also included apart from provisions for in patient.
- Rights of the patients are protected as discussed in the earlier section of the article, further they are also provided with emergency facilities like normal patients.[25]
- Duty of the government to draft, design and implement programmes for mentally ill people development[26], further due to the paucity of qualified and skillful personnel's to look after the mental health hospital, it is mentioned in the Act that it is the duty of the government to address the human resource requirements of mental health services in the country.[27]
- Central mental health authority and state mental health authority to be established, further licensing of hospitals is to be stopped and registration is to be conceded.
- Establishment of mental health review board.
- Protection of minors is strictly ensured in this Act, further it is stated that minor is to be kept in a different atmosphere from that

---

24 Tabassum Barnagarwala, 'In urgent need of being humans – mental hospitals' *Indian Express* (India 23rd December2014)<http://indianexpress.com/article/cities/mumbai/in-urgent-need-of-being-human-mentalhospitals/> accessed 16th October 2017.

25 Mental Health Care Act 2017, S.2 (1) (i)
"Informed consent" means consent given for a specific intervention, without any force, undue influence, fraud, threat, mistake or misrepresentation, and obtained after disclosing to a person adequate information including risks and benefits of, and alternatives to, the specific intervention in a language and manner understood by the Person.

26 Mental Health Care Act 2017, S 21 (1) (b).

27 Mental Health Care Act 2017, S.29.

of adults, for his developmental needs.[28] Also in case of minor girls if the nominative representative is a male, a female attendant shall be appointed by the nominated representative.

- Decriminalization of suicide[29] and abolishing electro conclusive therapy.[30]
- The board has a duty to check on the prisoners as to whether they have been shifted from jail to mental health hospital, further if the patients are used for research purpose without informed consent then the concerned state authority has to look into the issue.
- Done away with the provision that police can take into custody a person suspected to be a mentally ill person by the police.

The provisions in this Act are definitely securing and protecting the rights of the mentally ill persons in a better way as compared to previous Act, which is being discussed above. But still the pompous and ostentatious provisions of this Act will in reality be able to fulfill the big promises made to the country by this Act. Certainly there are various hurdles in the implantation of this Act.

The biggest hurdle is the lack of government run hospitals for mentally ill persons and also the lack of staff including nurses and doctors/ psychiatrists. As according to the provisions laid down by union government there must be one psychiatrist and one medical officer per 100 patients, despite of that there is massive shortage of medical practitioners[31] There are 0·3 psychiatrists per 100,000 people in India while in China, there are 1·7 psychiatrists per 100,000 people[32] further there is lack of infrastructure, as it is seldom highlighted that there are lack of beds and capacity in the hospital to inhibit the patients, even the most famous mental hospital of India Yervada, it is one of the biggest run hospital in Asia and have

28 Mental Health Care Act 2017, S 31.

29 Mental Health Care Act 2017, S. 87 (4).

30 Mental Health Care Act 2017, S.115.

31 Mental Health Care Act 2017, S. 95.

32 Tabassum Barnagarwala, 'In urgent need of being humans – mental hospitals' *Indian Express (*India 23rd December2014)<http://indianexpress.com/article/cities/mumbai/in-urgent-need-of-being-human-mentalhospitals/> accessed 16th October 2017.

around 1864 patients but only 25 working toilets, open defecation is the norm.[33] Pavlov hospital of Pune has 250 beds for 500 patients[34] . Many are not able to access the health care services due to lack of transport and unavailability of facilities in their area, though the new Act provides for a clause that facilities are to be provided considering the geographic factor. Legal services given to them are also in vulnerable state for them, as though there is a provision that they will be given free legal aid but still there are some glitches like for instance if the mentally ill woman gets raped then allegations are being raised like if the women is not in a conscious mind how can she say she is being raped, and even if a suo motu case is being registered, if doctor says so that she is being raped, but if she will not be able to identify accused then it will become a false case and thus not be able to stand up in court. Many are being hide in their homes and their family members do not talk about their illness openly and further refused to provide them with the treatment.[35] A study in four districts of Gujarat found that people with disabilities were discouraged from attending weddings. Another study in Orissa found that only 27 percent of women with intellectual disabilities leave their homes and 19 percent can take part in social activities.[36] Even doctors and psychiatrists in this field are ostracized from society, for example it was revealed in human rights watch report that a psychiatrists who have been working for more than 9 years in this field felt –

"My job here makes my family tense; they worry about me. If I talk too loudly or I crack a joke that my family doesn't understand, they look at

33 Anuradha Mascarenhas, 'Mental illness India's ticking bomb, only 1 in 10 treated: Lancet study' *Indian Express* (India 19th May 2016) <http://indianexpress.com/article/india/india-news-india/mental-illness-indias-ticking-bomb-only-1-in-10-treated-lancet-study-2807987/> accessed 18th October 2017.

34 Kumkum Dasgupta, 'India faces massive challenge to get mental healthcare right' *The Gaurdian (India* 29th December2014),<https://www.theguardian.com/global-development/2014/dec/29/india-mental-healthcare challenges> accessed 19th October 2017.

35 Gunjan Sharma , 'Mentally ill suffer a horrible fate in India' *Duetsche Velle* (Germany 23rd August 2013) <http://www.dw.com/en/mentally-ill-suffer-a-horrible-fate-in-india/a-17007499 > accessed 19th October 2017 .

36 Vikram Patel, 'Legislating the right to care for mental illness' [2013], 48 EPW 73.

each other and say I have lost my mind working at a mental hospital. Even the bus driver looks at me strangely when I ask him to drop me off at the hospital every morning"[37]

There are no rehabilitation facilities for the patients[38] they are deprived of job opportunities, i.e. once branded as mentally ill then no one is ready to take them back or give them new job even after they attain sanity or get cured.

So it is a tough call for the new Act to cover up for the faults or lacunae in the previous Act and to further resolve the issues discussed above in minimum period of time, so that a mentally ill person no longer be considered as stigma in our society and not only on paper but in reality is able to access his or her inalienable natural and human rights. The Act will not only address the curative but also preventive, promotive and rehabilitative aspects.[39] Thus mentally ill person will be brought at same stature like other human beings, if the Act is properly implemented.[40]

DECRIMINALIZATION OF SUICIDE AND BANNING OF ACT

When men became detached from society and when they loosen the bonds that previously had tied them to their fellows they are prone to individualistic suicide[41]Mentally ill persons are thus prone to this type of suicide and sometimes to anomic suicide as well when kept in excessive regulation,

37 Treated worse than animals, < https://www.hrw.org/report/2014/12/03/treated-worse-animals/abuses-against-women-and-girls-psychosocial-or-intellectual> accessed 11th October 2017.

38 *Ibid.*

39 'Are mental health facilities in India adequate?'*Times of India* (India 23rd December 2014) https://timesofindia.indiatimes.com/life-style/health-fitness/health-news/Are-mental-health-facilities-in-India-adequate/articleshow/40190993.cms, accessed 17th October 2017.

40 Suresh Bada Nath and D Nagaraja, 'Mental Health Legislative – An Indian perspective 'in D Nagraja and Pratima Murthy (eds.), *Mental Health Care and Human Rights* (NHRC New Delhi 2008).

41 Declarations on rights of mentally retarded person, resolution 2856 (XXVI), 28th December 2017, http://www.ohchr.org/EN/ProfessionalInterest/Pages/RightsOfMentallyRetardedPersons.aspx accessed 17th October 2017.

they resort to anomic type of suicide. The legitimacy of S.309[42] is being challenged a lot of times before honorable Supreme and High Court in number of cases, in cases like *Maruti Shripati v. State of Maharashtra*[43] and *P.Rathinam v. Union of India*[44] the High Court and Supreme Court respectively held that this section is violating the Articles 14 and 21 of Indian Constitution and thus this section must be struck down, and the same was observed in 42nd report of law commission where it was stated that the person who attempts to commit suicide deserves sympathy and not harsh punishment. But with the case of *Gian Kaur v. State of Punjab*[45] the Supreme Court overruled the decision give in the above two cases and also the law commission report released after this judgment i.e. 156th , it also upheld the same that is the S.309 is not to be repealed. But with the Mental Health Care Act 2017, suicide is decriminalized for mentally ill person, this is a step forward in understanding them as human beings and trying to secure their rights, as they might commit suicide under severe mental stress and thus cannot be double punished for their Act i.e. attempt to commit suicide and the pain they went through while attempting to commit suicide. Further mentally ill person are not able to sometimes judge their Acts or know the consequences of their Act thus imposing the harsh punishment under S.309 for them is unjustified.

Electric convulsive therapy is completely banned for performing on minors and further if electric convulsive therapy is performed on adults then it cannot be performed without muscle relaxants and anaesthesia. Sterilization is also banned when it is intended as a treatment for mental illness[46] though the provisions are stricter but still there are certain glitches like ECT can be performed if necessary in case of minor then it can be performed with informed consent of guardian. This is a bit risky and might override the right given to minors, and thus if informed consent is obtained from guardian then minor should also be present at the time of decision

42 Lewis A coser, *Masters of Sociological thought* (2nd ed., New Printing Press, 2015) 134.

43 Indian Penal Code 1960, S. 309.

44 *Maruti Shripati v. State of Maharashtra* [1987] (1) BOMCR 499.

45 *P. Rathinam v. Union of India* [1994] SCC (3) 394.

46 *Gian Kaur v. State of Punjab* [1996] AIR 946.

making[47] and they must be informed and properly explained about the therapy by the concerned doctors. Moreover the ECT gives short term benefit and is not an effective measure to cure the depression or mental illness of the patient in a long term, - "It's not difficult to get artificial changes in the brain, you could do it with cocaine, but it doesn't last and three or four weeks later the person is either back at the same level of depression or many studies show worse levels of depression." [48] Before the implementation of this Act, ECT was used casually in India. Some examples - Sara, a 25-year-old woman with schizophrenia, remembered with a shudder what happened to her:

"Nobody told me what was happening...They took me to another room; I didn't want to go but they still made me. There they gave me a nashainjection [anesthesia] and suddenly my stomach lurched. I felt like vomiting but I didn't"[49]

Devika also has the same experience –

"I said to the doctor that I've had enough of shocks, I can't take it anymore. I told the doctor again today but I still got shocks. He won't feel bad if I tell him again, no? Because of the shocks, my memory is suppressed"[50]

Thus with the stricter provision of regulating the ECT therapy was the dire need in our country and with the enactment of this Act, probably the use of that therapy is going to be under control and only in special circumstances.

CONCLUSION AND SUGGESTIONS

Mental Health Care Act 2017 is patient and right based or centric Act, it is bringing with a lot of hopes for mentally ill persons in India. This Act contains a lot of provisions which were not thought of earlier like

47 Mental Health Care Act 2017, S.95.

48 A P Rajkumar, B Saravanan and K S Jacob, 'Voices of people who have received ECT' (2007) 4 Indian Journal of medical ethics < http://ijme.in/articles/voices-of-people-who-have-received-ect/?galley=html> accessed 19th October 2017.

49 Jim Reed, 'Why are we still using electroconvulsive therapy', *British Broadcasting Corporation* (London 24th July 2013)< http://www.bbc.com/news/health-23414888> accessed 17th October 2017.

50 Treated worse than animals, < https://www.hrw.org/report/2014/12/03/treated-worse-animals/abuses-against-women-and-girls-psychosocial-or-intellectual> accessed 11th October 2017.

child should not be separated from her mother who is a patient unless it is necessary, police cannot take into custody if they suspect the person to be mentally ill, ECT banned for minors and the most important among all is decriminalization of suicide, though these are just a few examples but this Act contains a lot of provisions benefitting the patients and bringing them to the stature of a human being.

In order to fulfill the promises made in this Act, government has to take a step further and has to try their best to ensure rights to mentally ill persons. A few suggestions –

- As mentioned in the Act the services are to be provided by taking into consideration the geographical factor, therefore government must try to ensure facilities to treat mentally ill patients in each and every district of India.
- Funding must be proper and government must give priority in budget for securing funding for fulfilling the provisions of this Act.
- To establish a complaint mechanism for the mentally ill persons and to further to make the legal aid provision strong, a separate court can be established to listen to the cases related to them in each state.
- Focus on educating them, though the provision is given for giving them proper recreation and education facilities but still a proper monitoring system should be established that they are engaged into the same.
- Provision of informed consent should be evaluated further and made more patient centric.
- Private run hospitals should also contain provisions which are economically feasible for patients.
- Rehabilitation centre must be established for the patients who after treatment or gaining back the sanity must before starting back their normal life needs rehabilitation.
- Not to be discriminated on the basis of their past disease i.e. they should not be labeled as mentally ill person if they earlier were and thus should not be stopped from getting back their job or discouraged from joining the same.

Thus it can be concluded that the Act is acting as a ray of hope for protecting the rights of mentally ill person and finally trying to give them back what they were denied for ages that is their inalienable right – right to life with dignity.

1. Dhawani Himanshi, 'Indian women in mental hospitals 'treated worse than animals" *Times of India* (India 4th December2014).
2. Mascarenhas Anuradha, 'Mental illness India's ticking bomb, only 1 in 10 treated: Lancet study' *Indian Express* (India 19th May 2016).
3. Reed Jim, 'Why are we still using electroconvulsive therapy', *British Broadcasting Corporation* (London 24th July 2013).
4. Sharma Gunjan , 'Mentally ill suffer a horrible fate in India' *Duetsche Velle* (Germany 23rd August 2013).

BIBLIOGRAPHY

Books

1. Jain MP, *Indian Constitutional law* (7th ed., lexis nexis Gurgaon, Haryana 2014).
2. Lewis A coser , *Masters of Sociological thought* (2nd ed., New Printing Press, New Delhi, 2015).
3. Nagraja D and Murthy Pratima (eds.), *Mental Health Care and Human Rights* (NHRC New Delhi 2008).
4. Rajender Mangari, *The protection of Human Rights Act and relating Laws* (1st ed., Law book agency, Hyderabad 2000).

Articles

1. Bada Nath Suresh and Nagaraja D, 'Mental Health Legislative – An Indian perspective 'in D Nagraja and Pratima Murthy (eds.), *Mental Health Care and Human Rights* (NHRC New Delhi 2008).
2. Lakshmidhar Mishra, 'Human Rights in Mental Health Care- an Introduction' in D Nagraja and Pratima Murthy (eds.), *Mental Health Care and Human Rights* (NHRC New Delhi 2008).

3. Rajkumar A, Saravanan B and Jacob K, 'Voices of people who have received ECT'(2007) 4 Indian Journal of medical ethics.
4. Sadath Anvar, Mysore Vranda, Narasimha, Rao Mukand , Kumar Vijay and D Muralidhar, *Human Rights Violation. in Mental Health: A Case Report from India* (2014) Journal of Psychiatry.
5. Vikram Patel , 'Legislating the right to care for mental illness' [2013], 48 EPW 73.

Newspaper Articles and Magazines

1. Are mental health facilities in India adequate?'*Times of India* (India 23rd December 2014).
2. Barnagarwala Tabassum, 'In urgent need of being humans – mental hospitals' *Indian Express (*India 23rd December2014).
3. Dasgupta Kumkum, 'India faces massive challenge to get mental healthcare right' *The Gaurdian (* India 29th December2014).

Websites

1. http://ijme.in/articles/voices-of-people-who-have-received-ect/?galley=html.
2. http://indianexpress.com/article/cities/mumbai/in-urgent-need-of-being-human-mentalhospitals/.
3. http://indianexpress.com/article/india/india-news-india/mental-illness-indias-ticking-bomb-only-1-in-10-treated-lancet-study-2807987/.
4. http://www.bbc.com/news/health-23414888.
5. http://www.dw.com/en/mentally-ill-suffer-a-horrible-fate-in-india/a-17007499.
6. http://www.ohchr.org/EN/ProfessionalInterest/Pages/RightsofMentallyRetardedPersons.aspx.
7. https://timesofindia.indiatimes.com/india/Indian-women-in-mental-hospitals-treated-worse-than animals/articleshow/45368067.cms.
8. https://timesofindia.indiatimes.com/life-style/health-fitness/health-news/Are-mentalhealth-facilities-in-India-adequate/articleshow/40190993.cms.

9. https://www.hrw.org/news/2014/12/03/india-women-disabilities-locked-away-and-abused.
10. https://www.hrw.org/report/2014/12/03/treated-worse-animals/abuses-against-women-and-girls-psychosocial-or-intellectual.
11. https://www.omicsonline.org/open-access/human-rights-violation-in-mental-health-a-case-report-fromindia.php? aid=27210.
12. https://www.theguardian.com/global-development/2014/dec/29/india-mental-healthcare challenges.

Surrogacy in India

Anjali Dixit

Abstract

The ever-rising prevalence of infertility world over has lead to advancement of assisted reproductive techniques (ART). Herein, surrogacy comes as an alternative when the infertile woman or couple is not able to reproduce. Surrogacy is an arrangement where a surrogate mother bears and delivers a child for another couple or person. In gestational surrogacy, an embryo, which is fertilized by in vitro fertilization, is implanted into the uterus of the surrogate mother who carries and delivers the baby. In traditional surrogacy, the surrogate mother is impregnated with the sperms of the intended father artificially, thus making her both genetic and gestational mother. Surrogacy may be commercial or altruistic, depending upon whether the surrogate receives financial reward for her pregnancy. Surrogacy refers to a contract in which a woman carries a pregnancy "for" another couple. Number of infertile couples from all over the World approach India where commercial surrogacy is legal. Although this arrangement appears to be beneficial for all parties concerned, there are certain delicate issues which need to be addressed through carefully framed laws in order to protect the rights of the surrogate mother and the intended parents. The aim of this writing is to establish whether there is anything intrinsically immoral about surrogacy arrangements from the perspective of the surrogate mother herself. Specific attention is paid to the claim that surrogacy is similar to prostitution in that it reduces women›s reproductive labour to a form of alienated and/or dehumanized labour.

"Motherhood is the biggest gamble in the world. It is the glorious life force. It's huge and scary—it's an act of infinite optimism."

– Gilda Radner

SURROGACY–MEANING

The word ‘surrogate’ has its origin in Latin ‘surrogatus’, past participle of ‘surrogare’, meaning a substitute, that is, a person appointed to act in the place of another. Thus a surrogate mother is a woman who bears a child on behalf of another woman, either from her own egg or from the implantation in her womb of a fertilized egg from other woman.

According to the Black’s Law Dictionary, surrogacy means the process of carrying and delivering a child for another person. The New Encyclopaedia Britannica defines ‘surrogate motherhood’ as the practice in which a woman bears a child for a couple unable to produce children in the usual 9 way.

The Report of the Committee of Inquiry into Human Fertilization and Embryology or the Warnock Report (1984) defines surrogacy as the practice whereby one woman carries a child for another with the intention that the child should be handed over after birth.

Categorizes of Surrogacy

The Black’ Law Dictionary categorizes surrogacy into two classes:

1. Gestational surrogacy’ and
2. ‘Traditional surrogacy’.

They are defined as follows:

1. **Gestational surrogacy**: A pregnancy in which one woman (the genetic mother) provides the egg, which is fertilized, and another woman (the surrogate mother) carries the fetus and gives birth to the child.
2. **Traditional surrogacy**: A pregnancy in which a woman provides her own egg, which is fertilized by artificial insemination, and carries the fetus and gives birth to a child for another person.

‘Gestational surrogacy’ is total in the sense that an embryo created by the process of IVF is implanted into the surrogate mother. ‘Traditional surrogacy’ may be called partial or genetically contracted motherhood because the surrogate mother is impregnated with the sperm of the intended father making her both the genetic and the gestational mother; the child shares make-up of the commissioning father and the surrogate mother.

Commercial or Altruistic Surrogacy

Surrogacy is commercial or altruistic depending on whether the surrogate receives financial reward for her pregnancy or the relinquishment of the child, or not.

COMMERCIAL SURROGACY IN INDIA

Commercial surrogacy in India was legalized in India in 2002. The availability of medical infrastructure and potential surrogates, combined with international demand, has fueled the growth of the industry. Surrogate mothers receive medical, nutritional and overall health care through surrogacy agreements. The economic scale of surrogacy in India is unknown, but study backed by the United Nations in July 2012 estimated the business at more than $400 million a year, with over 3,000 fertility clinics across India. India is the leader in making it a viable industry rather than a rare fertility treatment. Experts say it could take off for the same reasons outsourcing in other industries has been successful: a wide labor pool working for relatively low rates.

Critics say the couples are exploiting poor women in India - a country with an alarmingly high maternal death rate - by hiring them at a cut-rate cost to undergo the hardship, pain and risks of labor.

"It raises the factor of baby farms in developing countries," said John Lantos of the Center for Practical Bioethics in Kansas City, Mo. "It comes down to questions of voluntariness and risk."

INDIA – A REPRODUCTIVE TOURISM DESTINATION

In commercial surrogacy agreements, the surrogate mother enters into an agreement with the commissioning couple or a single parent to bear the burden of pregnancy. In return of her agreeing to carry the term of the pregnancy, she is paid by the commissioning agent for that. The usual fee is around $25,000 to $30,000 in India which is around 1/3rd of that in developed countries like the USA. This has made India a favourable destination for foreign couples who look for a cost-effective treatment for infertility and a whole branch of medical tourism has flourished on the surrogate practice. ART industry is now a 25,000 crore rupee pot of gold. Anand, a small town in Gujarat, has acquired a distinct reputation as a place for outsourcing commercial surrogacy. It seems that wombs in India are on rent which translates into babies for foreigners and dollars for Indian surrogate mothers.

LEGAL AND MORAL ISSUES

The moral issues associated with surrogacy are pretty obvious, yet of an eye-opening nature. This includes the criticism that surrogacy leads to commoditization of the child, breaks the bond between the mother and the child, interferes with nature and leads to exploitation of poor women in underdeveloped countries who sell their bodies for money. Sometimes, psychological considerations may come in the way of a successful surrogacy arrangement. As far as the legality of the concept of surrogacy is concerned it would be worthwhile to mention that **Article 16.1 of the Universal Declaration of Human Rights 1948** says, inter alia, that "men and women of full age without any limitation due to race, nationality or religion have the right to marry and found a family".

JUDICIAL DECISIONS REGARDS SURROGACY

The Judiciary in India too has recognized the reproductive right of humans as a basic right. For instance, in *B. K. Parthasarthi v. Government of Andhra Pradesh,*[1], the Andhra Pradesh High Court upheld "the right of reproductive autonomy" of an individual as a facet of his "right to privacy" and agreed with the decision of the US Supreme Court in *Jack T. Skinner v. State of Oklahoma,*[2] which characterised the right to reproduce as "one of the basic civil rights of man". Even in *Javed v. State of Haryana*[3], though the Supreme Court upheld the two living children norm to debar a person

1 *Ibid.*
2 AIR 2000 A. P. 156
3 316 US 535

from contesting a Panchayati Raj election it refrained from stating that the right to procreation is not a basic human right Now, if reproductive right gets constitutional protection, surrogacy which allows an infertile couple to exercise that right also gets the same constitutional protection. However, jurisdictions in various countries have held different views regarding the legalization of surrogacy. In England, surrogacy arrangements are legal and the Surrogacy Arrangements Act 1985 prohibits advertising and other aspects of commercial surrogacy. In the US also, commercial surrogacy seems prohibited in many states. In the famous *Baby M case*[4], the New Jersey Supreme Court, though allowed custody to commissioning parents in the "best interest of the child", came to the conclusion that surrogacy contract is against public policy.

MOTHERHOOD – AN ENIGMA

How surrogacy can lead to an array of legal complexities regarding motherhood was shown by *Jaycee B. v. Superior Court.*[5] A child was born to a surrogate mother using sperm and eggs from anonymous donors because the infertile couple was unable to create their own embryo using the in vitro fertilization techniques. The couple chose to use anonymous donors rather than asking the surrogate to use her own eggs because of the *Baby M case* in New Jersey in which the surrogate had eventually refused to hand over the baby saying that she was its biological mother and her right to raise the child pre-empted the commissioning parents'. The child thus had five people who could lay claim to parenthood – a genetic mother, a commissioning mother, a surrogate mother, a genetic father and a commissioning father. One month prior to the birth of the baby Jaycee the intended parents John and Luanne separated and John sought to rescind his obligations under the surrogacy contract so as to avoid having to pay child support for Jaycee. Luanne sought both custody and support from her ex-husband. The court battle continued and for three years Jaycee did not have a legal parent. A Californian court granted temporary custody of the baby Jaycee to Luanne and ordered John to pay for child-support.

4 (2003) 8 SCC 369.
5 537 A.2d 1227.

In India, according to the **National Guidelines for Accreditation, Supervision and Regulation of ART Clinics, evolved in 2005** by the Indian Council of Medical Research (ICMR) and the National Academy of Medical Sciences (NAMS), the surrogate mother is not considered to be the legal mother. The birth certificate is made in the name of the genetic parents. The US position as per the Gestational Surrogacy Act 2004 is pretty similar to that of India.

INDIAN COUNCIL FOR MEDICAL RESEARCH GUIDELINES FOR SURROGACY

The Indian Council for Medical Research has given Guidelines in the year 2005 regulating Assisted Reproductive Technology procedures. The Law Commission of India submitted the 228th report on Assisted Reproductive Technology procedures discussing the importance and need for surrogacy, and also the steps taken to control surrogacy arrangements. The following observations had been made by the Law Commission:

1. Surrogacy arrangement will continue to be governed by contract amongst parties, which will contain all the terms requiring consent of surrogate mother to bear child, agreement of her husband and other family members for the same, medical procedures of artificial insemination, reimbursement of all reasonable expenses for carrying child to full term, willingness to hand over the child born to the commissioning parent(s), etc. But such an arrangement should not be for commercial purposes.
2. A surrogacy arrangement should provide for financial support for surrogate child in the event of death of the commissioning couple or individual before delivery of the child, or divorce between the intended parents and subsequent willingness of none to take delivery of the child.
3. A surrogacy contract should necessarily take care of life insurance cover for surrogate mother.
4. One of the intended parents should be a donor as well, because the bond of love and affection with a child primarily emanates from biological relationship. Also, the chances of various kinds of

child-abuse, which have been noticed in cases of adoptions, will be reduced. In case the intended parent is single, he or she should be a donor to be able to have a surrogate child. Otherwise, adoption is the way to have a child which is resorted to if biological (natural) parents and adoptive parents are different.

5. Legislation itself should recognize a surrogate child to be the legitimate child of the commissioning parent(s) without there being any need for adoption or even declaration of guardian.
6. The birth certificate of the surrogate child should contain the name(s) of the commissioning parent(s) only.
7. Right to privacy of donor as well as surrogate mother should be protected.
8. Sex-selective surrogacy should be prohibited.
9. Cases of abortions should be governed by the Medical Termination of Pregnancy Act 1971 only.

SURROGACY RISK AND CONDITIONS IN INDIA

According to The Guardian, there was a mother who died because she didn't get the proper medical attention. Conservatives estimates show that more than 25,000 children are now being born through surrogates in India every year in an industry worth $2 billion. Domestic demand is increasing, but as fertility levels drop elsewhere, at least 50% of these are "commissioned" by overseas, mainly western, couples. Most of the industry is operating unchecked. India's medical research watchdog drafted regulations more than two years ago, yet they still await presentation in parliament, leaving the surrogates and baby factories open to abuse.

SURROGACY LAWS IN OTHER COUNTRIES

Australia

In Australia the surrogate mother is considered as a legal mother of the child. Commercial surrogacy in the states of Australia is considered as a criminal offence. But altruistic surrogacy has been legalized under Surrogacy Act, 2010. Usually couples prefer adoption rather than surrogate technology. It does not seem that commercial surrogacy can become legal in near future.

France

Since 1994 any surrogacy whether commercial or altruistic surrogacy is illegal in France.

Canada

In Canada altruistic surrogacy is legal but when it comes to commercial surrogacy it is illegal in Canada under Human Reproduction Act, 2004. Any contractual agreement that involve surrogacy is void and unenforceable.

Israel

Israel is the first country that legalizes all types of surrogacy and implemented state controlled surrogacy in which each and every agreement that involves surrogacy should be approved directly by the state.

SURROGACY IN INDIA LEGAL PROSPECTS

Commercial surrogacy has been legal in India since 2002, as it is in many other countries, including the United States. But India is the leader in making it a viable industry rather than a rare fertility treatment. Experts say it could take off for the same reasons outsourcing in other industries has been successful: a wide labor pool working for relatively low rates.

Critics say the couples are exploiting poor women in India - a country with an alarmingly high maternal death rate - by hiring them at a cut-rate cost to undergo the hardship, pain and risks of labor.

"It raises the factor of baby farms in developing countries," said John Lantos of the Center for Practical Bioethics in Kansas City, Mo. "It comes down to questions of voluntariness and risk."

Surrogacy has been legalized in United Kingdom in 2009. The relationship can be recognized under Section 30 of Human Fertilization and Embryology Act, 2009.

LAW RELATES AND FOR REGULATES OF SURROGACY IN INDIA

The Draft Assisted Reproductive Technology (Regulation) Bill and Rules 2008

The legal issues related with surrogacy, as we have seen, are very complex and need to be addressed by a comprehensive legislation. After a long wait for so many years, the Indian Council of Medical Research (ICMR) has come out with a draft Assisted Reproductive Technology (Regulation) Bill and Rules 2008. The draft Bill contains 50 clauses under nine chapters.

- The Bill acknowledges surrogacy agreements and their legal enforceability. This will ensure that surrogacy agreements are treated on par with other contracts and the principles of the Indian Contract Act 1872 and other laws will be applicable to these kinds of agreements.
- The Bill provides that single persons may also go for surrogacy arrangements.
- The Bill provides that a foreigner or foreign couple not resident in India or a non-resident Indian individual or couple, seeking surrogacy in India, shall appoint a local guardian who will be legally responsible for taking care of the surrogate during and after pregnancy till the child is delivered to the foreigner or foreign couple or the local guardian. It is further provided that the commissioning parents or parent shall be legally bound to accept the custody of the child irrespective of any abnormality that the child may have, and the refusal to do so shall constitute an offence. A surrogate mother shall relinquish all parental rights over the child. The birth certificate in respect of a baby born through surrogacy shall bear the name(s) of genetic parents/parent of the baby.
- The Bill also provides that a child born to a married couple or a single person through the use of ART shall be presumed to be the legitimate child of the couple or the single person, as the case may be. If the commissioning couple separates or gets divorced after going for surrogacy but before the child is born, then also the child shall be considered to be the legitimate child of the couple.
- The Bill further provides that a couple or an individual shall not have the service of more than one surrogate at any given time. A couple shall also not have simultaneous transfer of embryos in the woman and in a surrogate.

- Chapter I of the Bill contains definitions.
- Chapter II provides for constitution of a National Advisory Board for ART and State Boards for ART for laying down policies, regulations and guidelines, and Registration Authorities for registering ART clinics. Chapter III lays down procedure for registration of ART clinics.
- Chapter IV prescribes duties of ART clinics. One of the duties is to make couples or individuals, as the case may be, aware of the rights of a child born through the use of ART. The duties also include the obligation not to offer to provide a couple with a child of a pre-determined sex.
- Chapter V provides for sourcing, storage, handling and record-keeping for gametes, embryos and surrogates.
- Chapter VI regulates research on embryos.
- Chapter VII discusses rights and duties of patients, donors, surrogates and children.
- Chapter VIII deals with offences and penalties there for.
- Chapter IX is titled 'Miscellaneous' and includes power to search and seize records etc. and the power to make rules and regulations. This legislation is intended to be in addition to, and not in derogation of, other 18 relevant laws in force.
- The draft Bill prepared by the ICMR is full of lacunae, nay, it is incomplete.

However, it is a beacon to move forward in the direction of preparing legislation to regulate not only ART clinics but rights and obligations of all the parties to a surrogacy including rights of the surrogate child.

ASSISTED REPRODUCTIVE TECHNOLOGY BILL, 2013

The Assisted Reproductive Technology Bill, 2013 has a been pending for quite a while and it has not been presented in the Indian Parliament

The Assisted Reproductive Technology (Regulation) Bill - 2013 Describes procedures for:

1. Accreditation and supervision of Assisted Reproductive Technology Clinics & Banks, ensuring that services provided by the Assisted Reproductive Technology Clinics and Banks are ethical and that the medical, social and legal rights of all those concerned are protected with maximum benefit to the infertile couples or individuals within a recognized framework of ethics and good medical practice.
2. Authorities to Regulate ART Clinics and Banks Registration Authority State Board (within 6 months) National Board DHR, MOHFW (within 3 months) Advisory Committee National Registry of ART Clinics and Banks in India (ICMR) Established (within 3 months)
3. All ART Clinics a. Involve in infertility treatment – including IUI, AIH, AID b. Infertility treatment involving the use and creation of embryos outside the human body c. Processing or storage of gametes and embryos d. Research on embryos.
4. Steps for Registration under National Registry of Assisted Reproductive Technology (ART) Clinics and Banks in India, Confirmation of contact No. and details of ART Clinics/Banks. Obtaining the information regarding available infrastructure facilities, trained manpower and different ART procedure being followed at your ART Clinic/Bank through prescribed Performa. Verification of the information provided by the respective ART Clinic/Bank through a sight visit to be conducted by the competent experts in the field at the respective ART Clinic/Bank. On receipt of satisfactory report of the Site Visit Committee, the Unique Registration Number will be issued.
5. Application for Registration under State Board (*i*) Unique Registration Number Certificate from the National Registry of Assisted Reproductive Technology (ART) Clinics and Banks in India of the ICMR. (*ii*) Bio-data of all the faculty members of the clinic or bank including Director or in-charge of the clinic or bank. (*iii*) Copies of the degrees and certificates of all the faculty members of the clinic or bank including Director or in-charge of the clinic or bank. (*iv*) Such other information and documents as may be prescribed.

THE SURROGACY (REGULATION) BILL, 2016

The Surrogacy (Regulation) Bill, 2016 proposes to regulate surrogacy in India by establishing National Surrogacy Board at Central level, State Surrogacy Boards and Appropriate Authorities in States and Union Territories. The proposed legislation ensures effective regulation of surrogacy, prohibit commercial surrogacy and allow ethical surrogacy to the needy infertile Indian couples. The major objectives of the Bill are to regulate surrogacy services in the country, to provide altruistic ethical surrogacy to the needy infertile Indian couples, to prohibit commercial surrogacy including sale and purchase of human embryo and gametes, to prevent commercialization of surrogacy, to prohibit potential exploitation of surrogate mothers and protect the rights of children born through surrogacy. The salient features of the bill are :-

- To allow altruistic ethical surrogacy to intending infertile couple between the age of 23- 50 years and 26-55 years for female and male respectively.
- The intending couples should be legally married for at least five years and should be Indian citizens.
- The intending couples have not had any surviving child biologically or through adoption or through surrogacy earlier except when they have a child and who is mentally or physically challenged or suffer from life threatening disorder with no permanent cure.
- The intending couples shall not abandon the child, born out of a surrogacy procedure under any condition.
- The child born through surrogacy will have the same rights as are available for the Biological child.
- The surrogate mother should be a close relative of the intending couple and should be between the ages of 25-35 years. She can act as surrogate mother only once.
- The surrogate mother will carry a child which is genetically related to the Intending Couple.
- An order concerning the parentage and custody of the child to be born through surrogacy is to be passed by a court of the Magistrate of the first class.

- An insurance coverage of reasonable and adequate amount shall be ensured in favour of the surrogate mother.
- National Surrogacy Board shall exercise the powers and shall perform functions conferred on the Board under this Act.
- The Board shall consist of the Minister in-charge of the Ministry of Health and Family Welfare, as the Chairperson, Secretary to the Government of India in- charge of the Department dealing with the surrogacy matter, as Vice-Chairperson and three women Members of Parliament, of whom two shall be elected by the House of the People and one by the Council of State as Members. The National Surrogacy board and State Surrogacy board shall be the Policy making bodies and Appropriate Authority will be the Implementation body for the Act. The appropriate authority shall comprise of an officer of or above the rank of the Joint Director of Health and Family Welfare Department, as Chairperson, an eminent woman representing women's organization, as member, an officer of Law Department of the State or the Union territory concerned not below the rank of a Deputy Secretary, as member and an eminent registered medical practitioner, as a member.
- The surrogacy clinics shall be registered under this Act after the Appropriate Authority is satisfied that such clinics are in a position to provide facilities and can maintain equipments and standards including specialized manpower, physical infrastructure and diagnostic facilities as may be prescribed in the rules and regulations.
- No person, organization, surrogacy clinic, laboratory or clinical establishment of any kind shall undertake commercial surrogacy, abandon the child, exploit the surrogate mother, sell human embryo or import embryo for the purpose of surrogacy. Violation to the said provision shall be an offence punishable with imprisonment for a term which shall not be less than ten years and with fine which may extend to ten lakh rupees.
- The surrogacy clinics shall have to maintain all records for a period of 25 years Transitional provision-Subject to the provisions of this

Act, there shall be provided a gestation period of ten months from the date of coming into force of this act to protect the wellbeing of already existing surrogate mothers

REPORT NO. 228 OF LAW COMMISSION OF INDIA

Need For Legislation to Regulate Assisted Reproductive Technology Clinics As Well As Rights and Obligations of Parties to a Surrogacy

Most important points in regard to the rights and obligations of the parties to a surrogacy and rights of the surrogate child the proposed legislation should include may be stated as under:

1. Surrogacy arrangement will continue to be governed by contract amongst parties, which will contain all the terms requiring consent of surrogate mother to bear child, agreement of her husband and other family members for the same, medical procedures of artificial insemination, reimbursement of all reasonable expenses for carrying child to full term, willingness to hand over the child born to the commissioning parent(s), etc. But such an arrangement should not be for commercial purposes.
2. A surrogacy arrangement should provide for financial support for surrogate child in the event of death of the commissioning couple or individual before delivery of the child, or divorce between the intended parents and subsequent willingness of none to take delivery of the child.
3. A surrogacy contract should necessarily take care of life insurance cover for surrogate mother.
4. One of the intended parents should be a donor as well, because the bond of love and affection with a child primarily emanates from biological relationship. Also, the chances of various kinds of child-abuse, which have been noticed in cases of adoptions, will be reduced. In case the intended parent is single, he or she should be a donor to be able to have a surrogate child. Otherwise, adoption is the way to have a child which is resorted to if biological (natural) parents and adoptive parents are different.

5. Legislation itself should recognize a surrogate child to be the legitimate child of the commissioning parent(s) without there being any need for adoption or even declaration of guardian.
6. The birth certificate of the surrogate child should contain the name(s) of the commissioning parent(s) only.
7. Right to privacy of donor as well as surrogate mother should be protected. [8] Sex-selective surrogacy should be prohibited.
8. Cases of abortions should be governed by the Medical Termination of Pregnancy Act 1971 only.

CONCLUSION AND SUGGESTIONS

Gift of child is the most precious one for a couple. Those who are deprived of this wonderful gift always feel inferior and frustrated. There are thousands of couples across the world facing humiliation because of not having any child. Surrogacy is a wonderful gift that would bring the big smile on their face. The development in medical science and increased social awareness and acceptance has made it popular and more and more couples are getting benefitted by it every year. The number is ever increasing and countries like India are becoming a major centre for surrogacy due to availability of surrogate mothers and legal flexibility

The following measures are being suggested on the basis of the present study:

1. There should be legislation directly on the subject of surrogacy arrangement involving all the three parties i.e. the surrogate mother, the commissioning parents and the child.
2. There is a need of right-based legal framework for the surrogate mothers, as far as the ICMR guidelines are not enough.
3. A clearly defined law needs to be drafted immediately which will pronounce in detail the Indian government's stand on surrogacy; so that discrete activity leading to exploitation of the surrogate mother can be stopped.
4. Although it is not a crime to bear a child for another, and then relinquish it for adoption, it is not regulated by law and may raise

a number of confusions. It has to be regulated whether paying the mother a fee for adoption beyond medical expenses is a crime (like in some countries) or not. In case it is recognized as crime and one pays extra charges then it should prevent the adoption from being approved.

5. There should be a substantial regulation designed to protect the interests of the child. Legal recognition of termination and transfer of parenting rights.
6. Right to privacy of donor as well as surrogate mother should be protected. It is crucially important to maintain and monitor the anonymity of the surrogate mothers.
7. The surrogate mother should not undergo more than 3 trials for a pregnancy and it has to be monitored.
8. The surrogate mother should be provided by the copy of the contract as she is a party in the agreement and her interests should be taken into account. It happens that very often decision is taken by the intended parents and clinic, while surrogate mother does not have any say in this matter.
9. There should be an interpreter (other than doctor) for the communication linkage between the surrogate and intended parents in order to convey the message from surrogate mother time to time. As far as often doctors speak on behalf of surrogate mothers, but there is no guarantee that their interests are conveyed without any misinterpretation.
10. Typically, after the birth the surrogate mother is left without any medical support, it is recommended that there should be a provision of intensive care and medical check-ups of their reproductive organs during the 3 months after pregnancy.
11. In case surrogate mother gives birth to twins she should be paid double amount or at least 75% of the charges for the second child.
12. The commissioning couple should try to establish a relationship of trust with the surrogate, yet such a relationship creates reciprocal rights and duties and might create demands for an undesired relationship after the birth.

13. In case of foreign commissioning parents the citizenship right of the surrogate baby is also of crucial importance. The Indian government needs to take a stand in terms of conferring the surrogate baby a dual citizenship as he/she is born in the womb of an Indian (the surrogate mother) and in India, but commissioning parents belong to a foreign country.
14. The rights of the child should be protected and in case he/she is not taken by the foreign commissioning parents, then the child should be given Indian citizenship.
15. A guarantor should be appointed to take the custody of the child in case commissioning patents fail to do so.
16. Health Insurance for both the surrogate mother and the child is essential to ensure a healthy life.
17. A surrogacy contract should necessarily take care of life insurance cover for surrogate mother.
18. There is a need of debate and discussion of the stance that public policy and the law should take toward surrogate mothering. Actually, there exists a range of choices from prohibition and regulation to active encouragement.
19. The government needs to monitor the surrogacy clinics, which generally charge arbitrary prices for surrogacy arrangements. Regulations would enable the government to ensure that the clinics charge fair prices.
20. Surrogacy arrangement should be governed by a contract amongst parties, which will contain all the terms requiring consent of surrogate mother to bear child, agreement of her husband and other family members for the same, medical procedures of artificial insemination, reimbursement of all reasonable expenses for carrying child to full term, willingness to hand over the child born to the commissioning parent(s), etc.
21. The contract signed between the commissioning parents and the surrogate mother should mention something about insurance and emergency needs that the surrogate mother may require during the pregnancy; it has to mention something about her future after relinquishing the baby.

22. A specialized court called "Surrogacy Court" can be created. It can comprehensively look at all the problems relating to surrogacy arrangement for adjudicating disputes.
23. A surrogacy arrangement should provide for financial support for surrogate child in the event of death of the commissioning couple or individual before delivery of the child, or divorce between the intended parents and subsequent willingness of none to take delivery of the child.
24. One of the intended parents should be a donor as well, because the bond of love and affection with a child primarily emanates from biological relationship. Also, the chances of various kinds of child-abuse, which have been noticed in cases of adoptions, will be reduced. In case the intended parent is single, he or she should be a donor to be able to have a surrogate child. Otherwise, adoption is the way to have a child which is resorted to if biological (natural) parents and adoptive parents are different.
25. Legislation itself should recognize a surrogate child to be the legitimate child of the commissioning parent(s) without there being any need for adoption or even declaration of guardian.
26. The birth certificate of the surrogate child should contain the name(s) of the commissioning parent(s) only.
27. Sex-selective surrogacy should be prohibited.
28. Surrogacy Arrangements brokered by commercial or profit agencies should be outlawed. It emphasizes the greatest possible regulation and prevention of commercial arrangements with the goal of diminishing exploitation of the statutory scheme and the parties involved.
29. Foreigners visiting India for commissioning surrogacy must apply for medical visa and not tourist visa.
30. A letter from the embassy should be enclosed with visa application stating that the country recognizes surrogacy and the child born thereof will be treated as a biological child of the couple. The treatment should be done only at registered ART clinics recognized by Indian Council for Medical Research.

At the end it can be said that even if surrogacy oversteps the natural ways of procreation, only those who have been able to get children from it know the value of legitimacy of surrogacy. At times, in a society like India, where barrenness is considered incompleteness for a woman, people have no option, but to resort to it to live peacefully in society. We cannot consider it against the unity of marriage, as even adoption is legally permissible then why not surrogacy.

Let us Regulate Technology and not Human Lives

"Motherhood: All love begins and ends there."

– Robert Browning

Environmental Pollution and Bio-Medical Wastage in India: Issues and Concerns

Dr. Deepom Baruah

Abstract

Hospital wastes pose a significant impact on health and environment. From this study it can be said that there is an urgent need for raising awareness and education on medical waste issues. Proper waste management strategy is needed to ensure health and environmental safety. For further study, it is needed:

- *To collect more information on impacts, disposal and management to draw clear conclusion.*
- *Need to collect information and examples from developed country or the country, which has sound medical waste management system.*
- *Find alternatives and appropriate technologies for developing countries.*
- *Need extensive study on this medical waste and its management aspects as well.*

All over the world, there is an exodus of people from villages to cities, partly for education and employment and partly because agriculture has become less and less profitable. It is estimated that 65% of the world's population will live in cities by 2030. The infrastructure required for this lop-sided growth of the cities is resulting in mountains of garbage collecting in the unplanned extensions in larger cities, because of poor conservancy services and lack of civic amenities. It is estimated that the domestic garbage produced per day in Mumbai is of size of an eight stored building complex. The quality of air in the surroundings of the cities is so poor that it is estimated about two million children under five die each year from respiratory infections Falling in line with the general situation, we find certain public places like hospitals, vegetable, fish and other market places, Railway stations, Bus stands, Parks and Cinema halls are maintained in an unhygienic manner contributing to the spread of infectious diseases. It is wonder how the elite like doctors and higher officials who work in such public places and spend major part of their day time in these places are callous to the environment. Particularly, hospitals generate an enormous amount of dangerous waste. The amount of solid waste generated by hospitals has been increasing rapidly in developing countries like India and its management can no longer be ignored. Increasing concern for community health standards and pollution control requirements demand that the huge mass of infectious waste be rendered as harmless as possible before it is disposed. Against this background, an attempt is made in this paper to discuss the problem of disposal of wastes in Indian hospitals and various legislations relating to environmental protection in general and Bio-medical waste (Management and Handling) rules,1998 (amended in 2000) based on the environmental (protection)Act, 1986 in particular. This Paper also suggests a few measures for the effective management of waste disposal.

Keywords: *Environment, Biomedical wastage, Health*

"Pollution is nothing but the resources we are not harvesting. We allow them to be dispersed because we've been ignorant of their value."

– R. Buckminster Fuller.

INTRODUCTION

Serious questions are being raised about economic and environmental effects of Bio-medical waste (BMW) in developing countries in recent times. BMW although constitutes a small portion of the total municipal waste generated, needs special handling and treatment as it is highly infectious and can pose a serious threat to human health if not managed in a scientific manner. In fact, the problem of BMW is more a question of its hazardous nature rather than the quantity.[1] With this backdrop, the present study considers the existing trends of BMW management in India. With the expansion of tourism in tandem with IT/BT boom, the administration is struggling to provide improved infrastructure while trying to cope with its massive unplanned development. One such supportive infrastructure that needs a thorough streamlining is the management of BMW, an offshoot of a boom, in the number of medical clinics. Although several initiatives have been undertaken for managing hospital waste in the city, there are still exist several missing links that have serious implications on human health and ecology.[2]

Almost all the countries around the world are directing their efforts towards a proper disposal of BMW. The management of BMW, due to the use of disposable items, is one of the major problems faced by the developed countries. In the United States, the hospitals discard more than two million tons of waste annually and are the third largest source of medical waste. In the developing countries, the waste gets dumped in open areas where rag pickers and beggars involve in search of goods; risk their lives by contacting hazardous diseases. Many hospitals in the developed countries are recycling or donating the scraps to the developing countries, for instance, at least 50% of the US hospitals send their single-use items to the re-processors who in turn resell them at relatively low prices after sterilizing them.[3]

In the developing world, the problems associated with medical waste are linked to the lack of funding and national regulations for the sanitary disposal of waste. A UNDP survey says that most of the African countries lack proper sanitary landfills and legal policies for medical waste management. The lack of sanitary landfills has led to the use of incinerators to large extent and it is reported that more than 1000 incinerators are found in Africa most of which are not operating or under operating. The disposal

1 42 Cal. App. 4th 718 (1996).

2 Downloaded from http://www.tsijournals.com/abstract/biomedical-waste-management-3107.html retrieved on 26.10.2017 at 1.03 am.

3 Ale. livs (2013) World Health Organization. WHO Handbook on Health Care Waste Management.

of infectious sharps is one of the challenging risks faced by African healthcare facilities. As the safety boxes used for the disposal of sharps are very expensive, there is a limit to the use of these boxes. A study by the UNDP shows that all the countries have never disposed of the sharp waste at the dump sites and that a very few hospitals have separate pits for the disposal of sharp waste.[4]

MEANING

According to Biomedical Waste (Management and Handling) Rules, 1998 of India "Any waste which is generated during the diagnosis, treatment or immunization of human beings or animals or in research activities pertaining thereto or in the production or testing of biologicals.[5]

The Government of India (notification, 1998) specifies that Hospital Waste Management is a part of hospital hygiene and maintenance activities. This involves management of range of activities, which are mainly engineering functions, such as collection, transportation, operation or treatment of processing systems, and disposal of wastes.[6]

World Health Organization states that 85% of hospital wastes are actually non-hazardous, whereas 10% are infectious and 5% are non-infectious but they are included in hazardous wastes. About 15% to 35% of Hospital waste is regulated as infectious waste. This range is dependent on the total amount of waste generated (Glenn and Garwal, 1999).

TYPES OF BIO-MEDICAL WASTE

Bio-medical waste means "any solid and/or liquid waste including its container and any intermediate product, which is generated during the diagnosis, treatment or immunization of human beings or animals or research activities pertaining thereto or in the production or testing of biological or in health camps.[7]

---

4 Downloaded from http://www.downtoearth.org.in/news/new-rules-for-biomedical-waste-management-released-53330, retrieved on 26.10.2017 at 1.11 am.

5 *Ibid.*

6 Downloaded from http://vikaspedia.in/energy/environment/waste-management/bio-medical-waste-management/what-is-bio-medical-waste, retrieved on 26.10.2017 at 1.13 am.

7 *Ibid.*

Biomedical waste poses hazard due to two principal reasons – the first is infectivity and other toxicity.[8]

Bio Medical waste consists of

- Human anatomical waste like tissues, organs and body parts
- Animal wastes generated during research from veterinary hospitals
- Microbiology and biotechnology wastes
- Waste sharps like hypodermic needles, syringes, scalpels and broken glass
- Discarded medicines and cytotoxic drugs
- Soiled waste such as dressing, bandages, plaster casts, material contaminated with blood, tubes and catheters
- Liquid waste from any of the infected areas
- Incineration ash and other chemical wastes[9]

The biomedical waste (BMW) management requires its categorisation as a first step. The BMW Rules classify the BMW into following categories.

Categories of Biomedical Waste Schedule – I			
Category	**Type of waste**	**Type of bag or container to be used**	**Treatment and disposal option**
Yellow	Human tissues, organs, body parts and foetus below the viability period (as per the Medical Termination of Pregnancy Act 1971, amended from time to time).	Yellow coloured non-chlorinated plastic bags	Incineration or Plasma Pyrolysis or deep burial *
	Animal Anatomical Waste: Experimental animal carcasses, body parts, organs, tissues, including the waste generated from animals used in experiments or testing in veterinary hospitals or colleges or animal houses.		

Contd...

8 *Ibid.*

9 *Ibid.*

	Soiled Waste: Items contaminated with blood, body fluids like dressings, plaster casts, cotton swabs and bags containing residual or discarded blood and blood components.		Incineration or Plasma Pyrolysis or deep burial. In absence of above facilities, autoclaving or micro-waving/ hydroclaving followed by shredding or mutilation or combination of sterilization and shredding. Treated waste to be sent for energy recovery.
	Expired or Discarded Medicines: Pharmaceutical waste like antibiotics, cytotoxic drugs including all items contaminated with cytotoxic drugs along with glass or plastic ampoules, vials etc.	Yellow coloured non-chlorinated plastic bags or containers	Expired cytotoxic drugs and items contaminated with cytotoxic drugs to be returned back to the manufacturer or supplier for incineration at temperature >1200 0 C or to common bio - medical waste treatment facility or hazardous waste treatment, storage and disposal facility for incineration at >1200 0 C Or Encapsulation or Plasma Pyrolysis at >1200 0 C All other discarded medicines shall be either sent back to manufacturer or disposed by incineration.
	Chemical Waste: Chemicals used in production of biological and used or discarded disinfectants.	Yellow coloured containers or non-chlorinated plastic bags	Disposed of by incineration or Plasma Pyrolysis or Encapsulation in hazardous waste treatment, storage and disposal facility.
	Chemical Liquid Waste: Liquid waste generated due to use of chemicals in production of biological and used or discarded disinfectants, Silver X - ray film developing liquid, discarded Formalin, infected secretions, aspirated body fluids , liquid from laboratories an d floor washings, cleaning, house - keeping and disinfecting activities etc.	Separate collection system leading to effluent treatment system	After resource recovery, the chemical liquid waste shall be pre - treated before mixing with other wastewater. The combined discharge shall conform to the discharge norms given in Schedule - III.

Contd...

	Discarded linen, mattresses, beddings contaminated with blood or body fluid.	Non-chlorinated yellow plastic bags or suitable packing material	Non - chlorinated chemical disinfection followed by incineration or Plasma Pyrolysis or for energy recovery. In absence of above facilities, shredding or mutilation or combination of sterilization and shredding. Treated waste to be sent for energy recovery or incineration or Plasma Pyrolysis.
	Microbiology, Biotechnology and other clinical laboratory waste: Blood bags, Laboratory cultures, stocks or specimens of micro - organisms, live or attenuated vaccines, human and animal cell cultures used in research, industrial laboratories, production of biological, residual toxins, dishes and devices used for cultures.	Autoclave safe plastic bags or containers	Pre - treat to sterilize with non - chlorinated chemicals on - site as per National AIDS Control Organisation or World Health Organisation guidelines thereafter for Incineration.
Red	Contaminated Waste (Recyclable) Wastes generated from disposable items such as tubing, bottles, intravenous tubes and sets, catheters, urine bags, syringes (without needles and fixed needle syringes) and vaccutainers with their needles cut) and gloves.	Red coloured non-chlorinated plastic bags or containers	Autoclaving or micro - waving/ hydroclaving followed by shredding or mutilation or combination of sterilization and shredding. Treated waste to be sent to registered or authorized recyclers or for energy recovery or plastics to diesel or fuel oil or for road making, whichever is possible. Plastic waste should not be sent to landfill sites.
White (Translucent)	**Waste sharps including Metals:** Needles, syringes with fixed needles, needles from needle tip cutter or burner, scalpels, blades, or any other contaminated sharp object that may cause puncture and cuts. This includes both used, discarded and contaminated metal sharps	Puncture proof, Leak proof, tamper proof containers	Autoclaving or Dry Heat Sterilization followed by shredding or mutilation or encapsulation in metal container or cement concrete; combination of shredding cum autoclaving; and sent for final disposal to iron foundries (having consent to operate from the State Pollution Control Board s or Pollution Control Committee s) or sanitary landfill or designated concrete waste sharp pit.

Contd...

Blue	**Glassware:** Broken or discarded and contaminated glass including medicine vials and ampoules except those contaminated with cytotoxic wastes	Cardboard boxes with blue coloured marking	Disinfection (by soaking the washed glass waste after cleaning with detergent and Sodium Hypochlorite treatment) or through autoclaving or microwaving or hydroclaving and then sent for recycling.
	Metallic Body Implants		

Disposal by deep burial is permitted only in rural or remote areas where there is no access to common bio - medical waste treatment facility. This will be carried out with prior approval from the prescribed authority and as per the Standards specified in Schedule - III. The deep burial facility shall be located as per the provisions and guidelines issued by Central Pollution Control Board from time to time.

PROCESS OF BIOMEDICAL WASTE MANAGEMENT

Handling, segregation, mutilation, disinfection, storage, transportation and final disposal are vital steps for safe and scientific management of bio-medical waste in any establishment. There are various categories of Biomedical Wastes. They must carefully segregated, disinfected and disposed off. [10]

Segregation

Segregation refers to the basic separation of different categories of waste generated at source and thereby reducing the risks as well as cost of handling and disposal. Segregation is the most crucial step in bio-medical waste management. Effective segregation alone can ensure effective bio-medical waste management.[11]

How does segregation help?

- Segregation reduces the amount of waste needs special handling and treatment
- Effective segregation process prevents the mixture of medical waste like sharps with the general municipal waste.

10 *Ibid.*
11 *Ibid.*

- Prevents illegally reuse of certain components of medical waste like used syringes, needles and other plastics.
- Provides an opportunity for recycling certain components of medical waste like plastics after proper and thorough disinfection.
- Recycled plastic material can be used for non-food grade applications.
- Of the general waste, the biodegradable waste can be composted within the hospital premises and can be used for gardening purposes.
- Recycling is a good environmental practice, which can also double as a revenue generating activity.
- Reduces the cost of treatment and disposal (80 per cent of a hospital's waste is general waste, which does not require special treatment, provided it is not contaminated with other infectious waste)

Proper Labelling of Bins[12]

The bins and bags should carry the biohazard symbol indicating the nature of waste to the patients and public.

Collection[13]

The collection of biomedical waste involves use of different types of container from various sources of biomedical wastes like Operation Theatre, laboratory, wards, kitchen, corridor etc. The containers/ bins should be placed in such a way that 100 % collection is achieved. Sharps must always be kept in puncture-proof containers to avoid injuries and infection to the workers handling them.

Storage[14]

Once collection occurs then biomedical waste is stored in a proper place. Segregated wastes of different categories need to be collected in

---

12 *Ibid.*

13 *Ibid.*

14 *Ibid.*

identifiable containers. The duration of storage should not exceed for 8-10 hrs in big hospitals (more than 250 bedded) and 24 hrs in nursing homes. Each container may be clearly labelled to show the ward or room where it is kept. The reason for this labelling is that it may be necessary to trace the waste back to its source. Besides this, storage area should be marked with a caution sign.

Transportation[15]

The waste should be transported for treatment either in trolleys or in covered wheelbarrow. Manual loading should be avoided as far as for as possible. The bags / Container containing BMWs should be tied/ lidded before transportation. Before transporting the bag containing BMWs, it should be accompanied with a signed document by Nurse/ Doctor mentioning date, shift, quantity and destination.

Special vehicles must be used so as to prevent access to, and direct contact with, the waste by the transportation operators, the scavengers and the public. The transport containers should be properly enclosed. The effects of traffic accidents should be considered in the design, and the driver must be trained in the procedures he must follow in case of an accidental spillage. It should also be possible to wash the interior of the containers thoroughly.

Personnel Safety Devices[16]

The use of protective gears should be made mandatory for all the personnel handling waste.

Gloves: Heavy-duty rubber gloves should be used for waste handling by the waste retrievers. This should be bright yellow in colour. After handling the waste, the gloves should be washed twice. The gloves should be washed after every use with carbolic soap and a disinfectant. The size should fit the operator.[17]

15 *Ibid.*
16 *Ibid.*
17 *Ibid.*

Aprons, gowns, suits or other apparels: Apparel is worn to prevent contamination of clothing and protect skin. It could be made of cloth or impermeable material such as plastic. People working in incinerator chambers should have gowns or suits made of non-inflammable material.

Masks: Various types of masks, goggles, and face shields are worn alone or in combination, to provide a protective barrier. It is mandatory for personnel working in the incinerator chamber to wear a mask covering both nose and mouth, preferably a gas mask with filters.[18]

Boots: Leg coverings, boots or shoe-covers provide greater protection to the skin when splashes or large quantities of infected waste have to be handled. The boots should be rubber-soled and anti-skid type. They should cover the leg up to the ankle.[19]

Cleaning Devices[20]

Brooms: The broom shall be a minimum of 1.2 m long, such that the worker need not stoop to sweep. The diameter of the broom should be convenient to handle. The brush of the broom shall be soft or hard depending on the type of flooring.

Dustpans: The dustpans should be used to collect the dust from the sweeping operations. They may be either of plastic or enamelled metal. They should be free of ribs and should have smooth contours, to prevent dust from sticking to the surface. They should be washed with disinfectants and dried before every use.

Mops: Mops with long handles must be used for swabbing the floor. They shall be of either the cloth or the rubber variety. The mop has to be replaced depending on the wear and tear. The mechanical-screw type of mop is convenient for squeezing out the water.

Vacuum cleaners: Domestic vacuum cleaners or industrial vacuum cleaners can be used depending on the size of the rooms.

---

18 *Ibid.*

19 *Ibid.*

20 *Ibid.*

Storage Devices

Dustbins: It is very important to assess the quantity of waste generated at each point. Dustbins should be of such capacity that they do not overflow between each cycle of waste collection. Dustbins should be cleaned after every cycle of clearance of waste with disinfectants. Dustbins can be lined with plastic bags, which are chlorine-free, and colour coded as per the law.

Handling Devices

Trolleys: The use of trolleys will facilitate the removal of infectious waste at the source itself, instead of adding a new category of waste.

Wheelbarrows: Wheelbarrows are used to transfer the waste from the point source to the collection centres. There are two types of wheelbarrow – covered and open. Wheelbarrows are made of steel and provided with two wheels and a handle. Care should be taken not to directly dump waste into it. Only packed waste (in plastic bags) should be carried. Care should also be taken not to allow liquid waste from spilling into the wheelbarrow, as it will corrode. These are ideal for transferring debris within the institution. Wheelbarrows also come in various sizes depending on the utility.

Chutes: Chutes are vertical conduits provided for easy transportation of refuse vertically in case of institutions with more than two floors. Chutes should be fabricated from stainless steel. It should have a self-closing lid. These chutes should be fumigated everyday with formaldehyde vapours. The contaminated linen (contaminated with blood and or other body fluids) from each floor should be bundled in soiled linen or in plastic bags before ejecting into the chute.

Alternately, elevators with mechanical winches or electrical winches can be provided to bring down waste containers from each floor. Chutes are necessary to avoid horizontal transport of waste thereby minimizing the routing of the waste within the premises and hence reducing the risk of secondary contamination.

BIO-MEDICAL WASTE (MANAGEMENT AND HANDLING) RULES, 1998 — IMPLEMENTATION[21]

With a view to control the indiscriminate disposal of hospital waste/bio-medical waste, the Ministry of Environment and Forest, Govt. of India has issued a notification on Bio-medical Waste Management under the Environment (Protection) Act. Govt. of NCT of Delhi in its notification dated 6th July, 1999 has authorized Delhi Pollution Control Committee (DPCC) for the purpose of granting authorization for collection, reception, storage, treatment and disposal of bio-medical waste to implement the Bio-medical Waste Management Rules, 1998. Govt. of NCT of Delhi has also constituted advisory committee, appellate authority in exercise of powers conferred under Bio-medical rules.

The Ministry of Environment and Forests' new Biomedical Waste Management Rules 2016 "will change the way the country used to manage biomedical waste" and "make a big difference to the Clean India Mission," Union Minister of State for Environment, Forests and Climate Change, Prakash Javadekar, said, while releasing the rules recently.[22]

"Under the new regime, coverage has increased and (it) also provides for pre-treatment of lab waste, blood samples, etc. It mandates bar code system for proper control. It has simplified categorisation and authorization," Javadekar added.[23]

To understand how the new rules are an improvement over the draft 2011 rules, we must know the broad system that deals with biomedical waste. Health care facilities (HCFs) must segregate biomedical waste (the wastes involved in diagnosis, treatment and immunisation such as human and animal anatomical waste, treatment apparatus such as needles and syringes and cytotoxic drugs) at the individual level in colored bags—yellow, red, blue/white and black according to the category of the biomedical waste. They can store this waste for up to 48 hours after which they either treat it in-situ or a worker from a common biomedical waste treatment facility (CBMWF) comes to collect it. The CMBWF then treats the waste

21 *Ibid.*

22 *Ibid.*

23 The Hindu(2009) Waste Management Cells at Government Hospitals, Nov. 22.

according to the colour of the bag. Different colours call for different types of treatments—incineration, deep burial, autoclaving, shredding, chemical treatment, disposal in a landfill, etc.[24]

The first distinction between the new rules and those prescribed in 2011 is their range of application. While in 2011, the 1998 rules were amended to include all persons who generate, collect, receive, store and transport biomedical waste, the 2016 rules bring more clarity by specifying that vaccination camps, blood donation camps, surgical camps and all other HCFs have been included.[25]

The second distinction comes in the segregation, packaging, transport and storage of biomedical waste in an HCF. The 2011 draft demarcated eight categories of biomedical waste (down from ten categories in the 1998 notification). The 2016 notification further brings down the number of categories to four. "Reduction in categories does not mean that a particular kind of biomedical waste is not being adhered to. What it means is that all types of wastes have been compiled in four categories for ease of segregation at a healthcare facility," Tripti Arora, programme manager at the non-profit Toxics Link, said.[26]

The new rules also explicitly lay down the duties of an HCF in adhering to the segregation, packaging and transport rules for the four different categories. The HCF is now responsible for pre-treatment of laboratory and microbiological waste, blood samples and blood bags through disinfection/sterilization on-site in the manner prescribed by the World Health Organization (WHO) or National Aids Control Organization (NACO), regardless of whether final treatment and disposal happens on-site or at a common biomedical waste treatment facility. Use of chlorinated plastic bags, gloves and blood bags is to be phased out by the HCF within two years to eliminate emission of dioxins and furans from burning of such wastes. The new rules also call for a bar code system for bags/containers containing biomedical waste and immunization of health workers upon their induction and after every one year interval.[27]

24 *Ibid.*

25 *Ibid.*

26 *Ibid.*

27 *Ibid.*

"The bar code system can be used to track and identify bags better. But, it will be effective only when the onus for using barcodes is on CBMWFs. That again is possible only if CMBWFs provide bags to hospitals. This is not happening right now," Prem Agrawal of the National Solid Waste Association of India (NSWAI), who also works as an independent environment researcher, said.

The new rules also specify the duties of the operator of the CBMWFs: In addition to the duties of the occupier of an HCF, the operator of a CMBWF must ensure timely collection of biomedical waste from HCFs and assist them in training.[28]

Another distinction comes in the treatment and disposal of biomedical waste. According to the 2011 draft, every HCF shall set requisite bio-medical waste treatment facilities like incinerator, autoclave, microwave system for the treatment of waste, or, ensure requisite treatment at a common biomedical waste treatment facility. These rules do not state where an on-site treatment facility is necessary and where dependence on a CMBWF is justified. It also does not mention who will provide land for the setup of a CBMWF. The 2016 rules make the guideline more specific: The Department dealing with allocation of land in the state government shall provide land for setting up a common biomedical waste treatment and disposal facility but no occupier of an HCF shall establish an on-site treatment and disposal facility if a CBMWF is available within 75 km.[29]

The new rules also have stricter standards of emission from incinerators: In 2011, the acceptable SPM emission was 150 mg/Nm^3 at 12 per cent Carbon dioxide correction. This has been reduced to 50 mg/Nm^3 in the new rules. Similarly, the standard retention time in the secondary chamber has been increased from 1 second to 2 seconds. The secondary chamber in incineration is where the temperature is lowered to 100 or 200 degree Celsius. "This is done to reduce dioxins and furans as, at low temperature, incineration of biomedical waste leads to the production of carbon dioxide and water. Dioxins and furans are produced at temperatures greater than 600 degree Celsius," Arora said.[30]

28 *Ibid.*
29 *Ibid.*
30 *Ibid.*

Further, the new rules lay new criteria for authorization of a HCF. In 1998, the rules said that hospitals with more than 1,000 beds must obtain authorization from State Pollution Control Boards (SPCBs) while the 2011 draft expanded the ambit of institutions that require authorization to include all HCFs. The new rules make the procedure of getting an authorization very simple: Bedded hospitals will get automatic authorization and non-bedded hospitals will get a one-time authorization.

"Non-bedded hospitals are generally small scale clinics that do not keep a record of the waste generated and the number of beds. So, they cannot be charged on a per bed basis like bedded hospitals. That is why, they are authorized once and yearly/half-yearly/quarterly prices for treatment are fixed accordingly," Agrawal said.[31]

Another improvement in the new rules is in the monitoring sector. While the 2011 rules have no provision for a monitoring authority, the 2016 rules state that the MoEF will review HCFs once a year through state health secretaries, the SPCB and the CPCB. The SPCB, in its turn, will oversee implementation through district level monitoring committees that will report to the State advisory Committee or the SPCB. Moreover, according to the new rules, the advisory committee on biomedical waste management is now mandated to meet every six months.[32]

The total biomedical waste generated in the country is 484 Tonnes Per Day (TPD) from 1,68,869 HCF. 85 per cent of the hospital waste is non-hazardous, 15 per cent is infectious/hazardous. Mixing of hazardous results in to contamination and makes the entire waste hazardous. Hence, there is necessity to segregate and treat. Improper disposal increases risk of infection; encourages recycling of prohibited disposables and disposed drugs; and develops resistant microorganisms.[33]

Biomedical Waste Treatment and Disposal

Health care waste is a heterogeneous mixture, which is very difficult to manage as such. But the problem can be simplified and its dimension reduced considerably if a proper management system is planned.[34]

---

31 *Ibid.*

32 *Ibid.*

33 *Ibid.*

34 *Ibid.*

Incineration Technology

This is a high temperature thermal process employing combustion of the waste under controlled condition for converting them into inert material and gases. Incinerators can be oil fired or electrically powered or a combination thereof. Broadly, three types of incinerators are used for hospital waste: multiple hearth type, rotary kiln and controlled air types. All the types can have primary and secondary combustion chambers to ensure optimal combustion. These are refractory lined.[35]

Non-Incineration Technology

Non-incineration treatment includes four basic processes: thermal, chemical, irradiative, and biological. The majority of non-incineration technologies employ the thermal and chemical processes. The main purpose of the treatment technology is to decontaminate waste by destroying pathogens. Facilities should make certain that the technology could meet state criteria for disinfection. [36]

Autoclaving

The autoclave operates on the principle of the standard pressure cooker. The process involves using steam at high temperatures. The steam generated at high temperature penetrates waste material and kills all the micro organism. These are also of three types: Gravity type, Pre-vacuum type and Retort type.

In the first type (Gravity type), air is evacuated with the help of gravity alone. The system operates with temperature of 121 deg. C. and steam pressure of15 psi. for 60-90 minutes. Vacuum pumps are used to evacuate air from the Pre vacuum autoclave system so that the time cycle is reduced to 30-60 minutes. It operates at about 132 deg. C. Retort type autoclaves are designed much higher steam temperature and pressure. Autoclave treatment has been recommended for microbiology and biotechnology waste, waste sharps, soiled and solid wastes. This technology renders certain categories (mentioned in the rules) of bio-medical waste innocuous and unrecognizable so that the treated residue can be land filled.[37]

---

35 *Ibid.*

36 *Ibid.*

37 *Ibid.*

Microwave Irradiation

The microwave is based on the principle of generation of high frequency waves. These waves cause the particles within the waste material to vibrate, generating heat. This heat generated from within kills all pathogens.

Chemical Methods

1 % hypochlorite solution can be used for chemical disinfection[38]

Plasma Pyrolysis

Plasma pyrolysis is a state-of-the-art technology for safe disposal of medical waste. It is an environment-friendly technology, which converts organic waste into commercially useful by-products. The intense heat generated by the plasma enables it to dispose all types of waste including municipal solid waste, biomedical waste and hazardous waste in a safe and reliable manner. Medical waste is pyrolysed into CO, H2, and hydrocarbons when it comes in contact with the plasma-arc. These gases are burned and produce a high temperature (around 1200°C).[39]

BIOMEDICAL WASTE MANAGEMENT RULES

Safe disposal of biomedical waste is now a legal requirement in India. The Biomedical Waste Management & Handling) Rules, 1998 came into force on 1998. In accordance with these rules, it is the duty of every "occupier" i.e. a person who has the control over the institution or its premises, to take all steps to ensure that waste generated is handled without any adverse effect to human health and environment. It consists of six schedules.[40]

RECOMMENDATIONS

1. For the use of incinerator Training should be given to some number of persons from staff.
2. Specific fund should be allocated for the use of incinerator.

---

38 *Ibid.*

39 *Ibid.*

40 *Ibid.*

3. Every hospital should have special boxes to use as dustbin for bio-medical waste.
4. Bio-medical waste should not be mixed with other waste of Municipal Corporation.
5. Private hospitals should also be allowed to use incinerator, which is installed, in govt. hospital. For this purpose a specific fee can be charged from private hospitals.
6. Special vehicle i.e. bio-medical waste vehicle should be started to collect waste from private hospitals and private medical clinics and carry it up to the main incinerator.
7. As provided by bio-medical waste rules, the whole of the waste should be fragmented into colours due to their hazardous nature.
8. Bio-medical waste Management Board can be established in each District.
9. Either judicial powers should be given to the management board or special court should be established in the matters of environment pollution for imposing fines and awarding damages etc.
10. Housekeeping staff wear protective devices such as gloves, face masks, gowned, while handling the waste.
11. There is biomedical waste label on waste carry bags and waste carry trolley and also poster has put on the wall adjacent to the bins (waste) giving details about the type of waste that has to dispose in the baggage as per biomedical waste management rule. Carry bags also have the biohazard symbol on them.

CONCLUSION

Medical wastes should be classified according to their source, typology and risk factors associated with their handling, storage and ultimate disposal. The segregation of waste at source is the key step and reduction, reuse and recycling should be considered in proper perspectives. We need to consider innovative and radical measures to clean up the distressing picture of lack of civic concern on the part of hospitals and slackness in government implementation of bare minimum of rules, as waste generation particularly biomedical waste imposes increasing direct and indirect costs on society. The challenge before us, therefore, is to scientifically manage growing quantities of biomedical waste that go beyond past practices. If we want to protect our environment and health of community we must sensitize ourselves to this important issue not only in the interest of health managers but also in the interest of community.

REFERENCES

1. Ale. Livs (2013)World Health Organization. WHO Handbook on Health Care Waste Management.
2. Amitabh Srivastava(2011) Rich Trash Pickings.
3. Angad Abhishek (2012) Unlicensed clinics going scot free, Citizen Matters. 18th June.
4. Bekir Onursal, Health Care Waste Management in India. The world Bank (2003)
5. Biswas PS (2013) Audit: MPCB has failed to address veterinary bio-medical waste issue, Pune August 22.
6. CEET: Biomedical Waste Management-Burgeoning issue (2008).
7. Chitra VR (2012) Biomedical waste not Disposed Properly at Mavallipura. Bangalore July 2.
8. DhavalKulkarni (2013) PAC raises a stink over dumping grounds, DNA, 10th August.
9. Dr. Saurabh Sikka, Biomedical Waste in Indian Context.
10. Gaur A(1995) Disposal and Recycling of Waste, National seminar on hospital architecture, Planning and Engineering. IV: 46-50.
11. Glenn, Mc.R & Garwal, R. Clinical waste in Developing Countries. An analysis with a Case Study of India, and a Critique of the Basle TWG Guidelines (1999)
12. Govt. of India, Ministry of Environment and Forests Gazette notification No 460 dated July 27, New Delhi: 1998: 10-20.
13. Gravers PD. Management of Hospital Wastes- An overview. Proceedings of National workshop on Management of Hospital Waste,(1998).

14. Hem Chandra, Hospital Waste an Environmental Hazard and Its Management, (1999).
15. Kela M, Nazareth S, Agarwal R (1997) Implementing hospital waste management; a guide for health care facilities, Shrishti 24-31.
16. Krishnan S (1997) Integrated Waste Management Plan, Hospital waste management plan, strategies for implementation.CEE South:10
17. Madhu Kumar Suwarna, Ramesh G (2012) International Journal of Basic Medical Science.Vol 3: 115.
18. Manasi S (2013) Challenges in Biomedical Waste management in Cities- A Ward level study of Bangalore 1-19.
19. Manasi S (2014) Biomedical Waste Management. 1-19.
20. Mandal S. K. and Dutta J. , Integrated Bio-Medical Waste Management Plan for Patna City, Institute of Town Planners, India Journal 6-2: 01-25 (2009).
21. Ministry of Environment and Forests (2011) Environment Management and Policy Research Institute, State of Karnataka Report.
22. Nirmala MN (2009) The Times of India - Medical tourism, 28 March.
23. Pruthvish S, Gopinath D, Jayachandra Rao M, Girish N, Bineesha P, et al.(1997) Health care waste disposal - an exploration, Department of Community Medicine, M S Ramaiah Medical College.1-11.
24. Ramky Enviro Engineers Ltd (2004) Waste Management.1-7.
25. RiyanRamanath V (2013) Bio-waste litters Bhubaneswar as hospitals flout norms, TNN, 7 August.
26. Shakil S(2013) National Green Tribunal says nine Delhi hospitals flout bio-medical waste disposal rules, New Delhi, July 25.
27. Shalini Sharma and S.V.S.Chauhan, Assessment of bio-medical waste management in three apex Government hospitals of Agra, Journal of Environmental Biology, 29(2), p. p 159-162 (2008).
28. Singh V. P., Biswas G., and Sharma, J. J., Biomedical Waste Management – An Emerging Concern in Indian Hospitals Indian, Journal of Forensic Medicine & Toxicology, Vol. 1, No. 1. (2007-12).
29. Sneha Mankikar (2013) Emerging Business Opportunities & Challenges.1-15.

30. Surjit S. Katoch Biomedical Waste Classification and Prevailing Management Strategies, Proceedings of the International Conference on Sustainable Solid Waste Management, p. p.169-175 (2007).
31. The Bio Medical Waste (Management and Handling) Rules, (1998).
32. The Hindu(2009) Waste Management Cells at Government Hospitals, Nov 22.
33. Thornton J., Tally MC, Orris P., Wentreg J. Hospitals and plastics Dioxin prevention and Medical Waste Incineration; Public Health Reports. 1996; 1:299- 313.
34. Times News Network (2013) Goa state pollution control board finds AlodnaPHC polluting, 22 August.
35. Yamini Ugender (2000) Biomedical waste Definition.

Abortion and Indian Law

Sridip S. Nambiar

Abstract

This chapter surveys the Indian law governing abortion. Several issues have been dragged to the court, especially those relating to length of pregnancy. Indian law is on the brink of change from the 20 weeks ceiling. It is suggested that owing to advancements in medical technology, the ceiling should be revised immediately to enable better access to abortion services. The chapter also argues that Supreme Court decision in Suchita Srivastava may not have been based on sound reasoning.

INTRODUCTION

Abortion is the deliberate ending of pregnancy before childbirth. It has been the subject of debates for a long time. Religions have had strong opinions on abortion. The Roman Catholic view is that abortion is 'gravely contrary to the moral law'.[1] This view is based on the belief that human life begins when the woman's egg is fertilized by a male sperm. Causing or having abortion led to excommunication.[2] Islam considers abortion as *haram* (forbidden) if it is done because the parents think they will not be able to provide for the child. Generally, Islam allows choosing the lesser of two evils which may mean that it permits abortion to save the life of the mother.[3] Classical Hindu texts say that a woman who aborts will lose her caste.[4] Ironically, in India there is a practice of carrying out abortions because of the preference for male children.

There are two prominent sets of opinions on the moral nature of abortion - one group says that foetus is a person from the point of conception and

1 http://www.bbc.co.uk/religion/religions/christianity/christianethics/abortion_1.shtml, last accessed on 21.10.2017, 10 PM.

2 Code of Canon Law (1983).

3 http://www.bbc.co.uk/religion/religions/islam/islamethics/abortion_1.shtml , last accessed on 21.10.2017, 10 PM

4 http://www.bbc.co.uk/religion/religions/hinduism/hinduethics/abortion_1.shtml, last accessed on 21.10.2017, 10 PM

abortion is nothing but murder. These pro-life advocates argue that 'life' should be protected as soon as it begins i.e. after conception. They do not support abortion in any circumstance. 'Sanctity of life' is paramount. Religious groups and some natural law scholars are part of this group. Some countries even uphold a doctor's decision not to participate in abortion procedures based on a conscientious objection.[5]However, courts have clarified that foetus has no rights until it is born.[6] In India, explanation 2 to section 299, Indian Penal Code provides that, only after any part of a child is out of the mother's womb, it will be considered as a person, whether it is breathing or not.

On the other hand, the pro-choice camp supports the right of a woman to control her body including the right to decide what happens to the foetus. Some argue that even if the foetus has a right to life, the woman's right to autonomy overrides it. Autonomy of a woman is linked to her reproductive choices. Various human rights instruments provide for specific reproductive rights. A woman has a right to privacy which includes right to timing and spacing of children. In the classic case of *Roe* v. *Wade,* the US Supreme Court struck down a law that criminalized abortion because it violates a woman's constitutional right to privacy. It was held that right to privacy includes right to take abortion decisions, though it is not to be considered as an absolute right.[7]It placed the point of regulation "at approximately the end of first trimester of pregnancy". Till that point, a woman's access to abortion services could not be limited.

Abortion is also linked to family planning and population control regimes. Many developing countries encourage contraceptives, sterilization and limited abortion for containing the population growth.

The middle path seems to be in accepting that a pregnant woman does have a right to autonomy, but as the pregnancy progresses, decisions cannot be wholly left to the woman alone. This is why an absolute right is not given to any woman anywhere to carry out abortion.[8] Legal systems need to balance the reproductive rights of a woman and that of an unborn

5 UK Abortion Act, 1967, Section 4(1).

6 *Attorney General's Reference*, [1997] 3 All ER 936.

7 410 U.S. 113, 93 S. Ct. 705, 35 L. Ed. 2d 147, 1973 U.S.

8 There are countries which punish miscarriage even if it is not the woman's fault.

child. It is also a fact that unsafe abortions contribute to 8% of the total maternal deaths in India.[9] Thus, law has to intervene in abortion decisions to protect the interests of the woman or foetus. This chapter surveys the law applicable in abortion cases and issues arising from the application of laws.

INDIAN LAW

In India, abortion has been regulated through the Medical Termination of Pregnancy Act. If abortion is not carried out as provided under the Act, it will be a criminal offence in India. Sections 312 to 316 of the Indian Penal Code, 1860 defines the various offences.

Section	Offence	Punishment
312	Causing miscarriage	Maximum 3 years imprisonment or 7 years (in case of advanced stage of pregnancy)
313	Causing miscarriage without women's consent	Imprisonment for life or imprisonment for maximum 10 years
314	Causing death by an act done with intent to cause miscarriage.	Imprisonment for life (if it is without women's consent) or imprisonment for maximum 10 years
315	Act done to prevent the child from being born alive or cause it to die after birth	Imprisonment for maximum 10 years or fine or both
316	Causing death of an unborn child, when in an advanced stage of pregnancy, by an act amounting to culpable homicide.	Imprisonment for maximum ten years and fine.

Exception to s.312 makes it clear that the woman herself can be an accused person under that section. Causing miscarriage without the woman's consent is a more serious offence. Advanced stage of pregnancy is referred to that stage when a woman can experience the motion of the foetus. A person who attempts or abets the causing of miscarriage will be punished whether miscarriage happens or not.[10]Importantly, section 312 provides a defence for a doctor. He will not be guilty if the act was done

9 http://www.thehindu.com/news/national/the-hindu-explains-medical-termination-of-pregnancy-amendment-bill-2014/article18474057.ece

10 Section 107 of Indian Penal Code defines abetment. Section 511, IPC generally criminalizes attempts.

in good faith for the purpose of saving the woman's life (therapeutic). Section 52 of the IPC defines an action in good faith as one which is done with due care and attention.

All therapeutic abortions were considered to be lawful. However, lack of regulations and the inability of penal provisions to prevent them led to an increase in illegal abortions. Complications during abortion led to increase in post-surgery deaths of women. This led the Parliament to enact the Medical Termination of Pregnancy Act, 1971.[11]

The MTP Act consists of eight sections and is considered to be an important social legislation. The object of the Act is to provide for termination of certain pregnancies by registered medical practitioners. A woman, therefore, cannot be said to have a right to abort. It is ultimately dependent on the opinion of the doctor.

FEATURES OF THE MTP ACT

(*i*) A doctor will not be liable for offences under the IPC if he is acting in accordance with the MTP Act. However, termination of pregnancy by a doctor who is not a registered medical practitioner is an offence.[12] However, no civil proceeding will lie against a doctor for damage caused due to anything done in good faith under the act.[13]

(*ii*) A pregnancy may be terminated by (i) one medical practitioner – if the pregnancy does not exceed twelve weeks and (ii) two or more medical practitioners – if the pregnancy exceeds twelve weeks but does not exceed twenty weeks. A medical practitioner is defined as a doctor who is registered with medical council and who has sufficient experience in gynecology or obstetrics.[14]

(*iii*) Doctor(s) can terminate pregnancy if he forms an opinion in good faith that[15]-

---

11 It came into force on 1 April, 1972 after the rules were framed. It is modeled on the British abortion law.

12 Section 5(2) of the MTP Act.

13 Section 8 of the MTP Act.

14 Section 2(d) of the MTP Act.

15 Section 3 of the MTP Act.

(*a*) It would pose a risk to life or of grave physical or mental injury to the woman.[16] Anguish caused by (i) pregnancy due to rape and (ii) failure of contraceptive methods used by a married woman, is presumed to be a grave mental injury. It is the opinion of the doctor(s) that counts.

(*b*) There is a substantial risk that, if the child is born, it may be seriously handicapped due to physical or mental abnormalities. There are debates on whether this ground devalues disability and perpetuates social stereotypes.[17]

(*iv*) The doctor may take into account actual or reasonably foreseeable scenarios to decide if there is a risk to the pregnant woman.

(*v*) Pregnancy cannot be terminated without the consent of the woman. If the woman is below the age of 18 years or mentally ill[18], the consent of the guardian[19] in writing is necessary.

(*vi*) Pregnancy may be terminated in a (a) hospital established or maintained by the government or (b) place approved for this purpose by the government or a district level committee.[20] The latter option is for improving access to health services in rural areas. Termination in any other place is an offence and the owner of that place will be prosecuted.[21]

(*vii*) The restrictions relating to conditions for termination or place of termination will not apply if a registered medical practitioner is of the opinion that it is immediately necessary to save the life of a woman.[22]

---

16 In UK, pregnancy can be terminated if it poses a risk to the mental health of any existing children of her family.

17 See Claudia Karr, *Beginning Medical Law*, Routledge (2015), p.117.

18 The word 'lunatic' was replaced by the word 'mentally ill' by amendment in 2002. A mentally ill person is defined as a person who is need of treatment of any mental disorder other than mental retardation.

19 A guardian is defined as a person having the care of the minor or mentally ill person. Section 2(a) of the Act.

20 Section 4 of the MTP Act

21 Section 5(2) of the MTP Act.

22 Section 5 of the MTP Act.

ISSUES

(*i*) Abortion is Illegal, Not Contraception

There is a difference between contraception and abortion. Contraception is barely regulated by law. In *R v. Secretary of State for Health*[23], a group that advocated for rights of unborn children challenged the legality of a law that permitted over-the-counter sale of emergency contraceptive pills (morning after pills). It was argued that sale without a doctor's prescription amounted to causing miscarriage as it does not meet the requirements of abortion law.[24] It was held that as miscarriage happens only in the case of an established pregnancy, it is not illegal to sell emergency contraceptives without prescription. In India, it has been used in the family welfare programs and is also available as an over-the-counter drug. The objective is to prevent unskilled abortions for unwanted pregnancies.[25]

(*ii*) Length of Pregnancy

There is an increased demand from various quarters to amend the Act to change the 20 week ceiling for abortion. Modern technologies have made the 20 week ceiling redundant. In UK, there is a 24 week limit.[26] In cases where genetic abnormalities are identified after twenty weeks, the woman will have no option but to continue with the pregnancy in India. The Draft Medical Termination of Pregnancy (Amendment) Bill, 2014[27] proposes a 24 week limit. The Draft Bill further proposes that rule relating to length of pregnancy should not apply where a 'substantial foetal abnormality' is detected. In UK, there is no time limit in case of serious handicap of the child. What can be considered as 'substantial' or serious abnormality is a question of fact.

In several cases, Supreme Court of India had to tackle post-20 weeks' termination requests. The decisions in these cases have been taken primarily on the basis of Medical Boards' reports. In *Meera Santhosh*

---

23 [2002] 2 FCR 193.

24 In this case, The Abortion Act 1967 in the UK.

25 http://dhs.kerala.gov.in/docs/pdf/fwiec5.pdf, last accessed on 21.10.2017, 10 PM.

26 Abortion Act, 1967.

27 Hereinafter 'Draft Bill'. It was drafted by the Ministry of Health and Family Welfare.

Pal v. *Union of India*[28], the foetus was without a skull and could not survive. The court considered the danger to the life of the woman and the inability of the foetus to survive extra-uterine life to allow termination of 24 weeks pregnancy. In *Mrs. X* v. *Union of India,*[29] termination of a 22 week pregnancy of a 22 year old was allowed because the foetus had a condition known as bilateral foetal agenesis (kidney failure). In *Sheetal Shankar Shelvi* v *Union of India,*[30] it was disallowed on medical grounds. In *Indu Devi* v. *State of Bihar*,[31] delay on the part of authorities and courts led to non-feasibility of abortion of a rape victim who contracted HIV/AIDS. The Supreme Court directed the State to pay compensation of ten lakhs rupees for the mental torture suffered by the woman.

(*iii*) Registered Health Providers(?)

Only allopathic practitioners are covered under the present MTP Act. The Draft Bill proposes inclusion of alternative medical professionals (Ayurveda or Siddha or Unani) or registered nurses/midwife.[32] This proposal is for increasing access to healthcare services.

(*iv*) Unwed pregnant woman

In India, only a married woman can seek to terminate pregnancy on the ground of failure of contraceptives. The Draft Bill proposes to extend it to pregnancies out of all kinds of relationships.

(*v*) Incompetent pregnant woman

In the case of a mentally ill person, as noted above, the guardian's consent is necessary. Even if there is consent, medical opinion may be against abortion. In such a situation and also when no guardian is available, it is the court which might be asked to take a decision. Courts usually apply the 'best interest' rule. A schizophrenic mother, who was 24 weeks pregnant,

28 2017 SCC Online SC 39.

29 Writ Petition(Civil) No. 81 of 2017.

30 Writ Petition(Civil) No. 174 of 2017.

31 2017 SCC Online SC 560.

32 In *Royal College of Nursing v. DHSS,* [1981] AC 800, it was held that registered medical practitioner includes a nurse.

was denied permission to abort based on the best interest rule.[33] But, in another case, a woman with bipolar disorder was permitted as she was able to articulate why she wanted abortion.[34]

The leading Indian authority on this issue is *Suchita Srivastava* v. *Chandigarh Administration.* A mentally retarded was allegedly raped in a government institution and became pregnant. The administration moved the courts for termination of pregnancy. The expert committee that was appointed observed that the woman had no general idea about pregnancy and it's effects. She, however, did not consent to termination. The Supreme Court of India held that termination without the consent of the 'mentally retarded' woman could not be permitted. The court drew a distinction between 'mentally ill' and 'mentally retarded' based on how these words are defined in disability statutes and stated that mentally retarded women have the right to make reproductive choices. The court further stated that termination of pregnancy would not be in the best interest of the woman.

This decision of the Supreme Court has to be reconsidered because the woman was not clearly able to understand the social implications of child-rearing without family support. Though an NGO undertook to take care of the woman and the child, it would have been ideal to terminate the pregnancy in the best interests of the woman. The only reason that the court has in it's favour is that the woman consented to continuation of pregnancy. But the interviews with the women clearly indicate that she had no idea about pregnancy generally. The High Court decision which permitted termination based on *parenspatriae* doctrine seems to be a more reasonable decision.

(*vi*) Rights of the Father

It was clarified in *Paton* v. *British Pregnancy Advisory Service Trustees* that father-to-be has no right to insist that the woman should continue with her pregnancy.[35] In India, the MTP Act does not provide for the father's role in abortion decisions.

33 *Re SS[An Adult: Medical Treatment],* [2002] 1 FLR 445.

34 *In Re SB(A Patient)(Capacity to Consent to Termination),* [2013]EWHC 1417.

35 [1978]2 All ER 98.

CONCLUSION

India has to wait till it passes the amendment bill that removes the 20 weeks ceiling to replace it with a 24 weeks one. Till then, women have to take recourse to courts for termination. Advancements in medical technology enable identification of foetal abnormalities even in advanced stages of pregnancy. It is unfair to restrict the abortion services when such techniques are available. If it will not affect the life or health of the mother in any way, law has to keep up with the new techniques that are available.

The Transplantation of Human Organs and Tissues: Law and Policy in India

*Dr. Radheshyam Prasad**

Abstract

Human organ transplantation is a boon to medical industry as it has helped in saving the lives of those who would have died otherwise. There is a great need for human organs for transplantation. In fact, the need far exceeds the supply of transplantable organs. At the same time, illegal organ trafficking has also developed rapidly in India. This is likely to exploit the poor for organ donation to rich people. This has now become a major problem because of rise in organ stealing rackets and corrupt health care system. To check such illegal organ transplantation, India passed legislation the Transplantation of Human Organs and Tissues Act, 1994(THOA)and Rules, 2014.There are two main objectives of the Act, first to regulate removal, storage and transplantation of human organs for therapeutic purposes and to prevent commercial dealings of organs and second is to promote organ donation. Now it is over two decades, THOA has neither able to curb commerce of organs nor helped in promotion of organ donation program to overcome the shortage of organ. These all aspect has been critically discussed in this chapter.

Keywords: *transplantation, trafficking, human organ, tissues, donation*

INTRODUCTION

We believe that the God is the creator of the world and human beings are the creation of the God. Life and death thus resume being into the hands of the God. This was the belief until now. Time has changed with the advancement of science, technology and in medical science. The humankind is progressing with rapid pace. Preservation and protecting the life has become the concern of medical fraternity. Life is a dynamic process. It starts from birth and ends with the death of the individuals. In between come different stages of life with different diseases and its problems. The body is the site of increasing disputes relating to the collection and distribution of human tissue and organs. An organ transplant is a surgical operation where a failing or damaged organ in the human body is replaced with the sound organ of another person. Organ transplantation done to replace the recipient's damaged organ with the working organ of the donor so that the recipient could function normally. Human organs that mainly donated are kidney, eyes, liver, heart, lung, pancreas, small bowel and sometimes skin along with the other things. There are mainly two types of organ donations:

1. **Live donation:** Where organ transplant takes place between the patient and his close friend or a family member
2. **Cadaveric donation:** Where a person pledges his organs for harvesting and donated after his death.

Organ transplantation has been part of medical science and technology for over six decades. The first case of successful organ (kidney) transplantation took place in 1954 in Peter Brigham Hospital, Boston where, a kidney of a young living person was removed and successfully implanted in his twin brother. Later on kidney transplantation, become a viable alternative to painful hemodialysis. In India, the first consistent successes in kidney transplantation was held in 1970 and liver transplantation on 15 November 1998. Since then organ transplantation technology

Now, a transplant is the standard method of treatment. At the same time illegal organ trafficking developed rapidly in India. It has now become a major problem because of rise in organ stealing rackets and corrupt health care system. Unethical organ transplant commerce is growing in India and has become a safe tourism for foreigners. Success rates for such surgeries of organ transplants in India are very high. "In January 2008, multi-billion rupee kidney scandal came into light when police arrested several people for running a kidney transplant racket in Gurgaon an industrial township near New Delhi. Kidneys from most of the victims, who were the poor hailing from the nearby western Uttar Pradesh, were transplanted into clients from the United States, United Kingdom, Canada, Saudi Arabia and Greece."[1]Similarly, several cases of illegal organ transplantations were came in light. Recently in September 2017, Dehradun police busted the racket on September 11 in Gangotri Charitable Hospital, 30 km from the city with allegation of 600 illegal kidney transplantation across the India.[2]The Government of India was serious with such illegal organ transplantation as it was likely to exploit the poor for organ donation to rich people. So, passed a legislation "The Transplantation of Human Organs and Tissues Act (hereinafter called THOA), 1994," which laid down certain rules and regulations that were to be followed while conducting organ transplant. The main aims of the Act are-

(*a*) Regulating removal, storage and transplantation of human organs for therapeutic purposes

(*b*) Accepting brain death and making it possible to use these patients as potential organ donors

(*c*) Preventing commercial dealings of organs

This Act is the only legislation and the Transplantation of Human Organs and Tissues Rules, 2014 provides policies to regulate organ transplantation in India. However, due to lack of implementation of policies and ignorance of government in this area gives rise to lots of problem. The major reasons for poor performance of organ transplant program is lack of awareness amongst public which has generally contributed for poor donor pool, but also lack of awareness of positive attitude and motivation amongst medical professionals. The Organ transplantation is boon to medical industries it has helped in saving the lives of those who would have died otherwise. In *Vijay kumar Hariram Sahu* v. *State of Maharastra*[3], the Bombay High Court discussed the principles of public interest stating that there is a need to allow transplantation as an instrument of saving lives. Transplantation has an important element in

1 The Times of India (ed. New Delhi) dated 25/01/2008,*"Kidney racket busted in Gurgaon."*

2 Indian Express (ed. New Delhi) available at *http://indianexpress.com/article/india/surgery-racket-held-in-dehradun-probed-for-600-kidney-transplants-across-country/* *(Last accessed on 30 September, 2017)*

3 (2013) 2 Mah LJ 927 (Bom)

the protection of public health. There is a need to ensure that trafficking in human organs does not take place by exploiting poverty, illiteracy and ignorance of a large section of Indian society. In developed countries, legislations are very clear and precise in dealing with problem of organ transplantation than India.

ORGAN TRANSPLANTAION: MEANING AND NEED

The transplantation of an organ from one's body to another person is known as the organ transplant. The person who gives the organ called the donor while the one who receives is the recipient. This is done to replace the recipient's damaged organ with the sound working organ of the donor so that the recipient could function normally and can live healthy life. The age of donor must be above eighteen years. The term transplantation means the grafting of any human organ from any living person or deceased person to some other living person for therapeutic purposes.[4]

Organ Transplantation is a boon to medical industry as it has helped in saving the lives of those who would have died otherwise. There is a great need for human organs for transplantation. In fact, the need far exceeds the supply of transplantable organs. This disparity has led to the formulation of various legislations, attempting to regulate the scare resources (transplantable human organs) and to help establish an equitable system to allocate the organs where they can do the most good.

Legally, organ donation can take place from living, genetically related individuals; from living, unrelated individuals in special circumstances where no unauthorized payment is made to the donor or from cadavers. Live donation of a kidney was the first done in 1954, but live donation of parts of other organs is a relatively recent innovation in the 1990s. Today the major source of organs and tissues transplantation in the west has been from cadaveric donors. Living tissue deteriorates rapidly when it loses its blood supply, and organs need to be cooled and transported for

4 Section 2(p) of the Transplantation of Human Organs and Tissues Act (hereinafter called THOA).

implantation into the recipient within a limited number of hours.[5] Short transfer time, entailing removal of organs from 'beating heart' donors was made possible by the acceptance of 'brain stem death' as death.

"Worldwide, the demand for organs is growing, as the supply of organs and tissues for transplantation have not kept pace with demand. In the UK only approximately 900 individuals become organ donors each year, while over 6000 people are waiting for suitable organs. In the US much the same situation exists, with 70 000 presently on the waiting list and only approximately 5500 cadaveric donors per year. There are several reasons for the shortage of organs. Perhaps the most common reason is that people are hesitant to donate organs. There are other reasons as well: for example, physicians may neglect to inquire of family members whether they would consent to donating organs when their loved one dies"[6]. In other cases, the deceased's wishes to donate his or her organs may not be known by those in the position to act on those wishes.

"Presently three major legal frameworks govern the donation of organs worldwide. The UK, along with a number of European countries, e.g. Germany and Italy, and Canada, Australia, and New Zealand has 'opting-in' systems. This means that the person in lawful possession of the body may authorize the removal of organs and tissues. In practice donation is usually requested from the next-of-kin of the deceased. Many other countries, including e.g. Austria, Belgium, and Singapore, have introduced 'opt-out' or 'presumed consent' systems that assume individuals have granted permission for their organs to be donated, unless they specify otherwise, in advance of their death. 'Required request' or routine enquiry of the next-of-kin of a potential donor, forms part of state law in the US. It provides for hospitals that fail to adopt 'required request' polices to be denied support from healthcare funding agencies".[7] World Health organization (WHO)

5 *How to stop organ trafficking? A Critique of the Transplantation of Human Organs Act in India,* Practical Lawyer, http://www.supremecourtcases.com/index2.php?option=com_content&itemid=1&do_pdf=1&id=15820(last accessed on 20 October 2017).

6 *Ibid.*

7 *Ibid.*

has also, now, approved organ transplantation as a well-established therapy. A Harvard Medical School committee made a historic proposal in 1968, recommending the criteria of death based on brain activity. In 1976, the Royal College of the UK published a comprehensive code for determination of 'Brain Death'. Now most countries, including India in 1994, redefine death as cessation of brain stem activity and organs can legally be removed after brain death.

To attempt to overcome the uncontrollable trade in organs the Indian parliament passed a bill in 1994, in keeping with the WHO guiding principles, prohibiting commercial dealings. There are restrictions for removal and retrieval of human organs and also regulations of hospitals involved to ensure transparency by all concerned. The aim of the THOA is to provide for the regulation of removal, storage and transplantation of human organs for therapeutic purposes and for the prevention of commercial dealings in human organs.

The passing of THOA heralded a new era in Indian medical science. This legislation is written on similar likes as the UK Transplant Act.[8] The essence of this legislation was threefold:

(*i*) To accept brain death as also a definition of death.

(*ii*) To stop commercial dealing in organs

(*iii*) To define the first relative (father, mother, brother, sister, son, daughter and wife) who could donate organs without permission from the government.

Organ transplant law does not allow exchange of money with organ between the donor and the recipient. According to the Act, the unrelated donor has to file an affidavit in the court of a magistrate stating that the organ is being donated out of affection. After which the donor has to undergo number of tests before the actual transplant takes place. The Authorization Committee set up for the purpose ensures that all the documents required under the Act have been supplied. If it is found that the money has been exchanged in the process then both the recipient as well as the donor is considered as prime offenders under the law. The multi-billion rupee Gurgaon kidney

8 *Ibid.*

scandal came into light in January 2008 when police arrested several people for running a kidney transplant racket in Gurgaon an industrial township near New Delhi, India. Kidneys from most of the victims, who were the poor hailing from the nearby western Uttar Pradesh, were transplanted into clients from the United States, United Kingdom, Canada, Saudi Arabia and Greece.[9] Recently in 2017, Dehradun police busted the racket on September 11 in Gangotri Charitable Hospital, 30 km from the town, and arrested Amit from Panchkula in Haryana four days later, along with brother Jeevan, 50. There is a middle brother, Ganesh Raut, 55, who worked with the other two at their Mumbai clinic in the 1990s. There is allegation of 600 illegal kidney transplantation across the India by them[10]. According to THOA Act, organ sale is banned and therefore no foreigner can get a local donor. Human organ transplant laws are very strict in India and the penalty incurred for organ trade is very high.

THE TRANSPLANTATION OF HUMAN ORGANS AND TISSUES: LAW AND POLICY

As stated earlier, THOA is the only legislation, in present, in India to regulate the human organ and tissues transplantation and "Transplantation of Human organs and tissues Rules, 2014" prescribes various rules governing transplantation. Chapter II of the Act prescribes the authority for the removal of organs and tissues, chapter III deals with the regulation of hospitals conducting the removal, storage or transplantation of organs and tissues. Chapter IV describes the appointment of Appropriate Authority to check the storage, distribution and transplantation of organs and their powers. Chapter VI prescribes the offences and penalties for removal of organs and tissues without authority, commercial dealings and contraventions of other provisions of the THOA.

9 The Times of India (ed. New Delhi) dated 25/01/2008,"Kidney racket busted in Gurgaon."

10 Indian Express dated 30 September 2017 (ed. New Delhi) available at *http://indianexpress.com/article/india/surgery-racket-held-in-dehradun-probed-for-600-kidney-transplants-across-country/ (accessed on 30 September, 2017).*

AUTHORITY FOR THE REMOVAL OF HUMAN ORGANS AND TISSUES

Section 3 of THOA states that only registered medical practioners are authorized to remove, store and transplantation of the human organs and tissues from donor for therapeutic purposes. The Act provides with guideline that minimum three qualified medical practitioners should be present at the time of removal and transplantation of organ.[11]If any donor had, in writing and in the presence of two or more witnesses (at least one of whom is a near relative of such person), unequivocally authorized at any time before his death, the removal of any human organ of his body, after his death, for therapeutic purposes, the person lawfully in possession of the dead body of the donor should, unless he has any reason to believe that the donor had subsequently revoked the authority aforesaid, grant to a registered medical practitioner all reasonable facilities for the removal, for therapeutic purposes, of that human organ or tissue or both from the dead body of the donor.[12]No authority to remove any organ or tissues from the deceased person is given by a person to whom such body has been entrusted solely for the purpose of interment, cremation or other disposal.

AUTHORITY FOR REMOVAL OF ORGANS OF UNCLAIMED BODIES

The Act provides that in the case of a dead body lying in a hospital or prison and not claimed by any of the near relatives of the deceased person within forty-eight hours from the time of the death of the concerned person, the authority for the removal of any human organ or tissue or both from such dead body may be given, in the prescribed form, by the person in charge, for the time being, of the management or control of the hospital or prison, or by an employee of such hospital or prison authorized in this behalf by the person in charge of the management or control thereof.[13]

---

11 S. 6 of the Act.

12 S.3(2).

13 S. 5 of the Act.

RESTRICTIONS ON REMOVAL AND TRANSPLANTATION OF ORGANS OR TISSUES OR BOTH

The Act has put restrictions for removal of organs or tissues or both from the body of a donor before his death and transplantation into a recipient unless the donor is a near relative of the recipient. In case of the donor or the recipient being near relative is a foreign national, prior approval of the Authorization Committee is necessary before removing or transplanting human organ or tissue or both.[14]No human organs is to be removed from the body of minor, mentally retarded, mental ill and mentally challenged person before his death for the purpose of transplantation except in the manner prescribed by the Authorization Committee constituted under section 9 of the Act. Where donor and recipient both are near relatives as defined above, there need to be no enquiry by the Authorization Committee to ascertain whether there is any commercial element and the Court is satisfied that the person is not mentally retarded, transplantation of kidney is permissible.[15]

REGULATION OF HOSPITALS CONDUCTING THE REMOVAL, STORAGE OR TRANSPLANTATION

Only registered hospitals registered under THOA are authorized to conduct, or associate with, or help in, the removal, storage or transplantation of any human organ or tissues or both. Medical practitioners are authorized to remove, store or transplant of any organ or tissue or both only in such registered hospitals for therapeutic use.[16] Before undertaking removal or transplanting the RMP should explain all possible effects, complications and hazards connected with this procedure to donor and the recipient respectively.

APPOINTMENT OF APPROPRIATE AUTHORITY AND ITS FUNCTIONS

---

14 S. 9

15 *Sonia Ajit Vayklip* v.*Lilawati Hospital and Research Centre*, (2012) 3 Mah LJ 31 (Bom)

16 S. 10

Chapter IV of Act has provided appointment for Appropriate Authorities. The Central Government is empowered to appoint one or more officers as Appropriate Authorities for each of the Union territories and State Government for their respective State for the performance of following functions.[17] They have the powers of a civil court trying a suit under the Code of Civil Procedure.

(*a*) To grant registration of hospitals engaged in removal, storage or transplantation of organs or tissues or both under section 15 of the THOA.

(*b*) To suspend or cancel registration of registered hospitals *suo motu* or on complaint under section 16 of the Act

(*c*) To enforce standards for hospitals and tissues banks engaged in removal, storage, testing or transplantation of organs or tissues or both.

(*d*) To investigate any complaint of breach of any of the provisions of this Act or any of the rules made there under and take appropriate action.

(*e*) To inspect periodically Tissue Banks and hospitals

(*f*) To inspect periodically hospitals for examination of the quality of transplantation and the follow-up medical care to persons who have undergone transplantation and persons from whom organs are removed.

(*g*) To undertake such other measures as may be prescribed by the Central Government or State Government.

POWERS OF APPROPRIATE AUTHORITIES

Appropriate Authorities is empowered with following powers

(*a*) Power to grant certificate of registration to the hospitals engaged in the removal, storage or transplantation of organs or tissues or both under the THOA.

---

17 S. 13 of THOA, 1994

(*b*) Power to grant certificate of registration to the tissues Bank engaged in activities relating to the recovery, screening, testing, processing, storage and distribution of tissues unless it is duly registered under this Act.

(*c*) Power to suspend or cancel registration of registered hospitals *suo motu* or on complaint, as prescribed in section 16 of the Act.

APPELLATE AUTHORITY

Any person aggrieved by an order of the Authorization Committee may prefer an appeal, within thirty days from the date of the receipt of the order[18], in such manner as may be prescribed, against such order to-

(*i*) the Central Government where the appeal is against the order of the Authorization Committee constituted by the Central Government; or

(*ii*) the State Government, where the appeal is against the order of the Authorization Committee constituted by the State Government.

PUNISHMENT FOR REMOVAL OF HUMAN ORGAN WITHOUT AUTHORITY

The Act prescribes very stringent punishment for removal of human organ without authority to prevent illegal trafficking by the Amendment Act, 2011. Now, any person who renders his services to or at any hospital and who, for purposes of transplantation, conducts, associates with, or helps in any manner in, the removal of any human organ without authority will be punished with imprisonment for a term, which may extend to **ten years and with fine, which may extend to twenty lakh rupees**.

PUNISHMENT FOR COMMERCIAL DEALINGS IN HUMAN ORGANS

There is complete ban on commercial dealings of human organs in India. Section 19 of the Act prescribes comprehensively on such ban. Any person who makes or receives any payment for the supply of or for an offer to

18 S. 17.

supply any human organ is punished with imprisonment with minimum term of **five years but may be extended to ten years and liable to fine with minimum twenty lakh rupees but may be extended to one crore**. In case of illegal dealings in human tissues the minimum punishment will be one year but which may be extended to three years and liable to fine with minimum five lakh rupees but may be extended to twenty five lakh rupees.[19]

PUNISHMENT FOR CONTRAVENTION OF ANY OTHER PROVISION OF THIS ACT

Whoever contravenes any provision of this Act or any rule made, or any condition of the registration granted, there under for which no punishment is separately provided in this Act, shall be punishable with imprisonment for a term which may extend to **five years or with fine which may extend to twenty lakh rupees**.[20]

COMPOSITION OF AUTHORISATION COMMITTEE

The Transplantation of Human Organs and Tissues Rules, 2014 provides composition of State level; District level and hospital based Authorization Committee to decide the matters related removal and all other type of transplantation and its procedure. Rule 18 describes procedure of proposed transplantation in case of near relatives and rules 19 in case of transplant other than near relatives. Rule 20 laid down rules for transplantation procedure when the proposed donor or the recipient is foreigner.

CRITICAL ANALYSIS OF THOA, 1994

The organ trafficking is not new to the world and India is considered to be one of the biggest center for this market. Illegal organ transplants are on the rise in spite of having a special legislation in place to deal with the menace. The law for various reasons failed in its objective and implementation

---

19 S. 19-A

20 S.20

giving scope to make the ground fertile for organ scandals[21]. It is also creating hurdles for various philanthropic agencies, which are working to further the cause of transplantation and sometimes unwittingly helping the kingpins, and touts to easily circumvent the law. The law enacted on this subject some fifteen years ago is still in force, but it has miserably failed to control the corrupt practices of the unscrupulous elements that are running an illegal trade in the transplantation of human organs. A description is given herein first of the evolution of the system of organ transplantation and then an analysis is given of the provisions forming part of the famous legislation called the Organ Transplantation Act of 1994.

"In India for a long time there was no specific legislation regulating organ transplantation due to which many number of kidney scams were reported leaving number of poor people exploited by the middlemen and the unscrupulous doctors in the country which led to the enactment of a law that could punish and curb this practice. A committee was appointed by the Central Government to draft legislation on this subject".[22] As the main focus of the proposed legislation was kidney scams, the panel of doctors in the committee for framing the law were all kidney experts and thus, the Act has largely been framed keeping in view the kidney scams only. Finally the present Act dealing with regulation of organ transplantation called the THOA, 1994 has come into existence.

"The Act more or less resembles the Organ Transplantation Act of the UK. Due to inefficient and corrupt healthcare system, illegal trafficking of organs is really high in India. To stop illegal organ transplants, Indian Government has enacted the above legislation that criminalizes organ sales".[23] THOA, 1994 has laid down the law that needs to be followed while conducting organ transplantation.

21 The Report of Transplantation of Human Organ Act Review Committee, 2005 available at http://www.mohanfoundation.org/tho/thoa-review-committee.asp (Last accessed on 21 November 2017).

22 *How to stop organ trafficking? A Critique of the Transplantation of Human Organs Act in India,* Practical Lawyer, http://www.supremecourtcases.com/index2.php?option=com_content&itemid=1&do_pdf=1&id=15820(last accessed on 20 October 2017).

23 The Report of Transplantation of Human Organ Act Review Committee, 2005 available at http://www.mohanfoundation.org/tho/thoa-review-committee.asp (Last accessed on 21 November 2017).

This Act allows doctors to certify brain death, thus enabling the starting of cadaver transplantation[24]. The provision refers to donors who are not near relatives of the recipient. The expression near relatives is defined in Section 2(i) to mean spouse, son, daughter, father, mother, brother or sister. Chapter II deals with Authority for the removal of human Organs. Section 3(2) deals with removal of the organs after death for therapeutic purposes. Sub-section (1) however deals with authorization by any donor for removal of any human organ before his death for therapeutic purposes. Section 9 (4) deals with constitution of Authorization Committee consisting of such members as may be notified by the Central Government or the State Government, as the case may be. Under section 9 (5), application is required to be jointly made by the donor and the recipient in the prescribed manner.

"According to the Act, the unrelated donor has to file an affidavit in the Court of a Magistrate stating that the organ is being donated out of affection. The Authorization Committee set up for the purpose ensures that all the documents required under the Act have been supplied. It banned organ sales; therefore, no foreigner can get a local donor. The Committee is required to hold an enquiry and if after such an enquiry it is certified that the applicants have complied with the requirements of the Act and the Rules, it can grant the applicants approval for the removal and transplantation of the human organs concerned. Section 11 prohibits removal or transplantation of human organs for any purpose other than therapeutic purposes".[25]

Chapter VI deals with Offences and penalties. Section 18 provides for punishment for removal of human organs without authority and section 19 provides for punishment for commercial dealings in human organs up to the extent of ten years imprisonment and with fine up to rupees twenty lakhs. This law does not allow exchange of money between the donor and the recipient. The Authorization Committee has to be satisfied

24 *How to stop organ trafficking? A Critique of the Transplantation of Human Organs Act in India,* Practical Lawyer, http://www.supremecourtcases.com/index2.php?option=com_content&itemid=1&do_pdf=1&id=15820(last accessed on 20 October 2017).

25 *Ibid.*

that the authorization for removal is not for commercial consideration. Since some amount of urgency has to be exhibited because of the need for transplantation, expeditious disposal of the application would be appropriate.

The law failed miserably in achieving the goal on two counts. Firstly, it did not register much success which is evident mainly from the kidney scams reported in the years 2002, 2003 and 2004 through the fortuitous fact of it being the only lucrative human organ accessible illegally from live donors. Numerous instances of kidney trade were highlighted by the media from the States of Kerala, Karnataka, Tamil Nadu and Punjab.[26] The story is more or less the same every time. The donor is lured by promise of a handsome monetary reward sometimes accompanied with an additional promise of a job.

"The debate came to forefront again when a press reports brought to light kidneys being bought and sold in Tamil Nadu, Andhra Pradesh and many other parts of India including the State capital, Delhi. In this incident the kidney transplantation racket was operated on national and international basis by a quack doctor, Dr. Amit Kumar involving three hospitals, five diagnostic centers and ten laboratories, and more than fifty accomplices, including doctors and nurses, carried for years across Uttar Pradesh."[27]

Secondly, the 1994 Act did nothing to ensure that hospitals would create protocols for retrieving the full range of retrievable organs that could be donated by the public and transplanted to save lives.[28] The result was a market-driven lucrative focus on the only organ that could be donated by live donor's viz. kidneys.

"Medical Tourism is another gateway to organ trade. The medical faculty of India in collaboration with the tourism industry has worked together

26 *How to stop organ trafficking? A Critique of the Transplantation of Human Organs Act in India,* Practical Lawyer, http://www.supremecourtcases.com/index2.php?option=com_content&itemid=1&do_pdf=1&id=15820(last accessed on 22 November 2017).

27 *Ibid.*

28 Smrithi Surendranath aryaand Aswini Anjana, "Organ donation and Transplant Torism- A Legal Perspective available at, http://ijldai.thelawbrigade.com/wp-content/uploads/2016/03/smrithi.pdf.(last accessed on 22November 2017).

to provide cost-effective treatment to people across the globe. With the privatization of medical care in India evolved the recent and popular trend of treatment along with the fun of a vacation, better known as medical tourism in India wherein the international kidney bazaar penetrated its tentacles and were highly evolved with extensive cross-border transactions and a hierarchy of preferences and prices."[29]

There are certain demerits of THOA, 1994 such as-

(*i*) A near absence of commitment on the part of Indian hospital managements and the Government to provide for brain death declaration and creation of reliable hospital infrastructure to counsel families of potential organ donors and retrieve offered organs in spite of proven successes of post-death counseling as a tool to motivate cadaver organ donation;

(*ii*) The inclusion of loopholes either by design or default permitting the continued access (often illegally) to one of two human kidneys (viz. the proviso that a person not related to the patient could donate a kidney by reason of affection and the inclusion of the spouse as near relative so that people can marry for organ donation

(*iii*) The availability of enough poor people ready to sell a part of themselves

(*iv*) A medical social ethos which permits justification of the trade as good for both the seller and buyer

(*v*) A medical establishment willing to accept such commercial concepts and, perhaps most importantly, even ready to terminate successful cadaver organ retrieval programs in hospitals without assigning reasons for doing so.

The Act has not defined the term organ, which need to define with clarity. The definition of organ as provided in the statute is not exhaustive and was

29 *How to stop organ trafficking? A Critique of the Transplantation of Human Organs Act in India,* Practical Lawyer, http://www.supremecourtcases.com/index2.php?option=com_content&itemid=1&do_pdf=1&id=15820(last accessed on 22 November 2017).

a preliminary attempt to introduce the concept of organ transplantation. The present Act says that any part of the human body, which is not replicated is called as organ. It mainly considered internal organs like kidneys, liver, etc. as an extension of brain death definition and the eyes (corneas)/ears as they were covered by earlier legislations.[30] The scope of the definition of organ has to be widened and the aim of the proposed section is to list out as clearly as possible the tissues/organs for transplantation, though this is not an exhaustive list. The contents of the list are contingent on the kinds of transplants possible in India.

The Act is also silent about live donation and related other issues. There is need to review the provision whether it allows live donation of organs freely. Should the fiduciary relationship of love and affection be removed or retained, keeping in view the instances of its abuse in the recent past. What are the other measures which will help in curbing the menace of illegal kidney rackets? The Authorization Committees are not working satisfactorily and most of the times they are obliging the rich and wealthy. The parameters to justify the love and affection clause is the major ambiguity which makes the provision all the more exploitative whereby a poor person donates his organ to a rich man out of love and affection.

Another issue is whether the non-governmental organizations (NGOs) working for the cause of organ transplantation should be recognized by the Act. Organ retrieval agencies (OROs) i.e. non-governmental organizations play a major role in counseling the family members or relatives of the brain dead patient or cadavers.[31] Since the awareness about the organ transplantation is abysmal in India this role being played by the NGOs/ organ retrieval organizations gains lot of importance and their absence would virtually make the whole object of the Act futile. But now these NGOs do not find any place in the statute so not formally recognized by the Government. Whether non-governmental organizations (NGOs) working to counsel the relatives of the patients and playing an important role in

30 *How to stop organ trafficking? A Critique of the Transplantation of Human Organs Act in India,* Practical Lawyer, http://www.supremecourtcases.com/index2.php?option=com_content&itemid=1&do_pdf=1&id=15820(last accessed on 30 November 2017).

31 *Ibid.*

forwarding the cause of transplantation shall be recognized by the Act and also be provided with financial assistance?[32] According to the present Act, the State does not have any network of its own for conducting counseling of the families of brain dead patients or dead patients for cadaver donation. Due to various inhibitions, religious or personal, relatives of the dead patient and brain dead patient show reluctance to donate the organs and the entire transplantation or cadaver donation comes to a standstill. Then the entire transplantation system falls back on the transplant counselor. The transplant counselor (usually a social worker) and the function performed by such a counselor are the basic fundamental key components in motivating donation of corneas, skin, heart valves, etc. from donors in hospital wards. They serve to obtain timely consent for organ/tissue donation from donor's relatives in a sensitive manner, after occurrence of normal deaths.

It is high time that India should think of establishing a centralized system, which takes care of organ retrieval, and organ distribution, which shall be impartial and transparent in its execution. Presently, there is no such system in place giving rise to a number of problems like lack of coordination between the organizations of different States. For example if a patient who is in need of liver transplantation in one State, he cannot get from another State. The waiting list of organ seeking patients is not maintained properly by the transplant organizations. The whole system also lacks transparency. Since such a planned system does not exist currently, every new organ scandal which is reported in the press raises fresh doubts in the mind of the public about the ethics and controls being followed in organ retrieval, distribution and transplantation. This affects the efforts of the Government and NGOs to increase cadaver organ donations. This prime responsibility is required to shoulder by the Government of India to ensure transparent and fair organ transplantation in the country.

To sum up, the THOA Act, 1994 needs to be improved upon and adjusted to the current scenario. The need for an overhaul of the Act is felt because

32 *How to stop organ trafficking? A Critique of the Transplantation of Human Organs Act in India,* Practical Lawyer, http://www.supremecourtcases.com/index2.php?option=com_content&itemid=1&do_pdf=1&id=15820(last accessed on 28November 2017)

when the legislators came up with this Act, they had envisaged something else in their minds. The main benefit of the Act was its focus on definition of brain death to allow legal retrieval of internal organs (kidney, liver, heart, etc.) and punitive steps to control illegal organ dealing. But this was nullified by lack of corresponding legal measures to make it obligatory for hospitals to declare brain death and create protocols with our vibrant social work community to retrieve organs as mandated in the US legislation. The Act also did not facilitate the post-death retrieval of various other types of transplantable tissues (cornea, bone, artery, skin, tendon, ligaments, heart valves, etc.) that are not limited to brain dead donors. We, thus, keeping this in mind have to go ahead and make the Act more amenable to the present situation.

CONCLUSION

Organ donation is one of the noblest forms of charity and the advancements in medical sciences have made organ transplantation a successful technique to save the lives of many. The deed of organ donation is however not popular amongst the public as it involves several ethical, social, cultural and psychological issues attached to it. Susceptible laws, variable interpretation of their provisions and their ineffective implementation have been a major cause for illegal organ trade and increase in commercialization of organ transplantation. Lack of awareness amongst the public, lack of governmental participation in monitoring hospitals and institutions involved in the cause of organ transplantations, indulgence of middlemen for procurement of organs and tissues poses challenges to the effective implementation of the Act. THOA, 1994 was amended in 2011 enabling to have deterrent impact on illegal trafficking of human organ. Transplantation is based on the principles of public interest to allow transplantation as an instrument of saving lives. Transplantation has an important element in the protection of public health. There is a need to ensure that trafficking in human organs does not take place by exploiting poverty, illiteracy and ignorance of a large section of Indian society. Now it is over two decades, THO Act has neither able to curb commerce of organs nor helped in promotion of organ donation program to overcome the shortage of organ. The requirement to establish a centralized registry with a hierarchical setup can help curb illegal organ trade as well as face organ shortage problems. Transplant tourism and organ trafficking are international threats which are likely to affect people in developing countries. Hence, the law needs to be reformed according to the dynamic needs of the society to promote and conduct legal organ transplantations. Finally, organ transplantation is an issue that must be dealt with sensitivity. Orienting society to accepting the 'value of life after death' will go a long way in strengthening transplantation as medical treatment.

BIBLIOGRAPHY

BOOKS

1. David Hamilton, *A History of Organ Transplantation: Ancient Legends to Modern Practice,* (University of Pittsburgh Press, 2012)
2. David Price, *Legal and Ethical Aspects of Organ Transplantation,* (Cambridge University Press, 2000)
3. Allan D. Kirk, Stuart J. Knechtle, Christian P. Larsen, Joren C. Madsen, Thomas C. Pearson, Steven A. Webber, *Textbook of Organ Transplantation, 2014*

Articles

1. Patel Jayant Prakesh, *Organ Transplantation And Its Legal Prospects,* http://www.legalserviceindia.com/article/l279-Organ-Transplantation.html
2. Nadir Nupur, *Law and Medicine: an Analysis of the Organ Transplantation Law in India,* http://www.legalserviceindia.com/article/l224-Organ-Transplantation-Law-In-India.html.
3. *How to stop organ trafficking? A Critique of the Transplantation of Human Organs Act in India,* Practical Lawyer, http://www.supremecourtcases.com/index2.php?option=com_content&itemid=1&do_pdf=1&id=15820.
4. Shroff Sunil, Legal and Ethical Aspects of Organ Donation and Transplantation, (Sep 25, 2009), https://www.ncbi.nlm.nih.gov/pmc/articles/PMC2779960/.

5. Smrithi Surendranath arya and Aswini Anjana , Organ Donation And Transplant Tourism- A Legal Perspective.
6. http://ijldai.thelawbrigade.com/wp-content/uploads/2016/03/smrithi.pdf.
7. Jayshri K, *Organ Transplantation-Legal, Social and Ethical issues*, (Apr 5, 2011), http://www.legalservicesindia.com/article/article/organ-transplantation-legal-social-and-ethical-issues-618-

Reports

1. The Report of Transplantation of Human Organ Act Review Committee, 2005 visited http://www.mohanfoundation.org/tho/thoa-review-committee.asp.

Statues

1. Transplantation of Human Organ Act, 1994.
2. Transplantation of Human Organ Act, 2011.
3. Transplantation of Human Organs and Tissues Rules, 2014.

❑❑❑

www.ingramcontent.com/pod-product-compliance
Ingram Content Group UK Ltd.
Pitfield, Milton Keynes, MK11 3LW, UK
UKHW021306260926
475702UK00048B/690
* 9 7 8 1 0 3 2 3 7 9 8 5 2 *